Praise for A

'A stunning intellectual achievement
interested in the lesser-known aspect
and modern.'
– Anthony Peake, author of *Opening the Doors of Perception* and
The Infinite Mindfield

'A fascinating and well-researched study into a vanishing religion and how it
connects us with 2000 years of religious history.'
– Richard Smoley, author of *Forbidden Faith: The Secret History of Gnosticism*

'*A Dictionary of Gnosticism* is a valuable resource for any student of Gnosis. If you
need a helpful translator of the language, or a sympathetic guide to the beliefs
of these extraordinary women and men who lived a long time ago, in a world far,
far away, then this is the book for you. Think of it as the 'Lonely Cosmos Guide
to Gnosis', and always pack a copy when you are setting out for that strange and
exciting country. Have a great trip!'
—Timothy Freke and Peter Gandy, authors of *The Jesus Mysteries* and *The Gospel
of the Second Coming*

The Gospel of Philip
'Provides us with a wealth of insightful annotations, and the translation is the
most accessible to date. All of those with an interest in Gnostic tradition and its
sacraments will be happy to receive this splendid work!'
—Stephan A Hoeller, author of *Jung and The Lost Gospels* and *The Gnostic Jung*

'How refreshing to move from our contemporary culture of Christian literalism
to a spiritual world alive with symbol, metaphor and the poetry of the Divine.'
—Ron Miller, Religion Department chair, Lake Forest College, author of
The Gospel of Thomas: A Guidebook for Spiritual Practice

The Lost Sayings of Jesus
'If the gospels represent the tip [of Jesus's sayings], Andrew Phillip Smith has
provided the rest of the iceberg. Here is proof that [Jesus's] voice has never
fallen silent.'
—Robert M Price, professor of scriptural studies, Johnnie Colemon Theological
Seminary

'Marvellous ... Will provide spiritual seekers, committed Christians, and
academic scholars [insight into] sayings attributed to Jesus that they may not
know existed. A valuable sourcebook and significant contribution to the study of
the history of Christian ideas.'
—Stevan Davies, professor of religious studies, College Misericordia and author
of *The Gospel of Thomas: Annotated & Explained*

By the same author

The Gospel of Thomas: A New Version Based on its Inner Meaning
The Gospel of Philip: Annotated & Explained
The Lost Sayings Of Jesus: Teachings from Ancient Christian,
    Jewish, Gnostic and Islamic Sources – Annotated & Explained
Gnostic Writings on the Soul: Annotated & Explained
A Dictionary of Gnosticism
The Gnostics: History Tradition Scriptures Influence
The Secret History of the Gnostics
The Gnostic: A Journal of Gnosticism, Western Esotericism and
    Spirituality, 1-6 (editor)
Lost Teachings of the Cathars

ANDREW PHILLIP SMITH

JOHN THE BAPTIST AND THE LAST GNOSTICS

THE SECRET HISTORY OF THE MANDAEANS

WATKINS

Sharing Wisdom Since 1893

This edition published in the UK and USA 2016 by
Watkins, an imprint of Watkins Media Limited
19 Cecil Court, London WC2N 4EZ

enquiries@watkinspublishing.com

Design and typography copyright © Watkins Media Limited 2016
Text copyright © Andrew Phillip Smith 2016

1 3 5 7 9 10 8 6 4 2

Designed and typeset by Gail Jones

Printed and bound in Finland

A CIP record for this book is available from the British Library

ISBN: 978-1-78028-913-7

www.watkinspublishing.com

Contents

In the Name of the Great Life!

******

Introduction

His pure white robes contrast with the muddied waters as the white-bearded baptiser, his staff propped against him, dunks the head of the baptised into the river. It could be a biblical scene. The river is the Jordan. This could be John the Baptist immersing Jesus, the Holy Spirit about to descend in the form of a dove, the voice from above about to announce that, 'Thou art my beloved Son; with thee I am well pleased.'[1]

Yet it is not Jesus who is being baptised and it is not John who is doing the baptising. I am looking at a photograph, from around 2002. This river is 'Yardna' in the dialect of Aramaic that the baptiser speaks, literally 'Jordan'. But this is not the physical and geographical River Jordan that runs through the countries of Jordan and Israel. This river is in Iraq, and it is likely to be the Euphrates. But it could be a river in New Jersey, USA, or the River Nepean running through a public park in Sydney, Australia. Every clean-running river in the entire world could potentially be the Yardna – the Jordan – if it is used for this purpose. Neither is this baptism a milestone event in the life of a Christian, which admits him or her into the Church. These baptisms occur every week. And these people are not Christians, Jews or Muslims. They are the Mandaeans.

Keepers of an ancient minority religious tradition, victims of sectarian violence and ethnic cleansing, these peace-loving people have been fleeing to Syria and to the West and may be found in small numbers in such unlikely locations as Sydney, New Jersey or Manchester. They are among the casualties of the Western intervention in Iraq and the recent activities of ISIS. Although they are eager to blend in with their local cultures and are often happy to be perceived as Christians, their religion is very distinctive, with priests (known as *tarmidas*) holding dramatic river baptisms in white robes. They may also lay claim to being the last Gnostics. They are the only surviving remnant of the ancient

Christian-related sects who taught *gnosis*, the direct knowledge of God, created their own gospels and myths, and were persecuted as heretical by the Church in the 2nd and 3rd centuries. The Mandaeans place these weekly river baptisms at the centre of their religious life, and the most important prophet, although not the founder of their religion, is claimed to be none other than John the Baptist (Yahia in Mandaic). For this reason they became known, inaccurately, as 'St John Christians' to the first Westerners who encountered them.

Could this really be true? Could an obscure Middle Eastern ethnic religion really stretch all the way back to the Gnostics and John the Baptist? Surely the Gnostics – an umbrella term for a range of heterodox religious groups known to scholars as Sethians, Valentinians and the like – died out in antiquity, marginalized and persecuted by the Church? The medieval Cathars, generally recognized as the very last group of successors to dualistic Gnostic Christianity, were eradicated in the series of bloodthirsty massacres known as the Albigensian Crusade. How could a little-known sect in Iraq and Iran be related to heretical Gnostic groups, who had thrived in Egypt, Syria, Italy and France?

And could they really lay historical claim to John the Baptist as their prophet? All Christians know that John's role was merely as the forerunner to the Christian revelation, a function that was fulfilled once he had baptised Jesus. John himself was beheaded by Herod Antipas before Jesus was crucified. Surely that was an end to his story?[2] Are we now in the realms of alternative history? In some ways, yes. Much of alternative history involves a radical reconsideration of the origins of Christianity, the validity of its transmission through the centuries and the possibility of underground traditions. There is a strong feeling in the post-Christian West that mainstream Christianity is missing some element that it must have had at the beginning; that something has been left out of the story. Hence the proliferation of alternative research and popular books on the divine feminine within Christianity; the relationship of Jesus and Mary Magdalene; the importance of apostles other than Peter and Paul; and the significance of vanquished or heterodox Christianities such as the Gnostics, the Cathars and the Knights Templar. These notions of lost

Christianities, ignored disciples and underground continuities meet spectacularly in the conspiracy theory of the bloodline Jesus, best known in the English-speaking world via *The Holy Blood and the Holy Grail* and *The Da Vinci Code*.

Most of these theories, fascinating though they are, have problems. For one, they strike me as being a triumph of literalism. The hypotheses of these books are very much wedded to physical, material events. The focus is on bloodlines and babies and marriages, secret societies and lost treasures; on the authenticity of relics, mysterious buildings and lost manuscripts. In mainstream Christianity, what has truly been submerged or, to use a more Gnostic metaphor, buried, is its inner meaning – the element of genuine spiritual experience or gnosis. The real underground transmission is the communication of *gnosis*, not of some hereditary descent that terminates in some dodgy secret society. Of what use would it be to discover the secret heir of Jesus if he turned out to be a paranoid, seedy, right-wing Frenchman?

I once sketched out a short story intended to parody the fascination with secret societies and alternative history. The protagonist would discover a society that had spread all over the world, to every continent. Its adepts placed great importance on lineage, which they received in an initiation ceremony that could only be conducted by those who were near the top of their hierarchy. They could track their initiation generation by generation, through the decades and centuries, from each individual to his predecessor. As their history is traced back it began to converge on a few holy places, and one city in particular. As the centuries are peeled away the lineage stands firm, all the way back to the 2nd century and – who knows! – even the 1st. It is the mother of all conspiracy theories, the epitome of the powerful organization that controls civilization behind the scenes. The twist was to be that this was not some obscure sect or esoteric inner circle but the Roman Catholic Church. (Of course, there are indeed a number of conspiracies about the Catholic Church and the Vatican Library, which holds – we would like to think – copies of every lost gospel and autograph editions of Jesus' very own writings, all of which contain secrets that, should the Church allow them to be known, would destroy Christianity forever.)

But, for all their faults, alternative visions of Christianity are correct in their recognition that self-designated official Church bodies have no exclusive claim to the truth and authority, and that they have at various stages in the history persecuted and eliminated those who have had a greater spiritual veracity. In their questioning of the official origin stories of Christianity and the early development of the Church, and in their understanding that there are other ways to relate to the past than by academic history, these alternative visions are spot on.

The story of the Mandaeans is true alternative history. They have represented an alternative to the giant imperial faiths of Christianity and Islam, although – as we shall see in Chapter 1 – they are not alone in this. They offer an alternative to the tale of the Church triumphant, which eliminated the nasty heresy of Gnosticism. They offer an alternative to the tragic history of the ancient Gnostics: the Mandaeans are Gnostics who didn't die out. Previously I had been slightly sceptical of these claims about the Mandaean religion. Much recent scholarship on Gnosticism has emphasized that it is not a coherent academic category, or that, in a more positive appraisal, the only people we should really call Gnostic are a single sect also known as the Sethians. However, in researching and writing this book I was struck by how Gnostic Mandaean ideas are. Time and again as I sorted through material about them I could see, almost despite myself, how the overall worldview, major themes and even minute details of Gnosticism continually crop up in Mandaeaism.

They force us to question the Christian view of John the Baptist as a mere forerunner of Christ. The extraordinary survival of the Mandaeans is a tale that forces us to question the received view of Jesus. An alternative transmission over a period of 2,000 years is possible. Yet this is not a book crammed with off-the-wall speculation. For the most part the subjects discussed here are the same as those discussed by academics. To a large extent my conclusions are the same, and, like any other writer on historical subjects, it is to professional historians and academics that I owe the groundwork and graft of translation, collation and analysis.

Some of the few scholars who have been involved in Mandaean studies have been true friends to the Mandaeans, offering material support and, most recently, help for refugees affected by the crises in Iraq and Syria. In the story of the Mandaeans, alternative history and careful academic study converge. The Mandaeans are a living alternative history of Gnosticism.

This book is not about the living experience of the modern Mandaeans, but about their extraordinary history and the fascinating possibilities of their encounters with and their influence on the Knights Templar and the Harranians, and their origins as disciples of John the Baptist. Yet, as I wrote the book, I always tried to bear in mind that the Mandaeans are a real, living ethnic group and not some ancient disappeared race.

The mythology of the Mandaeans is perhaps not quite as important as their ritual practices, yet the stories are the metaphysical foundation of the religion. These are not literary myths but part of the reality of devout Mandaeans. Scholar Jorunn Buckley described how Mamoon Aldulaimi, a Mandaean originally from Baghdad but living in New York working as an engineer, would call on the divine figure Hibil Ziwa (Abel) for extra strength when it was needed. Once he called on both Hibil Ziwa and Manda d-Hayyi (the Mandaean saviour figure) to help move his car successfully on an icy driveway.[3]

Although they are a living people and religion, their survival is not assured. It is increasingly difficult for them to maintain the strictures of their religion and the conditions through which the esoteric knowledge of the priests and educated lay people is passed on. Yet the Mandaeans have through the centuries faced up to crisis after crisis with tenacity and have endured.

Assailed on one side by the chaos and violence of the Middle East and on the other by the homogenizing pressure of the West, the Mandaeans are in danger of virtual extinction, both as an ethnic group and a religion.

Thus this book begins with the current plight of the Mandaeans. My method is to wind back the clock, spooling back through the ages along the unravelled thread of their history. For the convenience of the narrative I will have to dart back and forth occasionally, but essentially this is a reverse history, a life seen backwards, always looking towards the cradle and the womb. Although for the better part of their existence they have been confined to limited regions of Iraq and Iran, the Mandaeans have popped up in connection with the most unlikely aspects of history: Portuguese Jesuits, (possibly) the Knights Templar, the city of Harran in which pagan religion survived for centuries after the coming of Muhammad, Islam itself, right back to 1st-century Palestine and beyond. The Mandaeans have maintained their religion, ethnicity and culture down the centuries. Yet so much of their history is conjectural. The Mandaean literature sketches out a story that is well defined, if obtusely told. Critical history can show that some aspects of the Mandaean story are very unlikely to have taken place. Other aspects, such as the descent of the angelic entity Hibil Ziwa into 1st-century Judaea, are outside of history. Often there is virtually no trace of the Mandaeans for decades or centuries, at least in any way that is accessible for Westerners; but then they come into focus again, their white robes immersed in the river, beside their cult huts (the *manda*), baptising in the living water of the eternal Jordan.+

Strange Religion:
Minority Religions in
the Middle East

When we think of the Middle East, particularly in the 21st century, we think of Islam. It is probably the countries of Iran and Iraq that first come to mind for the average Westerner. The name Iran brings forth images of Ayatollah Khomeini, of long-bearded clerics, of *jihad* and *fatwa*. Iraq summons up Saddam Hussein and the chaotic aftermath of the Western-imposed regime change.

Beyond Iraq and Iran, the Middle East has been home to more recent developments such as the frightening machinations of ISIS/ISIL/Islamic State, the Assad regime in Syria, the Turkish bombing of Kurdistan, and the never-ending horrors of Israel and Palestine. The common theme is Islam. The West is the known, democratic, consumerist, Christian or secular post-Christian society. The Middle East is Islam. Islam is the Other.

Except this isn't true. Islam has indeed been a dominant force in the Middle East, and continues to be so. But, aside from the many Christian minorities spread through the area, and Jews who historically had communities in many Middle Eastern countries but are now mainly gathered in Israel, it is home to many minority religions. It may come as a shock to those of us who perceive the West as tolerant, but Islam has historically been more accommodating to other religions than Christianity ever has.[1]

The Quran specifically recommends toleration of three – four if a single mention of Zoroastrians is included – religious groups outside of Islam: the Christians, the Jews and the mysterious Sabians. This last category has allowed a number of minority religious groups to survive, although not thrive, down the centuries in the Middle East. It was always considered better for these people to convert to Islam. Non-Muslims had a special tax imposed on them at times in various countries. Yet, unlike pre-modern Christianity, Islam always recognized that there are other valid religions. It is a heritage that modern Islamist groups would do well to remember.

The Mandaeans are one of the groups that have been recognized as Sabians, conferring a status as 'people of the book'. We will look at the Sabians again later in the book and investigate whether this means that the Mandaeans could have been specifically referred to in the Quran.

The Mandaeans are not the only unusual minority religious–ethnic group in the Middle East. To understand the story of the Mandaeans we need to appreciate the surprising persistence of these other religions. None of them quite has a claim that stretches back to the time of Jesus, as the Mandaeans do; none can claim to be the last surviving Gnostics. But each of them has a fascinating story. These minority groups, which may also be mixed up with the Mandaeans, were not widely known in the West until recently, and even now most people's knowledge of them comes from violence and the refugee crisis.

Yazidis

Probably the most widely known of these groups are the Yazidis. The activities of ISIS in 2014 resulted in the Yazidis – also known as Yezidis or Ezidis – receiving extensive international attention for the first time in their long existence. The plight of the Mandaeans had also received a certain amount of occasional attention, mainly in newspapers. Their displacement as refugees and the human rights abuses they endured faded into the background of the chaos and violence that dominated the aftermath of the second Iraq war.

The Yazidis are spread around several countries in their hundreds of thousands: Syria, Georgia, Kurdish Armenia, northwestern Iran and northern Iraq, where their most sacred shrine is in the Yazidi town of Lalish. There are now even scattered individuals and families in the West. Although the Yazidis may be perceived as an ethnicity, they are primarily a religious group. Many Yazidis are ethnically Kurdish (although some deny this) and most speak Kurmanji, the Kurdish language. They have odd taboos: not to eat lettuce or fish and not to wear blue clothing. This prohibition of the colour blue was also upheld by Mandaeans in the past, and has not been explained satisfactorily.

Possibly their most famous taboo is their inability to move outside of a circle that has been drawn around them. This inspired the title of Bertolt Brecht's play *Caucasian Chalk Circle* and from G.I. Gurdjieff's 1888 account from Alexandropol in Armenia:

> *In the middle of a circle drawn on the ground stood one of the little boys, sobbing and making strange movements, and the others were standing at a certain distance laughing at him. I was puzzled and asked what it was all about.*

> *I learned that the boy in the middle was a Yezidi [sic], that the circle had been drawn round him and that he could not get out of it until it was rubbed away. The child was indeed trying with all his might to leave this magic circle, but he struggled in vain. I ran up to him and quickly rubbed out part of the circle, and immediately he dashed out and ran away as fast as he could.*

> *This so dumbfounded me that I stood rooted to the spot for a long time as if bewitched, until my usual ability to think returned. Although I had already heard something about these Yezidis, I had never given them any thought; but this astonishing incident, which I had seen with my own eyes, now compelled me to think seriously about them.*

... Many years after the incident just described, I made a special experimental verification of this phenomenon and found that, in fact, if a circle is drawn round a Yezidi, he cannot of his own volition escape from it. Within the circle he can move freely, and the larger the circle, the larger the space in which he can move, but get out of it he cannot. Some strange force, much more powerful than his normal strength, keeps him inside. I myself, although strong, could not pull a weak woman out of the circle; it needed yet another man as strong as I.

If a Yezidi is forcibly dragged out of a circle, he immediately falls into the state called catalepsy, from which he recovers the instant he is brought back inside. But if he is not brought back into the circle, he returns to a normal state, as we ascertained, only after either thirteen or twenty-one hours.[2]

Their sacred places are caves, or shrines with conical roofs. The four elements have an important role in their cosmology – particularly fire, which is represented by the fires lit in their shrines. Melek Taus, the Peacock Angel, is the central divine figure of the Yazidis. He is also called Iblis or Azazael, which are names for the devil in Islam. Thus the Yazidis are called devil-worshippers. However, they are no Satanists: even to say the name *Shaitan* is absolutely forbidden, and so offensive to Yazidis' ears that they were until modern times, at least in principle, compelled to kill anyone who said the name.[3] Like Lucifer, Melek Taus fell from grace but subsequently redeemed himself by repenting for his sins to such an extent that he wept for 7,000 years, filling seven jars with his tears, which were then used to extinguish the fires of hell. Melek Taus thus became the entity who is worshipped by the Yazidis.

Sheikh Adi bin Musafir, a Sufi born around 1075, is credited as a reformer of Yazidism, although not as the founder. That may be a mysterious figure named Sultan Ezid or Yezid. Ezid has been identified with a number of figures, from God himself to Caliph Yezid, an early Sunni ruler from whom Yazidis in Shia-dominated areas have been keen to distance themselves. These explanations have the ring of after-the-fact rationalization about them.

To Western scholars, little seems certain about Yazidism. The supposed sacred texts of the Yazidis, which were translated from Kurdish and published early in the 20th century, appear to have been fakes invented to satisfy Western curiosity. That is, although they may represent Yazidi beliefs, they are not actually the sacred scriptures of the Yazidis. It seems that, like the Mandaeans, Yazidis have often told outsiders what they want to hear.

Yazidi religion, in common with Mandaeism and other long-lived minority Middle Eastern religions, has an esoteric inner circle priesthood and a laity who are not privy to the true mysteries of their faith.

The intervention of Sheikh Adi bin Musafir in Yazidi history is somewhat reminiscent of that of John the Baptist in Mandaeism. Just as John gives the Mandaeans a Christian connection, so the sheikh gives the Yazidis a Muslim lineage. Further, the connection may be a real, historical one, although the Yazidis also preserve pre-Islamic beliefs and rituals with Kurdish, Mesopotamian and Zoroastrian features. These aspects may stretch back thousands of years earlier than the association with Sufism.

The Yazidis are not usually classified as Gnostic, after the type of religion that emerged out of the Judaeo–Hellenistic world, although the distant transcendent God about whom little can be said and the similarity of Melek Taus to a hybrid Sophia and redeemed–redeemer figure suggests some affinity with Gnosticism. In the redemption of the devil and his conversion into a redeemer figure perhaps we find an example of the inverse exegesis that is familiar in Gnosticism.

Although the Yazidis and Mandaeans mostly lived in different areas of Iraq, they certainly encountered each other. In one extraordinary collision of religions, a Mandaean told Lady Drower, the English scholar and friend of Mandaeans, that Melek Taus wrote the Jewish Torah.[4] This must be an adaptation of the idea that the devil wrote the Torah, with the devil then being translated into Yazidi terms, although inaccurately.

Alawites

The most prominent of the region's minority religions are probably the Alawites. In common with the Mandaeans and Yazidis, the Alawites reserve full knowledge of their teachings for an inner circle and the laity are not privy to the esoteric teachings. They also have the distinction – which has, alas, been a dubious one – of having some real political power via the Syrian leader Bashir al-Assad, who is Alawite.

The Alawites are Muslim, albeit a particularly distinctive branch of that major religion. They are Shia Muslims, the branch of Islam to which around one-fifth of the world's Muslims belong. Their own position within the world of Shia Islam is a quirky one. Shia Islam owes its existence to the schism in Islam that occurred after the murder of Ali, the cousin of Muhammad who was the fourth caliph and the first Shia Imam. Shiites are followers of Ali's branch of Islam. Most Shiites specifically acknowledge 12 Shia Imams, leading to them being known as Twelvers. A minority of Shiites acknowledge only the first six of the Imams and then trace an alternative lineage of Imams; these Shiites are known as Seveners, or Ismailis, because of their belief that Jafar al-Sadiq was the seventh Imam (rather than the Twelvers' Musa al-Kadhim).

The Alawites believe in reincarnation, as do the Druze and the Yazidis, but not the Mandaeans.[5] Like Christians, Alawites believe in a kind of trinity, but theirs has three divine beings who most recently incarnated as Ali, Muhammad and Salman the Persian. They also hold a form of communion using wine. Planetary observances have a vestigial role in Alawite religion. Their holy books are still largely secret and unseen by Westerners, but they are said to include a list of holy men that includes not only Muhammad and his successors, along with the preceding Abrahamic prophets honoured by Islam (such as Jesus, Moses and so on), but also Greek pagan figures such as Plato and Alexander the Great.

Assad has attempted to paper over these differences with mainstream Islam and to suppress the esoteric elements of Alawite religion, persecuting some of his own people. Were it not for the efforts of Alawites over the centuries to claim membership of the wider Muslim community, they would now be in the position of other minority religions in the Middle East. The Alawites have supported Assad in the civil war in Syria, resulting in around one-third of young Alawite men being killed. The actions of Assad have resulted in there being little sympathy for Alawites in the West and they have not figured prominently in reporting of the Syrian refugee crisis.

Druze

Sometimes confused with the Alawites, the Druze also believe in reincarnation and can also claim to be a heterodox form of Islam. The Druze have extensive communities in Syria (more than half their total population) and Lebanon (around one-quarter). They also have populations in Israel and Jordan, and some New World diaspora communities. They speak Arabic, as do most modern Mandaeans, apart from those in Iran who speak modern Persian (Farsi). For those of us in the English-speaking world it is perhaps difficult to appreciate the overlapping, converging and diverging aspects of identity in the Middle East. Language, location and religion may each provide commonality with or distinction from others living in the same country, which may be bolstered or diminished by changing politics.

A Druze living in Israel can speak Arabic, the language of the Quran, in common with masses of people in other Middle Eastern countries, yet serve in the Israel Defense Forces unlike their fellow Arabic-speaking Muslim Palestinians. A Mandaean in Iraq could also share the language of the Arab majority, be unable to understand an Iranian Mandaean who lives in a country that has regularly and recently been at war with his own, consider himself primarily an Iraqi and yet would share a strong religious and ethnic background with the Iranian Mandaean.

The Druze also self-define as a Muslim sect, although like the Alawites their religion contains syncretistic features. They give prominence not to Moses but to Jethro, a Midianite priest and the father-in-law of Moses, who appears chiefly in Exodus 18. He is seen as a divine revealer, a prophet and an ancestor of the Druze. The distinctive features of Druzism are a cosmology influenced by Pythagorean and Neoplatonic philosophy, combined with a liberal interpretation of the obligations of Islam, which are particularly lax for the laity. A local speciality dish of the Lebanese mountain Druze is a small pig cooked in wine, which would be absolutely anathema for any orthodox Muslim. Immediately before the Arab Muslim invasion of Syria, the area had been a longstanding part of the Hellenistic world, hence the legacy of Greek philosophy.

The Druze follow the now-familiar model of a laity defined more by their membership of an ethnic group or social community than by their beliefs or even their practices. The one important compulsion for lay people is to marry within the Druze community. There is considerable pressure on Mandaeans to marry other Mandaeans too, and those who marry outside the community may even be considered apostate. Many young Mandaean adults in Australia and Canada use the Internet to help them to marry within their own religious community.

The Druze clergy have considerably more religious knowledge than the laymen and there are secret esoteric teachings. Purity and religious discipline is particularly accentuated in the priestly caste, who maintain Islamic food laws (no pork in red wine for them) and practise asceticism. In earlier centuries, the Druze had a reputation as fierce warriors and they fought on the side of the Muslims during the Crusades.

With a total international population of more than 1,500,000, the Druze are a sizeable minority. When I asked the former British diplomat Gerard Russell, author of *Heirs to Forgotten Kingdoms*, which of the many minority religions he had encountered had most impressed him, it was this one:

> *The Druze are such an intact community. If you go into the Druze area you're in an area of hundreds of thousands of people who live in a sort of exclusive enclave now. Nearly always did, actually, but the Christians who lived there have mostly left.*

> *When you look at the Druze community, it still is cohesive. But you've really got the priests, as it were, bearing on their shoulders the whole weight of their religion. I don't think that can easily last when the communities are dispersed, when the sheikh doesn't any longer live down the road, but the sheikh lives 100 miles away in Los Angeles.* [6]

Zoroastrians

Zoroastrians are better documented in their history than any of the preceding groups, although the ultimate origin of their religion is as hazy as any other. Theirs is now a minority religion having once been a powerful state religion in Persia, or Iran, for centuries. The native Iranian religion of extreme antiquity was reformed by Zarathustra (Zoroaster is the Greek version of his name), probably around 1000 BC. The historical details of his life are very uncertain and scholarly assessments of the dates of the reform have ranged from 1200 to 500 BC and he is at least a semi-legendary figure. What came after the reform was an organized state religion in which a single god was supreme and a dualism of good and evil was believed to exist, not one of the more Gnostic matter and spirit or light and darkness.

Zoroastrianism had a resurgence in the 3rd century AD. At this time it came into contact with the new Manichaean religion and effectively defeated it as a rival candidate for the state religion of the Sasanian Persians in the 3rd century AD. As we shall see later, the prophet Mani was killed on account of the political influence the Zoroastrian magi had with the Persian king. The Mandaeans were already in Iraq by the Sasanian period. Could the dualism of the Zoroastrians have influenced Mandaeism? Did the Manichaean religion have a formative influence on Mandaeism, or could it be the other way around? What exactly is dualism, and is it compatible with monotheism?

Monotheism

Each of the religions described above may be described as monotheist, albeit with a great deal of variation in the understanding and meaning of this term. The Mandaean religion is monotheistic too. This is an important point, because in the Middle East this can be a matter of life and death. There is no polytheistic element in the Mandaean faith. There are many spiritual beings, but this is also true of Judaism, Christianity and Islam, each of which has a range of angels, archangels, demons, djinn and so on.[7] Mandaean beliefs, as we shall see, may also be classified as dualist – but dualist systems may be considered a variety of monotheism. Zoroastrianism itself is classified as a form of monotheistic dualism.

My own interests have moved away considerably from monotheistic religion, which I find rather overrated. Monotheism can't laugh at its gods, and neither do(es) the god(s) of monotheism laugh at anything. The kind of monotheism espoused by most Christians, Jews and Muslims has considerable difficulty with issues such as the existence of evil. When the creator of the world is identical with the transcendent God, the transcendent God has dirtied his hands, so to speak, with the sufferings, disasters and abominations of physical existence. Nor does monotheism allow for the equal validity of all the psychic powers that make up the human being: sexual love, romantic love, pleasure, curiosity, tolerance, transgression and other qualities are pressed down into sins and demonic impulses under the thumb of the one God. When the God who is the fount of all being dictates laws and scripture, and invests organizations with authority, you can be sure that there will be trouble down the line.

Yet monotheism does have a strength, which is its conception of a single correct goal for humanity. Polytheism acknowledges the diversity of human psychology and needs, and the diversity of nature in its gods. Yet without some transcendent or unifying principle pure polytheism may resemble humanity in its worst features: unintegrated, bickering, petty, defined by desire and conflict. Monotheism at its worst is the religious equivalent of the totalitarian state.

Thus my own interests are in more heterodox forms of religion and spirituality. The contents of this book reflect my focus. But I want to emphasize that the Mandaeans have every right to be acknowledged as a form of monotheism. It can be a matter of life or death for them.

Abrahamic religions

It is common to refer to Judaism, Christianity and Islam not only as monotheistic but also as Abrahamic religions. Moses may be considered to be the founder of Jewish Law, even the founder of Judaism. He is also revered as a prophet in Islam. Moses is common to all three religions but is an essentially Jewish figure, responsible for the Exodus. Abraham, however, reaches further back and may be considered the recipient of the first covenant with God. Abraham had two sons, Ishmael by his wife

Sarah's slave-girl Hagar, and Isaac by Sarah herself in her old age. Jews trace their descent through Isaac. Arabs trace themselves back to Ishmael and, as an Arab, Muhammad is therefore a descendant of Ishmael too. Spiritually, every Muslim – whether Arab or not – may be considered a descendant of Ishmael, and Hagar and Ishmael are traditionally buried in the Ka'aba at Mecca. The descent of Arabs from Ishmael is probably no more and no less literally true than that of Jews from Isaac.

Christianity became a separate religion from Judaism via its denial of an ethnic element – being available to male and female, gentile and Jew, free or enslaved. Paul argued allegorically in Galatians 4: 24–31 that although Abraham's son by Sarah, Isaac, whom Abraham was willing to sacrifice to God until Isaac was spared at the last moment, was the ancestor of the Jews, allegorically he represented Christians, and hence the new covenant from God to the gentiles, whereas Ishmael, born of a foreign slave woman, and not a freeman, represented the current state of the Jews and Jerusalem. Although few Christians place importance on this allegorical descent from Ishmael, it is nevertheless a factor because Abraham represents a commitment to monotheism. Thus the three Abrahamic religions[8] each claim a kind of legitimacy from the sons of Abraham and he is seen as the common denominator between them.

The Mandaean religion may arguably be counted as Abrahamic. Abraham is often not a popular figure in Mandaean legend, being considered the leader of the Jews, against whom there is often much hostility. Yet he does occur in at least one folktale told to Drower. In this story Bihram was a Mandaean of an important priestly family who discovered a sore on his foreskin and had to be circumcised.[9] Perhaps we might consider the broader category of Adamic religion, religions who honour the figure of Adam (although Eve often does not fare so well.) Adam is the first man in Mandaeism as well as Islam, Judaism, Christianity, Yazidism and other religions.

It is a discernible pattern with the ancient religions of the Middle East that they are credited as having historical founders in early medieval times. However, they also have elements that are anomalous if they are purely heterodox Islamic sects, even compared to the more extreme varieties of Shiism. The Druze have the Pythagorean and Neoplatonic influences. The Alawites have reincarnation, some Christian aspects and elements of planetary worship. The Yazidis have aspects to their religion that connect them with ancient Persia. Far from being founded by a Sufi in the second millennium AD, the Yazidis may go back in one form or another for thousands of years. Many of these religions have rituals that could not come from Muslim sources but may instead represent the continuing hegemony of ancient pagan practices.

The situation with the Mandaeans is somewhat different. Mandaeism does not have a Muslim founder or even a Muslim reformer to justify its continued existence. Instead it has John the Baptist as its final prophet. According to the received view, he was a 1st-century Jew who was the harbinger of Christianity and a prophet mentioned in the Quran. Yet perhaps elements of Mandaeism too precede even John.

Dualism: Two powers in the universe

Dualist religions posit or acknowledge two opposing powers in the universe. Light and dark, good and evil, spirit and matter are common ontological dichotomies. These are often lined up with each other, so that the spirit may come from the world of light, which is good, whereas the body may be made of matter from the world of darkness and be evil. The focus of the dualism and its implications may vary considerably, as may the mythical structure that supports it.

The somewhat haphazard and unstandardized nature of Mandaean myth means that we may be able to find most forms of dualism within its tales, from a fairly pure straight monotheism to the kind of absolute dualism positing that light and darkness have each existed since the beginning.

Yet in each variety of dualism, only one of the two powers may be considered equivalent to God. Dualist religions always see themselves on the side of God – as light, of spirit, of good. Nobody chooses which side to take, although a religion's enemies may be seen as on the side of evil, just as apostates may be. The idea of a good power and an evil power being at war with each other, or competing to influence humanity, might not seem all that strange: what about God and the devil in Christianity? It is true that there is a dualistic element in mainstream Christianity, yet neither Christianity nor Islam nor Judaism are classed as dualistic religions. The reason is probably something to do with the proportion of power possessed by God or Satan. While the devil is seen as an influence on the development of the world and a significant risk for human beings, that influence is relatively minor, as was his original role before his fall. In mainstream Christianity the Earth is not the work of the devil, nor are human beings created by the devil, nor is there any question whether the devil has usurped God, nor that God is diminished by the devil, nor that the devil might be as ancient as God.[10] In dualistic religions – a category to which Zoroastrianism, Manichaeism, most forms of Gnosticism, Catharism, Bogomilism and Mandaeism all belong – two powers are in opposition to each other and the arenas in which this contest is played out are the human soul and the world.

If there are two powers in the universe, certain questions come to mind. Are these two powers equal? Was the situation always like this, or has one of the forces seized power? To which power does the Earth owe its existence? Which of the powers created humanity? Is the Earth a good place? And so on.

Perhaps the most basic of these questions is whether the two powers have always existed. There are various logical possibilities available – for instance, the two powers may be the children of an earlier single power; the original nature of the universe may have been Chaos, from which came the good power; there may have been many other powers or gods at an earlier phase but now there are only two – but the most important distinction in practice is whether these two powers have each been there from the beginning, or if the evil power is a later development. If the powers are co-eternal, the dualism is called absolute dualism. If there was originally only God as a single, unique power, and the evil power has fallen or broken away or usurped part of the universe, or is a result of the action of an angel, then this is known as a moderate or monarchical dualism.

In many forms of Gnosticism the creation of the material world is due to Sophia leaving the pleroma and giving birth to the demiurge.

Thus the situation of humanity is of spirit imprisoned in matter. The god of matter is the demiurge; the god of spirit is the true God. Spirit and matter are in opposition, yet matter is not inherently real. The situation is a temporary one and eventually all of the spirit trapped in matter will be liberated and the pleroma will be restored to its original fullness.

When many people encounter the Gnostic myth in one of its many versions their response is often to feel it is gloomy or, to use some of the epithets popular in scholarship over the years, pessimistic, world-denying or anti-cosmic. Yet, perhaps paradoxically, what might be perceived as a negative worldview does not necessarily have a negative effect on the participant. The Cathars of the medieval Languedoc saw the world as the work of the devil, the result of a fall from a purely spiritual heaven into a world of matter. The Perfect, the Cathar elite, abstained from alcohol, meat and sex, as did the earlier Manichaeans. Yet, by all accounts, they were much loved by the ordinary people of the area, including many Catholic lay people, and as a result people were willing to protect them from the Inquisition at great personal cost.

Similarly, the Gnosticism of the Mandaeans has not produced a community that is disgusted with the material world. Even allowing for a considerable amount of accommodation made over the centuries to the practical demands of living in the world, the Mandaeans have the reputation of being gentle people who have good family relations and enjoy traditional ways of life.

One of the questions brought up by any Gnostic myth is the role of nature. If we are told that the material world is a prison and the main purpose of human life is to have the spirit or soul escape from that prison, one of our first responses might be, what about nature? Isn't nature beautiful and bountiful? Isn't nature *natural*? We might object that nature is also cruel and unforgiving, or that eulogizing nature is essentially a romantic urban response, but there is something to it. Perhaps Gnosticism is the response of people who live in cities.[11]

Yet Lady Drower was struck by the Mandaeans' love of nature (although some of the following comments may display a certain amount of Orientalism):

They possess a genuine love of nature... An Arab, although he admires beauty in a woman or a horse, sees personal comfort rather than actual loveliness in a natural scene: a tree to give him shade, running water at which he may drink, a garden in which he may entertain his friends. But the darawish of Mandaean tales behold nature in a mystic light. They delight in Nature as apart from man. The birds are praying to the Great Life, the stars and the sun chant His praises in harmonies which the pure can hear. This mysticism enters into the action of daily life. If I give a Mandaean a few flowers, he murmurs as he bends over them (from my experience) the beautiful formula 'Perfume of Life, joy of my Lord, Manda of Life!'...

The mortification, dirtiness, and self-deprivation of Christian asceticism in its medieval stage are unknown to these joyous mystics. All that the Spirit of Life sends is a good gift, to be used with praise... Death does not exist, since the living and the dead constantly meet at the table of the ritual meal.[12]

The dualism of the Mandaeans can be an absolute one. Light and dark each existed from the beginning in their separate kingdoms. But now they are mixed. How did the universe come to be this way, how will it end, and what is the ongoing process in which humans are involved? It is the role of Mandaean myth to explain these questions.

Chapter 2

The Mandaean Myth

Myths grow in a variety of ways and in answer to many needs. The first thing to note is that there are many versions of the central Mandaean myth, with many variations and contradictions.

Lady Drower commented that, for a Mandaean:

> *The immutable and sacrosanct elements of his religion are the ancient rituals, baptism and the various forms of the sacramental meal. It does not worry him that there are a number of creation stories, contradictory of one another or that there is confusion in his heterogeneous pantheon of spirits of light and darkness. What does matter is that no rule of ritual purity be broken, and that every gesture and action prescribed for ritual shall be rigidly observed.*[1]

Good scripture is self-contradictory and inconsistent. Successful scripture not only allows conflicting interpretations and revisionism, it requires them. From the Hebrew Bible to the New Testament to the Quran to the *Book of Mormon* to Aleister Crowley's *Book of the Law*, scripture can be used to justify any form of community structure and any kind of politics. Scriptures don't make sense by themselves. They need interpreters and scholars, and new prophets, poets and artists and lawyers to apply their meaning to contemporary times.

A systematic way of dealing with these would be to summarize the version of the myth in each source then show which elements are earlier and which later, and illustrate how the myth has changed, how characters have been combined and emphases varied. This is well beyond the scope of this book. Thus what appears below is a composite myth, with a nod to some of the major variations. Elements of the myth will crop up again and again as we look at the history of the Mandaeans. What will become obvious is the myth's similarity in structure and outlook to the standard Gnostic myth described in Chapter 1.

Worlds and lives

Broadly speaking, Mandaean cosmology consists of four worlds: the Lightworld; the world of darkness; our world, the physical world, known as Tibil; and the world of ideal forms, the *mshunia kushta*. The Lightworld is there from the beginning, although further layers of it emanate as the cosmic process develops, and it is of day-to-day importance in Mandaean religion. The world of darkness is given little importance until it comes into contact with beings from the Lightworld. The physical world is a result of this. The *mshunia kushta* is also at a folk level a worldly paradise: it acts as a spiritual counterpart to Tibil.

This fourfold structure of worlds, while not terribly systematic, is evident in most Mandaean stories. It can also accommodate many various approaches to religious cosmology from monotheism to emanationism and many forms of dualism, while allowing for the existence of spirits, demons, planetary deities, celestial counterparts, divine revealer figures and just about anything short of actual polytheism. (There are also other worlds and other ways to divide up the universe, including a series of purgatories with planetary associations and the four 'Lives' described below, which may each count as separate worlds too if one is so inclined.)

The first book of the collection of scripture known as the *Right Ginza* (part of the great *Ginza Rabba*, better known simply as the *Ginza*) contains an extended elegy to the Great Life, which is very monotheistic in its approach. The Great Life, or First Life, is all powerful, all knowing and all loving. Everything comes from him. Yet the Great Life may be considered secondary to the Great Mana, who was in existence from the very beginning, 'When the fruit was still inside the fruit, and the ether was still inside the Ether, the glorious Great Mana was there'.[2] Sometimes the Great Life is seen as equivalent to the Great Mana, sometimes the Great Life is seen as an entity who has a separate existence in a way in which the Great Mana, within the great fruit, does not. The Great Life 'formed himself in the likeness of the Great Mana, from which he emerged, and made a request to Himself.'[3]

From this request an *uthra* (a heavenly light being, plural *uthri*) emerged called the Second Life. Also present at the beginning is the Yardna – the Jordan – a river of light, flowing endlessly. Through regular baptism every Mandaean maintains their connection with the Lightworld.

What is being addressed, in mythical terms, is the problem of how to obtain diversity out of unity: the relationship between the myriad aspects of the world we live in and the single source whence everything arises.

When there is only one thing, a unity (the world of darkness does not enter the story until later), all is complete and perfect – but all is static. Without the multiplication of entities, nothing happens; there is no story. And if there is no story, there are no human beings, who in every mythology are the dynamic aspect of the universe, through whom and in whom the cosmic drama is played out.

The mechanics of going from one entity to two must involve a willed division by the unique being. (I am putting aside for the moment the pre-existence of a world of darkness.) In some versions of Gnosticism this involves the One seeing himself as if in a mirror; the result is the existence of an observer and an observed – that is, of two beings where previously there was one. In the Mandaean story the Great Life made a request to himself – and it is from this action that all further beings emerge in the Lightworld. This process is known as emanationism. The second being is not created, nor does it have any existence independent from God: it has emanated from him. From that second being, further beings can emanate, and so on. Paradoxically, the Great Life has not lost anything of his unity in this process, but now a Second Life exists too.

Yoshamin, the Second Life[4], is also a realm within which the 'limitless and countless'[5] *uthri* emerge. These beings of light, who are somewhat equivalent to angels, are also known as *malki* ('kings' – *malka*, 'king'). A version of the Yardna flows through this world too, and the Second Life has dwellings in which the *uthri* live. Thus the Second Life resembles an ideal version of the Mandaean existence, with *uthri* living by the Yardna, just as Mandaeans hold their baptisms in their cult huts by the river. However, these *uthri* start plotting once they have looked towards the land of darkness and the great Sea of Suf.[6] The Second Life gives them permission to prepare another world but the Great Life, or the First Life, is not pleased by this decision. He brings into being Manda d-Hayyi, the 'knowledge of life', who has many other names and epithets. Manda d-Hayyi is declared the king of all the *uthri* and is without imperfection. He is tasked by the Great Life with rescuing the *uthri* from their attraction to the darkness. Manda d-Hayyi must descend into the world of darkness (described as being below the Lightworld) before the rest of the *uthri* do.

The Third Life is Abathur, who becomes associated with the progress of the soul after death, when purgatories must be journeyed through. He emanates, and is sometimes described as a father to, Ptahil, the Fourth Life, who is the creator God.

The material world enters the story

Abathur, the Third Life, ordered Ptahil, the Fourth Life, to create the material world, known as Tibil. Thus Ptahil is the actual demiurge but he is interpreting the directions of a level higher than himself, rather than creating a new world as an act of rebellion against divine authority. Yet it all goes wrong, as the creation of the material world always does in Gnosticism. Each of the second, third and fourth lives may be considered a demiurge to some extent, because each had a role in the creation of our world. Each is subsequently censured in the *Ginza* for his role in the unsuccessful creation.

The Great Life and the lord of light continues to be indirectly involved with the unfolding of the universe and the development of the world. He cannot act directly and cannot undo the creation of the world, but he can try to limit the influence of the darkness, which is why he sends Manda d-Hayyi to bind the ruler of darkness and limit his action. Ptahil – also at the bidding of the Great Life – created Adam from the material of darkness, but Adam was inanimate until Manda d-Hayyi helped to bring forth his soul Adakas, an abbreviated form of Adam Kasya ('hidden Adam'), from the Lightworld.

Thus the Mandaean view of the demiurge is generally somewhat softer than many Gnostic views. It is certainly more dispersed, with the blame being shared out among Yoshamin, Abathur, Ptahil and other *uthri*. In classical Gnosticism the demiurge is identified with the God of Judaism, or, to put it another way, the God of the Old Testament, the jealous God of Genesis. Ptahil is never treated this way.[7] However, in a parallel tradition somewhat separate from the cosmogonical myths, we find in the shape of Adonai something more like a nasty biblical demiurge. Adonai is the Hebrew word translated as 'the Lord' in the Old Testament. In the Mandaean collection of stories and discourses relating to John the Baptist, commonly known as the *Book of John* or *Book of the Kings*, Adonai is the God of the Jews and is in league with Ruha, the evil female spirit. Yet in other stories Adonai was at one time more benign and was worshipped by the Mandaeans. It isn't possible to tie each of these strands together to get them to make sense. It is in this way that these Mandaean stories are truly myths because they express the life of a community through story in a non-literal manner.

Uthri from the Lightworld

It is difficult to know how to categorize the *uthri*. Although they are entities from the Lightworld – the Second Life, the Third Life and the Fourth Life is an *uthra* – they are also realms in which lesser *uthri* live. This is one of those aspects of mythical thought that seems very odd to us. They may also hesitantly be described as deities, some of them as hypostases, embodying concepts such as life, light or image, each in a divine form. The tendency of the Mandaeans to create divine figures that are personifications of everyday items has led to entities that are palm trees, fruit, vines, garments and even half-man half-book. No modern Mandaean would describe any of these figures, apart from the Great Life, as a god. But one man's angel is another man's god; one religion's god is another faith's demon.

The interventionist saviour entities who are involved with the history of the Mandaeans and take their names from some of the earliest figures in the Bible – such as Hibil, Shitil and Anush – are also *uthri*. By the 20th century these *uthri* had kept pace with the times and 'mounted vehicles like ships that moved by electricity' in the words of one Mandaean storyteller.[8]

Darkness

Whether the darkness has existed as long as the light, or even came into being before the light, is difficult to determine in Mandaean mythology, which contains many irreconcilable discrepancies. The Mandaean myths always begin with the formation of the Lightworld, with the world of darkness only entering the story later on. The myths explain that Malka Dhshuka, the lord of darkness, self-generated and emerged from the dark waters, which might be interpreted as polluted water. This lion-headed king of darkness – reminiscent of the Gnostic demiurge Ialdabaoth – has the power to create demons and other evil creatures. Although descriptions of the underworld draw on many sources, they derive in part from the geography of Iraq. As an oil-bearing land, beneath the surface is dark and the water is polluted. 'Pitch and oil are the sap of the trees of the underworld.'[9]

Into this darkness falls the evil spirit Ruha, who gives birth to a dragon or monster known as Ur. In the realm of darkness, monsters emerge and evil angels are born as Ruha mates with her offspring Ur, and the malign astrological influences are felt of the Seven (the planets) and the Twelve (the zodiac). Ruha means 'spirit' and she is the intermediate entity who has fallen from grace and the light.

How is it that spirit – in the form of Ruha – can be seen in such a negative light? In Valentinian Gnosticism the human being consists of three parts: body, soul and spirit. The body is, of course, from the physical world; the soul is the intermediary; and spirit is the part that comes from the pleroma. In Valentinian Gnosticism the soul may be compelled to stoop down to the level of the body, which is attached to base physical needs, or it may ascend to be married with the spirit in the bridal chamber.

In Mandaeism, soul and spirit have the reverse values. *Nishimta* is 'soul', which is interpreted as the highest part of the human. Ruha is cognate with the Hebrew *ruach* (in the sense of living breath or spirit). It is possible that the choice of 'spirit' is a typically Gnostic inversion of meaning. Since the Holy Spirit is one of the members of the Trinity in Christianity, the positioning of Ruha as queen of darkness may be commenting on Christianity, at least in part. Another aspect of Ruha, apart from a personification of darkness, is the fallen soul. There are variations on the myth in which Ruha is partially raised up from the world of darkness by Hibil.[10] It seems that she has a vestigial role as the fallen soul who can be turned around by a messenger from the Lightworld and oriented towards it, even if she cannot ascend there properly herself. To a small extent she resembles Sophia of ancient Gnosticism, who falls from the pleroma, gives birth to the demiurge and is partly trapped in the material world.

Ruha has very much been a living presence in the world of the Mandaeans, playing a malign part in the ongoing drama of the world, including the tale of John the Baptist and Jesus and the destruction of Jerusalem and the migration of the Mandaeans. Ruha's colour is blue, which goes some way to explaining the former prohibition on Mandaeans to not wear blue (although not the Yazidis' taboo against the colour). A special reed hut known as a *mandi* built in the courtyard of the *ganzibra's* house in order to ordain priests is covered with a blue cloth (the *ganzibra* is a Mandaean priest of rank, somewhat like a bishop). The association is with Ruha, but its usage is an oddity in this context. One Mandaean told Drower:

> *Once a candidate for priesthood refused to put the blue 'aba above the reed hut, saying, 'Why should one put Ruha's mantle above all?' When he went down to the river to cleanse dates before eating them, something came and struck him to the ground. They picked him up*

and took him back, and he told them before he died that it was Ruha
herself who struck him. Yes, he died, although no sign of illness had
been upon him previously.[11]

There are other demonic, dark or evil beings in Mandaean myth. One
of these is Krun, 'the great hill of flesh who has no bones.'[12] Ruha was
responsible for giving birth to the planets too.

Revealing, redeeming and repairing

It was the task of Manda d-Hayyi to descend into the world of darkness
on a reconnaissance mission. He sees black waters, the 'woman Hiwath'
(Ruha) who 'speaks sophistry', the gates of darkness, dragons of all
shapes and sizes, the chariots of the sons of darkness and evil rebels with
weapons that they will use against the Place of Light. Manda d-Hayyi is
armed by the Great Life with the ritual garb and tokens of the Mandaean
baptism: the robe, the staff and weapons.

Adam and Eve

Adam Kasya ('hidden Adam') is the 'secret Adam', as Lady Drower put
it, the Lightworld counterpart of Adam Pagria, who is the material,
physical Adam. Adam Kasya may be thought of as imprisoned within
Adam Pagria – another example of a Gnostic use of Plato's idea of the
body being the prison of the soul. The creation of man is the culmination
of the process of creation – or begetting or emanation – that began with
the Second Life, Yoshamin.

Adam himself does not sin and fall, nor is Hawwa/Eve to blame.
The Gnostic understanding is always that the fault has occurred further
up the chain, and the great universal error or fall was made even before
humankind came into existence.

Adam is less important in Mandaeism than his sons Abel and Seth,
who appear as Hibil and Shitil and have an identity as *uthri* who answer
directly to the First Life. Adam is most notable for refusing to die when
his time has come. Shitil/Seth takes his place and becomes the first to die.

However, Hibil, Shitil and Anosh have exceedingly important
roles in the ongoing myth-history of the Mandaeans. Note that the first

two names end in the -il, suffix, cognate to the –el, which signifies divinity in other Semitic traditions. Hibil is often associated with Manda d-Hayyi as a revealer figure who assists the First Life and aids humankind.

Ascent of the soul

After death, the soul journeys through several spheres associated with the planets and Ruha, where there are purgatories in which the soul might become detained. The ascent of the soul features not only in ancient Gnostic texts, but also in Neoplatonism, Jewish mysticism and in mystery traditions. It occurs after death, but can also be experienced in a preliminary form during life. Again, this is a typical Gnostic feature familiar as the ascent of the soul. If the soul succeeds in negotiating these obstacles, the final stage involves being weighed on the balance of Abathur. This immediately brings to mind Egyptian tradition, but in the Mandaean version it must be proved (to Abathur) that the soul, including the weight of the spirit, has the correct weight, rather than that it is as light as a feather.

Not every soul can ascend through all the spheres/planes. Mandaeans believed that the soul descends into the foetus at five months,[13] so what of the souls of unbaptised children? In Mandaeism unbaptised children are sent to the realm of Ptahil, the Fourth Life and demiurgic figure, rather than to the Lightworld. It is not a purgatory for the infants but a kind of earthly paradise. Charmingly, this land has trees from which hang fruitlike milk-bearing teats for the babies to suckle at.[14] A lilith (female demon) named Zahar'il is responsible for children during childbirth. Her name probably derives from Venus/Ishtar, and as such she is a survival of pagan belief, but Zahar'il is believed to be married to the divine figure Hibil Ziwa (Abel).

It appears that the Mandaeans believed that this ascent of the soul only applied to their own people.

Apocalypse and exodus

In Mandaean myth the first humans of the first epoch are Adam and Hawwa. (Some Mandaean traditions refer to each epoch beginning with a single man and woman who have survived the previous age, and these variations will be discussed more fully in the section on Mandaean astrology.) At the end of this world and time there will be an apocalyptic judgment, when everyone will either be admitted into the realm of light or will be cast into a fire or the Sea of Suf – the 'Sea of Reeds' in Exodus, commonly known in English as the Red Sea.

The Exodus story seems to be important to the Mandaeans, but their version is subject to a twist. It is questionable whether this may be interpreted as inverse exegesis, which is a typically Gnostic way of dealing with Old Testament stories. To the Mandaeans, Moses and the migrating Israelites are the bad guys. Pharaoh and Moses were brothers but fell out with each other. The Jews suffered in Egypt and were led out by their god and Ruha. The twist is this: each year Mandaeans commemorate the Egyptians who died when the Red Sea closed about them.

Living myth

Ideas such as Adam Pagria and Adam Kasria, and of Hibil being Abel but having a spiritual existence before the Earth is even formed, may strike many readers as strange. These ideas are mythic. We no longer think in mythic terms or see the world in that way. In the Western secular mainstream, stories are fictional and history is factual. In popular Christianity the life of Jesus is seen as part myth, although conservative Christians believe that the annunciation of the coming of the Messiah by Gabriel in Luke 1: 26–38 is literally true. It is considered to have happened not metaphorically nor in a mythic dreamtime but in a way that is as literally true as the everyday act of buying bread in a bakery. However, aspects of the life of Jesus can also be used as examples of the life that the Christian lives, not just intellectually or emotionally but in reality and spiritually. Thus the Christian who undergoes persecution or suffering is reliving the passion of Christ in a small way. The Christian who at some point doubts or denies is reliving the actions of Thomas or Peter, and so on. One aspect of myth is therefore that of a living pattern, one which repeats throughout history and individual lives.

Myth uses story to understand the world. Carl Gustav Jung believed that mythopoeia, or the creation myths, was a largely unconscious process in which archetypes from the unconscious mind found expression through religious activity, creative activity, psychosis and so on. Although a place can be found in his system for all kinds of spiritual experience and phenomena, these are seen as the result of unconscious archetypes. These myths were not dead on the page. When Lady Drower lived among the Mandaeans, the myths were told orally, combining adaptations of the scriptural accounts with folktale elements.

Despite the complexity of the story I have given, it is in fact a simplified and streamlined version that combines elements from various versions. Over centuries Mandaeans told and retold their myths, which resulted in quite contradictory versions. Lady Drower records several examples of Mandaean storytelling in the 20th century in which new accounts of the myths were still emerging and diverging from written versions. This is a process common to all cultures. The story of Jesus' life exists in canonical versions only in the four gospels. But Christians continued to come up with new stories about Jesus and new retellings of those gospel stories for centuries. Medieval legends continued to add their own interests: not only were characters like Mary Magdalene and Joseph of Arimathea associated with the South of France and England, even the true cross on which Jesus was crucified had its tale told, retconned to link in with other biblical stories.

Even today, any children's version of the story of Jesus will harmonize and simplify the gospel story. Yet the life of Jesus is essentially enshrined in the four gospels of the New Testament, no matter how contradictory these might be. This is not quite the case in Mandaeism. Although some Mandaean scriptures may be considered canonical – such as the *Ginza*, *Qolasta* and the *Book of John* – there is no definitive version. As Nathaniel Deutsch put it, 'What's extraordinary about Mandaeism is that here you have this very small community living, really, in one place, they're producing this enormous variety of views that, if you were to take it all together, would show the whole spectrum of dualistic traditions, all produced by this one community over time.'[15]

This fluidity is common to most forms of Gnosticism. I have wondered whether the Gnostics of antiquity, such as the Sethians and

Valentinians or medieval movements such as the Bogomils and Cathars, simply didn't survive long enough to produce a static myth or definitive story. But this isn't true of the Mandaeans, whose religion is close to 2,000 years old or perhaps older, but at least 1,700 years old even by the most conservative modern scholarly estimates. It seems to be something in the nature of the Gnostic approach to the universe that resists etching scripture in stone. Writing was sacred – so too was the alphabet, which is unique to the Mandaeans, albeit with a close resemblance to other Aramaic alphabets. The myths were sacred but did not need to have their exact form preserved.

On the other hand, Mandaean ritual is very strictly defined, carefully practised and believed to be central to Mandaeaism – the sun around which the planets representing different myths revolve.

Myth enacted, ritual practised

Through myth, Mandaean ritual allows the participants to play their part in the cosmic drama. These practices and prohibitions are considered a matter of life and death. The weekly baptism renews the contact with the Lightworld. Breaking such prohibitions weakens or severs the bond to the Lightworld, so that repeated additional baptisms may be required.

Much of Mandaean practice is concerned directly with the body. The body has no part in the life after death, but as the vessel of the soul great care must be taken to discipline it and treat it correctly. As one scholar put it:

> *Adventitious pollution of the body both through its entrances and external contact is the subject of ritual care. What exits in the body, whether it is bodily wastes, semen, or a newborn, also pollute the body. The Mandaeans treat the body as if it is a beleaguered town and every ingress and exit is guarded by ritual purity devices. Consequently, a constant monitoring of the body's purity is the main religious preoccupation of the Mandaeans.*[16]

The most obviously notable aspects of Mandaean ritual are the river, the cult hut known as a *mandi*, the white ritual robe known as a *rasta* and other priestly garb and paraphernalia. The *rasta* is the distinctive white garment familiar from photographs of the Mandaeans. In Lady Drower's time the *rasta* was seldom pure white due to contact with river mud.[17]

The ritual implements and clothing are understood to have a direct connection to the Lightworld. The priest's staff is made of olivewood or willow. The rasta is of white cotton, but symbolically the rasta is a robe of light and the staff is a staff of living water. The priest makes two myrtle wreaths – one for his head, one to crown the staff.[18]

Death must be prepared for in the correct manner because this is essential for the progress of the soul; in particular, Mandaeans must not die in their lay clothes but in a special robe.

Some Mandaean books are made from lead, inscribed with a stylus. Buckley was shown one in Iraq – it was very heavy and its owner claimed that it was inscribed by John the Baptist himself. Books with pages of lead are not unknown in other traditions but for the Mandaeans this metal had a practical value: lead rolls and codices can be dipped in water without being ruined.

Baptism

Held on Sundays, with the crosslike *drabsha* standard planted in the ground, it is easy to see how the Mandaean weekly baptism ritual, known as the *masbuta*, could be mistaken for a Christian ceremony. In its full form the baptism is held by the *mandi*, around which is a reed fence enclosure. The water flows into an immersion pool via a channel, and out again back into the river via another channel, so that it may satisfy the condition of being living flowing water. In modern conditions the pool and surrounding area may be tiled and the water treated. The ceremony may be split into the actual baptism and the ritual meal that follows it. The baptised person first immerses himself or herself three times and then is immersed three times by the *tarmida*. Then he or she eats specially prepared pitta bread and water and is anointed with sesame oil on the forehead and face. A ritual handshake known as the *kushta* is made between participants regularly during the ritual, which may last for hours. The priest must drink the river water while immersed in it, and there are all sorts of purity restrictions, the breaking of which will invalidate the baptism and require often extensive rebaptisms and ritual purifications. The priest is in a state of purity during the baptism and has additional strictures. When Peter Owen Jones, the Anglican vicar who presented the BBC series *Around the World in 80 Faiths*, encountered Mandaeans in Australia and attempted to shake the hand of the priest, the *tarmida* had to back away and explain that it was not possible because he was in a state of purity. This baptism is at the centre of Mandaean practice and community, and variations on it occur in different contexts aside from the weekly Sunday *masbuta*.[19]

Priestly demands

The circumcised, the impotent and eunuchs are all banned from serving in the priesthood. The consecration or initiation of a priest – and, more especially, a *ganzibra* – is a complex task beset with strictures and ritual remedies. For instance, the novice priest must make his own bread, must live apart from his family, and must for a period stay in a cult hut built specially for his initiation. The most serious pollution of his purity is having a nocturnal emission, or wet dream. If this were to occur during the crucial week of initiation, multiple baptisms of varying numbers must be conducted. If he were to have a nocturnal emission in the first three days a special set of 365 baptisms must be conducted at the end of the week.[20] There are varying numbers of baptisms to be conducted if this occurs on the other days, from a triple baptism by three priests to 60 baptisms. If the wet dream were to occur on the final night the consecration must be delayed for a whole year. For a *ganzibra* the set of specifications is even more complex and arduous.[21]

Following the first stage of consecration the priest must undertake 60 days of purity, during which he must be immersed three times a day, eat no meat, make his own bread, keep away from public markets or baths or public toilets, always wear his undergarment and observe strict conditions under which his hair may be combed or he may remove the headdress. Like other minority Middle Eastern faiths, the burden of ritual observance and the reward of esoteric knowledge is largely confined to the priesthood.

Dying into the Lightworld

After death the spirit wanders three days[22] before ascending through the realms of the planets and the purgatories.[23] The *masiqta* is a mass for the dead – a solemn meal that lasts for eight hours. Weeping is discouraged at death, as is the ancient practice of tearing out hair, because when the newly dead soul ascends any tears will form a river that has to be crossed and torn hair will tangle at the feet of the ascending soul and hinder its progress.[24] Drower met an old man whose brother had died that day, during the five sacred days of the Panja New Year festival, a time when the soul could ascend more easily. 'His white hair flew in the wind, and his face was shining and ecstatic. "My brother died this morning! Splendid, splendid! I have forbidden the women to weep!"'[25]

It is the ritual of the Mandaeans that defines them visually: those evocative photographs of white-robed priests wading in the murky waters or immersing other Mandaeans. Their myths define who they are and what the world is. But there is one particular document in their scriptures that is of particular interest to us: the *Haran Gawaita*.

Chapter 3

The Mandaeans
Emerge into History

Once the Mandaeans emerge into Western history they are already in crisis. It is an ongoing condition for them. But it is only to be expected – after all, they live in exile waiting to return to the Lightworld. Most outsider interest in minority peoples is generated because they are regarded as an oddity or because some catastrophe has happened, and this much is true of the Europeans who have encountered and reported on the Mandaeans over the last few centuries. Most are surprised at finding a people who claim descent from John the Baptist. Centuries of sporadic Western contact with the Mandaeans allows us to see them from the outside, albeit through a distorting lens. But first a word on their language, which is the medium of all their knowledge and, along with ritual, of all their legends and all their history.

The Mandaic language

Mandaic is a dialect of Aramaic. Technically it is an Eastern, or Southeastern, dialect, sharing many features with Jewish Babylonian Aramaic. Along with Hebrew Aramaic it belongs to the northwest branch of the Semitic language group. The Semitic languages cover a wide area of the Near- or Middle-East. Aside from Aramaic and Hebrew, Arabic is the best-known Semitic language, the language of the Quran, spoken by hundreds of millions of people today, including many modern Mandaeans.

If Aramaic is mentioned most people think of the language of Jesus. It was surely true that he spoke Aramaic (although Hebrew and Greek are also possibilities) but in doing so Jesus was speaking the language of the conqueror. Aramaic was the language of the Babylonian Empire and had for centuries been the lingua franca of the Near East. Aramaic itself was so widespread for so long that it developed into different dialects in an extensive range of areas. Among the western dialects were Galilean Aramaic, Samaritan and a Christian Aramaic dialect. The eastern dialects included Syriac, which was used extensively as a literary language in Christianity from the 2nd century onwards, Jewish Babylonian Aramaic and Mandaic.[1] Many non-Jewish people may be unaware that the Talmuds, the vast compilations of oral and legal tradition that defined post-Temple rabbinical Judaism, are written mostly in Aramaic. The Aramaic of the Palestinian Talmud is close to the dialect of Galilee. The Aramaic of the Babylonian Talmud is very close to Mandaic.[2]

At this point the reader may be wondering what the difference is between a language and a dialect? There is no clearly defined distinction. As some have put it, a language is a dialect with an army. A dialect may be said to be a child of a parent language. What defines one language as separate from another is mutual incomprehensibility. Thus we may consider French, Spanish and Italian each to be a dialect of Latin, the parent language – but because they are mutually incomprehensible, they are different languages.[3] We might therefore find ourselves discussing Syriac simultaneously as a distinct language and as a dialect of Aramaic. Similarly, Mandaic is a dialect of Aramaic and the language of the Mandaeans. Mandaic and Jewish Babylonian Aramaic are very close and hail from the same region, although they are different dialects.[4] Because Mandaic is eastern Aramaic some scholars have argued against a Mandaean migration from Palestine. One might similarly argue that Aramaic-speaking Babylonian Jews did not originate from Palestine, whereas we know that they were exiled from Palestine in the Babylonian captivity.

A variety of linguistic features show that the classical Mandaic language of the texts clearly had very ancient origins. But there was also a spoken language, known as *ratna*, that was distinct from the literary language – and in the 1950s this language was discovered to still be alive in Iran. In the 1990s it was Buckley's impression that *ratna* Mandaic was still commonly spoken among Iranian Mandaeans but rarely among Iraqi Mandaeans. Many aspects of culture are preserved in language, but while it is very admirable that Mandaean scriptures are being translated into Arabic and English – because these efforts might help to keep the Mandaean scriptures relevant to the Mandaean people – it is only thanks to the efforts of the most dedicated Mandaeans and a small handful of scholars.[5] Mandaean writings are said to be full of wordplay and puns, which makes it difficult to translate a text and retain the ambiguities and subtleties of meaning. As an example, the Semitic root *qdsh* means 'holy' to Jews and Christians, and the Mandaeans use the same root in some of the same phrases (such as *Ruha d-Qudsha*, 'Holy Spirit') but with exact opposite connotations. Thus although Ruha is evil, she is referred to as 'the Holy Spirit'. Translating it literally perhaps gives entirely the wrong idea, yet how else should it be translated? Any Mandaean priest would have known that the natural Mandaean meaning of the term was the opposite of its face value.[6]

From scribe to scribe

The Mandaean scriptures are full of mythologized versions of the Mandaeans' history. These texts were copied by hand and it is only relatively recently that they have come to be printed in academic editions and in translation for the Mandaean diaspora community. The manuscripts tell a story beyond that of the texts themselves: they give the lineage of the scribes who copied the manuscripts from generation to generation. The source of these scraps of information are colophons rather than histories or memoirs. Colophons are a common feature of manuscripts and usually occur at the very end. Colophons at their simplest consist only of the title of the text, but often the scribe will name himself and insert a comment. Mandaean colophons not only name the scribe who made that particular copy but also may include a more or less complete history of the scribes who copied the particular branch of that manuscript. This is potentially a goldmine of information for any scholar who is able to put in the painstaking effort required to record and collate the evidence.[7]

Lady Drower

An extraordinary Englishwoman, Lady Ethel Drower (E.S. Drower, 1879–1972), remains the most important Western scholar of Mandaeism. She was a novelist writing under her maiden name, E.S. Stevens, and also worked for the literary agency Curtis Brown. Many of her books were women's romances set in the Middle East and published by pulp romantic fiction company Mills & Boon. She also wrote two travel books on the Middle East. She lived in Iraq from 1921 to 1947, where her husband was posted in Baghdad as a governmental adviser in the 1920s and 1930s during the British Mandate of Iraq. She visited Mandaeans on and off over a period of four decades and worked on Mandaean scholarship into her 80s.

As well as a fieldworker, she was a manuscript collector and even commissioned new copies of manuscripts, bequeathing the Drower Collection at the Bodleian Library in Oxford, the largest Western collection of Mandaic manuscripts.

Mandaeans remembered her fondly and some considered her an honorary Mandaean. She also wrote *The Peacock Angel*, about Yazidis, whom she investigated and befriended to a lesser extent.[8] Her scholarship, dedication to helping the Mandaeans and her acceptance among Mandaeans is perhaps matched only by that of Jorunn Jacobsen Buckley. Originally from Norway, Buckley is Professor of Religion Emerita at Bowdoin College, Brunswick, Maine. She has published extensively on the Mandaeans and two of her books, *The Mandaeans: Ancient Texts and Modern People* and *The Great Stem of Souls*, address many aspects of Mandaean scholarship. She has lived and travelled with Mandaeans and been made welcome by many Mandaean families, and attempted to practise Mandaean religion, or at least to fit in with the purity requirements of partaking in Mandaean rituals. Beyond this she has been instrumental in helping Mandaean refugees to migrate to the USA in the aftermath of the Iraq War.

There have been other particularly influential scholars in the West, including Kurt Rudolph and Rudolf Macuch, and in the present day scholars such as James McGrath and others who are working on the Mandaean lexicon project. But the achievements of Lady Drower and Jorunn Buckley particularly stand out. Many people find academics to be limited in their approach, but it really is true that without the work of Western academics we would know next to nothing about the Mandaeans. The preservation of texts and the work being done on the Mandaic language may also feed back into Mandaean culture and allow modern Mandaeans, particularly among the diaspora, to rescue their own traditions.

An earlier important historic scholar was Nicolas Siouffi, a European-educated Syrian Christian who later became vice consul at Mosul in the French diplomatic corps in 1875. Much of Siouffi's information came from an apostate Mandaean named Adam, who had been in the process of becoming a Mandaean priest but had abandoned his religion and become a Catholic. In such cases it is clear that the Mandaean view of Jesus – as an apostate Mandaean who left behind the rigours of his faith to found Christianity – worked on one level as a cautionary tale to discourage Mandaeans from becoming Christians, because the disapproval of Jesus' actions was extended to those of any apostate. It also illustrates the difficulty often encountered in getting Mandaeans to talk openly about their religion. Siouffi could only get an apostate to talk to him; he had no success with current Mandaeans.

Earlier still, a Swedish scholar and adventurer Matthias Norberg translated Mandaic texts into Syriac letters and then into Latin. Norberg's activities straddled the last decades of the 18th century and the beginning of the 19th. His theories about the Mandaic language were reputedly so quirky that his translations convey little of the meaning of the originals.

Norberg believed that a branch of the Mandaeans had remained near Palestine while the rest migrated to Mesopotamia. This group he argued was the people known as the Nizaris. An important but inaccurate historic account of the Nizaris was produced by Germano Conti of Aleppo in Syria, the 'vicar of the Marionite Patriarch of Constantinople'. There was certainly some common ground between the Mandaeans and Nizaris: each included ritual use of myrtle, practised repeated handshakes, and made a surrogate ritual sweet wine from raisins and dried figs (dates in the Mandaean case) macerated in water.[9]

Decimation and revival in the 19th century

Mandaean culture and religion only survived into modern times by the skin of its teeth. In 1831 cholera spread through large swathes of what is now Iraq and Iran, decimating the Mandaean population. All the priests died. According to the only estimate, there were just 1,500 Mandaeans left.[10] Bear in mind that modern population estimates are usually between 70,000 and 100,000, although some sources claim that there are only 30,000 Mandaeans.

Yahia Bihram and his cousin (who was also his brother-in-law) Ram Zihrin were both *shgandia* – not priests but trainees who had received a certain amount of religious instruction, a position that might be likened to that of a deacon in Christian churches. Many of the *ialupia* had survived, including elders. The *ialupia* were laymen who were literate and highly educated in Mandaean tradition. Yahia and his cousin convened with the elders to gather as much of the surviving oral lore as possible and to study the sacred texts and rituals. They received permission from the Muslim Arab sheikh who ruled the area to construct a *manda*. In the presence of the elders Yahia and Ram ordained each other as priests, thus continuing the ancient line in a somewhat unorthodox way. It was a question of bending the rules a little or seeing the end of their religion. Without Yahia Mandaeism would be an extinct faith about which little would be known, a lost religion of the past like Manichaeism rather than a threatened but living faith.[11]

Why did Yahia and Ram and others survive while the entire priesthood did not? The answer lies in the baptisms. Cholera is a waterborne disease and all Mandaean priests spend long periods of time in rivers, drinking the river water itself as part of the baptism. Spiritually and mythically the river may have been the heavenly Jordan of the Lightworld, but in the physical realm of Tibil the great Tigris and Euphrates rivers were thoroughfares of cholera, enabling it to spread up and down Mesopotamia.[12] Yahia and Ram, and other non-priests, were not exposed to waterborne cholera to the same extent as the priests. We have Yahia's own words from a postscript to a manuscript that he copied:

> And now, O our brothers that shall succeed us, know that in the year of Friday [sic], the year AH 1 247,[13] the great plague came, and not one of the ganzibras or priests survived, and many people departed the body. Then, when the world was quieter and there was calm, (we) literates arose on the Day of Parwanaiia and we prayed the 'Devotions', and we consecrated a cult-hut. After the consecration, one esteemed yalufa (literate) set the crown on one of the yalufas in the cult-hut. He prayed the 'Devotions' for sixty days, and celebrated a masiqta for his teacher, and they consecrated one another, one by one (as priests).[14]

Yahia recorded – in the colophons to manuscripts that he copied – several accounts of the extreme difficulties of the Mandaeans and their fortunate survival as a religion. It is to scholars like Lady Drower and Jorunn Buckley that we owe our knowledge of these extraordinary sources, but it was a Mandaean in extreme circumstances who preserved both these historical accounts and his religion.[15]

Woe was piled upon woe. Many Mandaeans converted to Islam. The new priesthood fell out with local Mandaeans three or four years after the plague and Yahia and others had to leave their homes.[16] Carrying nearly all his belongings with him, Yahia was attacked by Arab robbers and ended up losing nearly everything. By 1837 Yahia's family had rejoined him but his daughter died and Yahia was unable to muster the four Mandaean bier-carriers that were required for a proper funeral (and for Mandaeans the correct funeral observations are essential for the deceased to travel properly to the Lightworld).

Yahia spent much time travelling – escaping troubles but also teaching surviving Mandaeans and doing his best to maintain the religion. Yahia worked mainly in southern Babylonia, Ram in Khuzestan over the modern-day border into Iran. In Margab, a year after Yahia had settled there, the local Bedouin sheikh ordered all of the Mandaeans to be circumcised: not just the men and boys, but the women and girls too. Mandaeans are uncircumcised and according to their traditions any mutilation traditionally barred them from the Mandaean community. Despite the religious taboo against the mutilated, the larger Mandaean community took the abused population of Margab back in and allowed them to be baptised. Yahia himself was fortunate enough not to suffer circumcision.

Yahia began to believe that he was living in the last of the four Mandaean ages, full of the harsh sufferings that would precede the apocalypse. He was oppressed by the seven, the twelve and the five, the malign astrological influences of the seven classical planets, the zodiac and the five planets that were, minus the sun and moon, sometimes counted as a separate group with their own origins and powers.

Yahia Bihram copied his final scroll in 1867, according to the surviving evidence. He had been born around 1800. His year of death does not seem to be recorded but he lived a long life considering the obstacles that he encountered. Without him the Mandaeans would probably not exist in a recognizable form today and most of them, lacking the structure so essential to their religion, would probably have succumbed to the pressure to convert to Islam.

Rudolf Macuch, a major 20th-century scholar of Mandaeism, opined 'the true nasiruta [*nasuraiia*] died in the 1832 cholera when the laypeople were compelled to take over the leadership'.[17] There is surely some truth in this: much of the esoteric side of the religion must have been lost. There is a whole class of Mandaean writings classified by scholars as esoteric texts, which describe the deeper significance of Mandaean ritual. Yet there were surely spiritual techniques and an oral tradition known only to the priesthood, or to its highest levels, that were exterminated by the cholera.

The Jesuits and India

Until Yahia's account there had been little substantial knowledge available to Westerners about the activities of the Mandaeans for centuries, since the first clearly documented encounters between the Mandaeans and Westerners had occurred during the great European age of exploration that began in the 15th century, when the Portuguese were in the vanguard.

Although the Middle East would remain off limits to European colonialism for a long time to come, the Mandaeans unexpectedly found themselves involved in early imperial ventures when the Portuguese captain Vasco da Gama arrived in India, at Calicut, in 1497 after his pioneering voyage around the then Cape of Storms (renamed the Cape of Good Hope).

Europeans were well prepared to expect groups of lost Christians sustaining, in isolation, their ancient traditions in distant parts of the world. In the mid-1290s Marco Polo was in India, returning from China via Ceylon. In Mylapore, now a district of Madras, he saw the tomb of St Thomas and discovered that there were 'St Thomas Christians' there who maintained the church, which was a pilgrimage site for both Christians and Muslims. Polo observed that these Christians took red earth from the place where the apostle was killed and gave it to anyone sick of a fever, 'and by the power of God and of St. Thomas' the sick were cured. (The use of earth from the apostle's tomb in the cathedral to work cures was reported as a continuing practice late in the 19th century.[18])

By 1498 the Portuguese had a presence in Goa, Diu, Malabar and other areas. The Portuguese began building forts and trading posts along the Malabar Coast and by 1515 they controlled the sea trade between India and the Persian Gulf, having established a series of bases between Ormuz (Hormuz) and the western coast of India. In 1542 Jesuits began to arrive in Goa.

The discovery of St Thomas Christians in India led Jesuits in 1555 to assume that the Mandaeans were Christians because of their association with John the Baptist. The Mandaeans were happy to be represented as the 'St John Christians' that they so essentially are not. Odd shards of history have survived over the centuries: in 1555 Mandaeans in Goa claimed to be in contact with the Syrian patriarch; in 1595 an Italian Jesuit mentioned the Mandaeans as Sabi – a version of Sabian, the name used by

Muslims for the Mandaeans; and in 1615 a Mandaean claimed that they were Christians who, 150 years earlier, had broken with the patriarch of Babylon.[19] The title of St John Christians would stick.[20] Lady Drower recalled: 'During the British occupation and the early days of the mandate, as one walked between the Subbi silver-shops in River Street, Baghdad, one sometimes saw a board announcing the proprietor to be a "St. John Christian".'[21] In possibly the earliest Western reference, in 1290 Ricoldo da Montecroce (a Tuscan Dominican, also known as Ricoldo Pennini) described Mandaeans in Mesopotamia:

> *A very strange and singular people, in terms of their rituals, lives in the desert near Baghdad; they are called Sabaeans. Many of them came to me and begged me insistently to go and visit them. They are a very simple people and they claim to possess a secret law of God, which they preserve in beautiful books. Their writing is a sort of middle way between Syriac and Arabic. They detest Abraham because of circumcision and they venerate John the Baptist above all. They live only near a few rivers in the desert. They wash day and night so as not to be condemned by God...*[22]

Such are the few references to an already ancient people. Although our story will take us away from Western sources and encounters, the first major contact between medieval western Europe and the Middle East must be examined. The Crusades led to a medieval Western Christian kingdom on the otherwise Muslim-dominated eastern shores of the Mediterranean. Could there have been an encounter with the Mandaeans at that time? Could the Mandaeans have met the Knights Templar?

Chapter 4

Those Ubiquitous
Knights Templar

The Knights Templar, or the Poor Fellow-Soldiers of Christ and of the Temple of Solomon, remain one of the most fascinating organizations of the medieval world. Founded as a religious military order around 1119, in the aftermath of the First Crusade, by Hugues de Payens and eight knights who were related to him, their initial purpose was stated to be the protection of pilgrims en route to the Holy Land. Jerusalem had been captured in 1099 during the First Crusade and was part of the newly established Christian kingdom of Outremer. King Baldwin II of Jerusalem gave the Knights Templar, or Templars, permission to establish a headquarters on the Temple Mount. The Templars were celibate and took vows of obedience and poverty; as warrior monks, they were unyielding soldiers and superb tacticians. Sanctioned by the Church and promoted by Bernard de Clairvaux, they soon became a powerful force in Western Christendom. The Templars owed allegiance to no one but the pope, owned extensive properties throughout western Europe and had established a banking system that accrued massive wealth.

After the loss of Jerusalem, the Holy Land and the end of the Crusades their star began to wane. On Friday 13 October 1307 the Grand Master Jacques de Molay and other leading Knights Templar were arrested at the behest of King Philip IV of France. Among the charges were heresy, seemingly confirmed by confessions from those interrogated, and the order was disbanded. The remaining Templars were arrested, the order's assets seized and its leaders burned alive at the stake. After the discovery of the Chinon Parchment in 2001, it was learned that Pope Clement V had absolved the order of heresy, and it is now the official line of the Roman Catholic Church that the Knights Templar were treated unjustly.

The Knights Templar have been blessed, or cursed, with a dramatic story arc. Their white mantle adorned with the large red cross, worn over chainmail armour, is as well known today as it ever was. When I was a child I had a plastic figure about an inch high of a Knights Templar Crusader. Now it is video games, like the extraordinarily popular *Assassin's Creed* series, which perpetuate the image of the Templars. Yet their main appeal lies in the fact that many researchers, usually outside of the mainstream of professional or academic history, maintain that there are unsolved mysteries concerning the Knights Templar and their beliefs and practices.

Why the Knights Templar?

So why should the Knights Templar have any part in the history of the Mandaeans? As Umberto Eco famously had his character Casaubon say in his conspiracy-theorizing spoof *Foucault's Pendulum*: 'The Templars have something to do with everything.'[1] One might add that as Eco's quote is now mentioned in almost every book on the Knights Templar, *Foucault's Pendulum* now has something to do with everything. If you look in the index of any academic work on the Mandaeans you will find no mention of the Knights Templar. The period during which the Templars were active in the East, up to around 1300, is several centuries before the Mandaeans' first notable historical encounter with Westerners. For the most part the Knights Templars clung to the Mediterranean Coast of Syria and the Holy Land, whereas the Mandaeans lived hundreds of miles away, a journey that involved crossing either mountain terrain – a substantial detour in itself – or harsh, seemingly endless desert. It would seem, initially, that trying to make a connection between the Mandaeans and the Knights Templar is as unpromising as the prospect of undertaking any of these journeys.

Yet there are odd little connections between the two groups. Additionally, some unorthodox theories have been proposed by alternative researchers. These are more suggestive than definitive and may prove unlikely in the final analysis, but they deserve to be explored.

Connecting to the sacred

Each Knights Templar wore a thin cord of linen outside his clothes[2] and had vowed never to remove this cord. It seems that the meaning of this practice changed over the generations. Initially, it had been connected with restrictions against nakedness, connected with the vow of chastity. While the knight wore this strip of linen he was symbolically clothed and would therefore be reminded of his vow of chastity (so the reasoning went). Eventually this meaning was forgotten and the threads became a kind of relic believed to have a connection with sacred sites, usually related to the life of Jesus. For example, linen would be pressed against the pillar in Nazareth that marked the spot where Mary received the annunciation from the angel Gabriel. During the trial of the Knights Templar witnesses claimed that these linen threads had been brought into contact with the mysterious bearded idol of the Knights Templar. This alleged practice is surely identical in its principles with the practice of sacralizing the linen by contact with the sacred sites of Christianity? The crucial difference is that one was perceived as acceptable, the other not.

The Knights Templar were obsessed with relics, a medieval trade that now seems ludicrous to those of a rationalist, or even a Protestant, bent; indeed, it is a humourless soul who is not tempted to mock the numerous foreskins of Jesus that were preserved in relic boxes around Christendom. Yet relics are silly as well as sacred.

Of course, despite the venality and cupidity and rapacity and dishonesty of the medieval trade in relics, there was a widespread appreciation of relics and they had a real power to them. Even today, contact with a relic is seen by the devout as sanctifying. Anyone who has ever had a lucky charm or a protective amulet might understand this belief.

In its essence, a devotion to relics is a form of magical practice. The only difference between the bone of a saint kept in a church and a pagan amulet worn to protect against a curse is that the former is approved of by the Church whereas the latter is prohibited by the same institution.

It was Ian Wilson, in his popular book *The Turin Shroud*, first published in 1978, who made the connection between the Turin Shroud and the Knights Templar.

There is no direct evidence that the Knights Templar ever possessed the linen cloth now known as the Turin Shroud. However, there is much that is suggestive, in the manner of the best historical detective story. As with the best mysteries the facts are enticing but inconclusive. What is not really in dispute is whether the Knights Templar owned mysterious artefacts and magical items: they did. What is controversial is whether these items were those that the Church approved of or not.

The Templars' strong interest in collecting relics is well established. So too is the earliest historical reference to the Turin Shroud, which was first displayed in 1357 by the widow of a French knight in the area of Troyes – renowned as a centre of Knights Templar activity. The link to the Templars is suggested by the name of the knight whose widow displayed the shroud: Geoffrey de Charny. Another Geoffrey de Charny was burned at the stake with Jacques de Molay, the last head of the Knights Templar, in 1314. It has been argued that the later Geoffrey was the nephew of the first. Thus the suggestion is that after the suppression of the Knights Templar it was the de Charnys who inherited the shroud.

A relic of 'the linen in which our lord Jesus Christ was wrapped after his death and before the resurrection' was looted from Constantinople during the Fourth Crusade in 1204. It is not certain that this shroud is identical to the Turin Shroud because several supposed shrouds of Jesus were in existence as relics during the medieval period. However, among the documents detailing the confessions of the Knights Templar is a testimony by Arnaut Sabbatier. He was taken to a secret room accessible only to Knights Templar. There he viewed 'a long linen cloth on which was impressed the figure of a man' and instructed to kiss its feet three times. This may have been some other relic in the large collections that the Knights Templar had dotted around western Europe, or it may have been the Turin Shroud itself.

A Mandaean shroud?

Once again, the reader might ask what all this material has to do with the Mandaeans? Extraordinarily, it has been argued that the Turin Shroud is a Mandaean burial shroud. The late Norma Weller, who was an art lecturer at the University of Brighton, proposed that the shroud was a Mandaean burial cloth. However, she didn't settle for the notion that this was simply a burial shroud that found its way into the relics market, either through a mistaken identity or through deliberate misrepresentation. Norma Weller believed that this was both a Mandaean shroud and the shroud of Jesus – because Jesus had been a Mandaean.

Her argument is to do with Jesus being a Nazarene and the Mandaeans being Nazarenes. We will look later at the complex web of Nazarenes, Nazarites and Nasoreans. Weller was arguing that the shroud is genuine and that Jesus was a Mandaean.

This is, of course, highly controversial. Not even the Mandaeans would accept this. They believe that Jesus was indeed one of their own but that he became an apostate. One of their accusations against him is that he didn't keep to their strict system of rituals and purity. If Jesus really was an apostate Mandaean – and they do not deny that he founded Christianity – why on Earth would he be buried in the traditional and required Mandaean style?[3] Putting that aside for a moment, why did Weller believe in the first place that the shroud resembles the Mandaean burial cloth? The shroud has marks on it that suggest a crown of thorns. Weller believed that this was actually the myrtle crown, the *klila*, worn by Mandaeans:

> *Myrtle was used in all ceremonies of birth, marriage and death, and to quote Helen Frenkley, Director of Neot Kedumin, the Biblical Landscape reserve in Israel, 'In Jewish tradition dating back at least to the Mishnaic period the myrtle symbolises immortality and success, because of its ability to withstand extended periods of drought and to remain green and fragrant throughout the year. Sprigs of myrtle were held by brides under the wedding canopy and conversely placed on the Shroud of the deceased before burial.'*

Myrtle grows wild in Judaea and contiguous regions and the plant is used in ritual in several different ways by the Mandaeans. The most important ritual uses to which it is put are the *klila*, the myrtle crown that is placed on the head of the Mandaean, and the sprig of myrtle that is entwined around the top of the *drabsha* banner that flutters when a Mandaean baptism is being held. Myrtle features in a wide variety of Middle Eastern traditions. It was claimed as being sacred to Aphrodite due to the 'yoni-form leaves'.[4]

Could there be a link between myrtle and Harran? Harran was the centre of an ancient copper industry and copper was sacred to Aphrodite/Venus/Ishtra, who, as we shall see, was one of the planetary gods worshipped at Harran. Myrtle also has its place in Jewish tradition, particularly during the festival of Tabernacles, the liturgy of which is referred to in Leviticus 23: 40, which prescribes the waving of the 'four species': willows, palm branches, myrtle and the fruit of the citron. According to the Talmud, which was a product of the Babylonian Jewish academies, Rabbi Johanan said, 'One who studies the Torah but does not teach it is like the myrtle in the wilderness'.[5] Norma Weller had also lectured in Colour Studies at Brighton Polytechnic and she applied a form of colour intensification to black-and-white photographs of the shroud:

> *The properties of this scale which uses no modifications but purely the spectrum of light has the effect when used methodically in relation to a monochromatic image, of so intensifying the tones as to make the face appear 'present' and 'alive'...*
>
> *It has shown that there is what would seem to be a wreath of foliage around the brow, particularly over the left side of the forehead. By a chance concatenation of circumstances, I happen also to have done, for my own purposes, extensive research on the Nazarenes and their traditions and have found some deeply fascinating facts about their customs of burial, particularly concerning the hierarchy of their community and the details of their rites, which at that time were completely sacrosanct, closely guarded secrets.*
> *The most elevated priestly leaders would be identified by a precise set of garments: (i) the Padân, or priestly Padama, a square cloth directly*

placed over the face, reminiscent of the Mandylion/Veronica; (ii)
the shroud itself, placed over the whole body; (iii) lastly, until now
unrecorded, and highly important to our considerations, a myrtle
wreath placed over the brow of the deceased so that it falls over the
left side of the brow.[6]

Weller also experimented with attempting to produce a shroud-like image using photographic means:

However it is to William Henry Fox-Talbot (1800–1877), one of the fathers of photography that I owe my methodology since his experiments in the coating of paper with silver nitrate and other substances to register an image, gave me my first insights into the workings of the Shroud.

By placing myrtle sprigs onto paper coated with a simple photographic solution and leaving them in sunlight, faint images appeared almost identical to those registered on the Shroud. What had happened was that the dark blue background of the paper had lightened, leaving the trace of an image fully visible.

Now the Shroud image was categorically not formed by a photographic process but by light and the presence of a three-dimensional solid body imprinting its form against a linen cloth.[7]

Weller was excited by the idea of testing this area of the shroud for myrtle pollen, but unfortunately only the periphery of the shroud was available for pollen tests. 'Regrettably all this will remain unproven unless the brow markings on the front and back of the Shroud could be examined for traces of myrtle.'[8] The clincher, she believed, was:

...the suspension on a cord of an iron ring attached to the myrtle
wreath and hanging down the side of the head (left on the positive
Secondo Pia photograph and right on the Shroud). This ring was
often attached to the bodies of the deceased as an emblem of the sect
and as protection for the soul on its journey into the beyond. It bore the
symbol of Lion, Bee, Scorpion and the Serpent of Eternity consuming
its own tail and was known as the Skandola.

Mandaean priests have two rings: the *skandola* and the *shom*. The *skandola* is made of iron with the symbols of lion, scorpion, bee (or wasp), and a serpent swallowing its own tail (or rather, mouth to tail). The other, the *shom* is of gold with the name of a great spirit of light inscribed on it. Some say that the lion is Krum and the scorpion is Hagh. These symbols are somewhat similar to those found in Mithraism but lack the bull, so central to the story of Mithra, and the dog. Any indication of this on the shroud image is of course very much in the eye of the beholder. The presence of 'certain unexplained findings of a metallic nature of particles of Iron on the Shroud described as 'exceptionally pure' in a former book by Ian Wilson' is, to Weller, confirmation that the iron *skandola* ring was present. Picknett and Prince's remarks on her theory are rather sharp but pertinent (see page 64). [9]

As intriguing as all this information is, and as beguiling as the thesis that Jesus the Mandaean had his shroud preserved and handed on down the centuries, I cannot find it in my heart to be convinced, much less in my head. According to the general consensus, we have an admittedly mysterious shroud for which there is no evidence that it is older than the medieval period and no evidence that it was in the possession of the Knights Templar, hence it could not be a product from the Middle East of the 1st century. Nor is there any evidence that it resembles a Mandaean burial shroud, nor that Mandaean shrouds were ever kept as relics. Any of the above might be disputed, but to me it looks like the possibility of Jesus' burial shroud being preserved by Mandaeans and acquired by the Knights Templar is thinner even than the worn linen cloth of the shroud itself.

The Templar head

Even if the shroud is unlikely to be a connection between the Knights Templar and the Mandaeans, no one can deny that both groups share a reverence for a particular figure: John the Baptist. Yet in one of those curious coincidences, Turin Cathedral is dedicated to John the Baptist.

Some pilgrims to the Holy Land were particularly attracted to being baptised in the River Jordan, reliving the baptism of Jesus by John. Such a baptism in the Jordan was also associated by the pilgrims with the healings of Jesus and the Jordan was resorted to by the sick.[10]

The Knights Templar's interest in John the Baptist is largely unexplained, and even downplayed. There was nothing intrinsically heretical at all in dedicating preceptories and churches to John, who was a saint of the Church and, after all, a major – if unique – figure in the New Testament.

Sacred skulls were part of the repertoire of medieval relics, with the purported skulls of many saints on display in shrines across Christendom, so a relic that both Knights Templar and Mandaeans could appreciate is the skull of John the Baptist in Damascus. It is reputed to be a place of pilgrimage for Mandaeans until recent times. Yet, as we shall see, the Mandaeans had no tradition of the beheading of John the Baptist. According to Mandaeans, when John died his head was squarely on his shoulders and, rather than being thrown to the dogs outside Herod's fortress, as we may presume would have been the outcome if the Baptist had been executed, the Mandaeans believed John had a full Mandaean funeral attended by his wife and children. On the other hand, we have seen that Mandaeism is able to contain different approaches to various matters without concern for contradiction. Mandaeans could well appreciate a shrine dedicated to their prophet despite a different understanding about the manner of his death in their scripture.

If the Knights Templar had had contact with Mandaeans, where could have it have happened? One of the stopping off points of the Mandaeans on their migration is said to have been Damascus. The crusaders had attempted to take Damascus during the Second Crusade in 1148, but had been unsuccessful. Nearly a century later, the Knights Templar policy was to support Damascus against their mutual enemy of Egypt, and in 1244 the barons of Outremer had backed the Muslim lord of Damascus against forces from Cairo. It turned out to be a disaster for the Templars and the Christian population – one of the great losses in the series of Crusades.[11] Yet these encounters illustrate that if the Mandaeans and the Knights Templar were to have encountered one another, then Damascus or its vicinity is a likely locale. As for the Knights Templar obtaining esoteric knowledge from the Mandaeans, the suggestion seems ambiguous. Mandaeans certainly had esoteric knowledge. They were also reluctant for even friendly outsiders to obtain much in the way of information about their religion. Yet we see from their documented encounters with Westerners that they were eager to make a good impression with Christians who might protect them against periodic persecution from the generally heavy hand of Islam. Once again, we can only speculate.

A ritual handshake

If we suppose that the two groups did meet, and that this influenced either's religious or ritual practices, what form might this have taken? We have seen that the importance of John the Baptist is one avenue. The shroud, if we are feeling exceedingly generous, might be considered another.

It has been pointed out that a ritual handshake is common both to the Mandaeans and the Freemasons. Who or what provides common ground between the two far-distant organizations, other than the Knights Templar? Freemasons claim a lineage from the Knights Templar, interpreted literally or legendarily according to one's lights.

It must be stated that a handshake is a very common form of greeting. I remember watching the Russian coup of 1991 on television in London with a Serbian friend of mine. Boris Yeltsin reached down from the tank on which he was standing to shake hands with a member of the crowd, an iconic picture. My friend explained to me that shaking hands is distinctively Slavic, seemingly unaware that handshaking is deeply embedded in British culture too. The point is that common human practices cannot necessarily be shown to be historically related.

However, handclasps are particularly associated with ritual, and there are several versions. The Mandaean *kushta* is intimately connected with the myth. For instance, Manda d-Hayyi receives the *kushta* from the Great Life and the *uthri* extend the *kushta* to one another. It is a symbol of faithfulness, truth and community. It was also known only to members of the Mandaean community. According to one scholar: 'This kusta [sic] is identical to the first Masonic hand-clasp. It is also reminiscent of the dexiosis seen on Greek and Roman funerary art, the art associated with the Eleusinian Mysteries, and the records preserved regarding the rituals of Mithraism.'[12] Yet it seems too much of a stretch to argue that the Mandaeans influenced the Knights Templar and that they influenced the Freemasons and directly transferred the secret of the handclasp down the centuries. The oldest attestation of the ancient Greek handshake is on a funeral stele from the 5th century BC, with two soldiers depicted shaking hands. Other roughly contemporaneous examples show couples shaking hands. The image of soldiers is interesting because followers of the Mithraic mystery religion, which was popular among soldiers in the Roman Empire, practised ritual handshakes and were known as 'those united by the handshake'.[13]

Mithraism was based upon worship of Mithra, the god of the sun in pre-Zoroastrian Iran. This element of Persian religion continued during the pre-Islamic Sasanian Empire, under which the Mandaeans existed from the 3rd century AD. Gerard Russell argues that the Yazidi handshake derived from, or had some connection with, the Mithraic one. He also believes the Yazidis bequeathed the handshake to the West, and it is thus their most notable and widespread cultural contribution: 'Unlike the Mandaeans, who lived in relative isolation in the Iraqi marshes, the Yazidis have been exposed to and influenced by many different religions and cultures over the past two thousand years.'

Russell sees more Babylonian than Jewish influence in Mandaean religious practices, so perhaps his conclusion is influenced by that. However, the Mandaeans have not lived all of their lives in the Iraqi marshes. They have also lived in Khuzestan in Iran, in Baghdad and Basra, and still do. As we shall see, their tradition of migration places them in a variety of locations. They were skilled silversmiths and goldsmiths – occupations linked to travellers and traders over the centuries. There is no compelling evidence that the Yazidis gave the handclasp to the West. Perhaps the Mandaeans are equally good candidates.

Many of the ancient minority religions of the Middle East have been tentatively linked with the Knights Templar. The logic behind this comes from the Templars' supposed heresy, which must have been contracted from somewhere – and because they were in the Middle East they must have been contaminated by some group from the region (since their 'heresy' is not distinctly Islamic, with the exception of the possibility of Baphomet being Muhammad).

A theory of Johannite heresy

A fascinating thesis is proposed by Lynn Picknett and Clive Prince, both good researchers, who have argued that a web of connections between the Knights Templar, Cathars and other mysterious groups amounted to a heretical underground Church centred around the figure of Mary Magdalene and including John the Baptist as Messiah. Influence originating from the Mandaeans has extended to this fascinating but rather hypothetical organization.

In many ways links between the Mandaeans and the Knights Templar turn out to be red herrings, false leads and false flags. The material itself is fascinating, even if for just about every putative association between the Templars and the Mandaeans there is a better solution just around the corner. If we allow ourselves – just for a moment – to suspend disbelief, what picture does it give us of the Mandaeans? A pacifist people who influenced the greatest warrior-monks of Christendom. A religion for whom the material world and body were a prison, yet which nevertheless revered the severed head of John the Baptist. The religion from which Jesus was an apostate, but which somehow gave him a full ritual burial and preserved a shroud that has miraculous properties. A people of which there is no trace in Europe prior to the 20th century yet it is claimed they are behind an underground Church that reveres John the Baptist.

There are mysteries enough in the other questions concerning the Mandaeans. Yet the Knights Templar can lead us forward to that next mystery. On 7 May 1104 an important battle was fought in the Balikh river valley in what is now southeastern Turkey. During the battle, the count of Edessa, one Baldwin of Bourcq, was captured by Seljuq soldiers. A ransom was paid and Baldwin was released. His fortunes improved and Baldwin went on to become king of Jerusalem, in which role he would grant the Knights Templar the right to base themselves on the Temple

Mount. The encounter was the Battle of Harran, a city that for centuries was known as a stronghold of the Sabians, the designation under which the Mandaeans attained some toleration under the rule of Islam.

The city of Harran would be destroyed in the middle of the next century by the invading Mongols. Some refugees from Harran are known to have settled in Damascus. Perhaps events are more connected than we realize? History sometimes only allows herself to be painted in broad strokes.

Chapter 5

Harran, the Hermetic City of the Sabians

If ever a city was destined to be the locus of romantic esotericism it is Harran. For centuries it has been a desolate ruin, populated only by a few Bedouin villagers, who have been moved in recent years to a nearby village. Most of the remains are merely ordinary houses, but even these are redolent of mystery: beehive houses, made entirely of clay to insulate effectively against the punishing sun, shaped like a combination of cone and elongated egg. Harran was an ancient city, a thriving centre of civilization even at the time of the biblical patriarchs. Abraham was there when he was still called Abram, having migrated north from Ur of the Chaldees farther down the Euphrates near the Gulf. He lived with his father Terah, his wife Sarai and his nephew Lot, until his father died and he received an instruction to go to Canaan, where the Lord would make a great nation of him (Genesis 12: 2). The beehive houses maintain relatively cool temperatures within despite the baking heat outside. The design is believed to go back to around the 3rd or 4th century BC, so Abraham, if he ever existed, would have beheld a different Harran. Historical Harran was destroyed by the Mongols in 1271.

Harran was particularly associated with the worship of the male moon god Sin. Conquered by the Assyrians in the 8th century BC, Harran would be the site of the last royal court of the Assyrian kings. In the 7th century BC it was the residence of Ashurbanipal after he lost Ninevah and later came under Babylonian control. Nabonidus, the last king of Babylon, was very supportive of the moon god Sin. Carved stone slabs depict him adoring Sin. These stones were used by Saladin – the same Saladin who recaptured Jerusalem for Islam – when he had a mosque built in Harran. The slabs were laid on the ground face up so that worshippers approaching the mosque were walking over the pagan images.[1] From one point of view Saladin's act confirmed the conquest of Islam. On the other hand, it allowed the cult of the moon god to persist through centuries in secret, the ancient pagan life of the city preserved beneath the facade of the new-fangled monotheism. The survival until the medieval period of the Harranians as a pagan people is in its way as remarkable as that of the Mandaeans to the present day.

Elusive Sabians

The association of the Mandaeans with Harran relies largely on their identity as Sabians, 'people of the book'. This term Sabian is intrinsic to the ability of the Mandaeans to survive Islam. Sabians are mentioned three times in the Quran: 'The [Muslim] believers, the Jews, the Christians, and the Sabians – all those who believe in God and the Last Day and do good – will have their rewards with their Lord' (Quran 2: 62).

In the second reference these other religions are specifically named as 'people of the book', who should look to 'the Torah, the Gospel, and that which has been sent down to you from your Lord'. For 'people of the book', 'there is no fear, they will not grieve' (Quran 5: 69). In the third reference Magians (Zoroastrians) are added to the list, but so are idolaters as 'God will judge between all these on the day of judgment' (Quran 22: 17).[2] The identity of the original Sabians[3] that Muhammad (or Allah, or the angel Gabriel) had in mind is unknown, or at least uncertain. Some scholars believe the people referred to were those of South Arabia, otherwise known as the kingdom of Sheba, famous for their Queen's encounter with Solomon in the Bible, which maintained a 'star-worshipping' religion until the coming of Islam. However, the Queen of Sheba is mentioned briefly elsewhere in the Quran, and because the Sabians are always mentioned in the company of the Jews and Christians, they are clearly considered to have some link to them as monotheistic or Abrahamic religions.

Sabian contradiction

The Mandaeans have often been known in Arabic in recent times as *subba* ('baptisers'). The 's-b' root comes from an Aramaic verb that exists both in Syriac and Mandaic, meaning 'to immerse' or 'to dip' and so on. Semitic languages have roots of usually three or four consonants. Variations on these roots, filled with differing vowels, give words that are etymologically connected in a way that is foreign to Indo-European languages. Thus it is possible that the original Sabians were baptisers known to Muhammad (or Allah, or Gabriel). It is entirely possible that the Mandaeans were the Sabians referred to in the Quran.

An examination of early Islamic writers on the subject of the Sabians produces a jumble of half-understood hearsay.[4] Among the contradictory things written about the Sabians is that their religion is halfway between Judaism and Zoroastrianism; that they pray five times daily, as Muslims do; that they are a Christian sect and that they are a separate religion. According to one writer they have Noah as a prophet; alternatively, they worship angels or worship the sun; according to another they have no cult, scripture or prophet, but if this were so they could hardly qualify as 'people of the book' in the first place. However, some of these points do match the Mandaeans: Noah is a figure in their stories; the sun, Shamash, often has a positive role; the Arabic for 'angel' is *malak*, the same word used in Mandaic for good and evil spirits alike, and in a cognate form *malka* is used to describe the *uthri* and the highest divinity. Given the nomadic nature of Arabic life and the location of the Mandaeans largely in the southeast of Iraq, it is not impossible that they really could be the Sabians from the Quran.

Harran had been part of the Byzantine Empire before the coming of Islam, and in 217 the Roman emperor Caracalla was murdered in Harran.[5] Its near neighbour Edessa had been a dynamic centre of activity for Syrian Christianity for centuries. Harran, by contrast, had been called Hellenopolis, 'Pagan City', by the Church Fathers.[6] A Christian named Egeria visited Harran in the 4th or 5th century, when it had had a Christian bishop for over a century, and complained, 'In the city itself, apart from a few clergy and lowly monks, who, however, stay outside its walls, I found not a single Christian; all were pagans'.[7] Julian the Apostate, who temporarily restored neopaganism as the official religion of the Roman Empire, visited in 363 and was happy to pay homage to the moon god Sin, as Caracalla had been doing when he was murdered. The people of Harran were clearly experienced in holding on to their pagan religion and temples.

With the Arab conquest of Syria and Mesopotamia in the 7th century (633–643) Harran became part of the Arab Islamic Empire. In 744 the Umayyad caliph Marwan II made Harran his capital instead of Damascus. Extraordinarily, although Harran was now in a sense a centre of the Muslim political world, the old paganism continued. The real intrigue begins in around the 9th century when Muslim writers begin to mention the Harranians as Sabians. The declaration goes back to a specific incident associated, as so often in human affairs, with violence. The Abbasid caliph al-Ma'mun visited Harran and threatened its pagan population with death unless they converted to Islam or could show that they belonged to another of the religions mentioned in the Quran.

Al-Ma'mun was initially displeased with their mode of dress, which involved short gowns and long hair with ringlets. 'Which of the subject people are you?' he asked.

'We are Harranians,' they answered.

'Are you Christians?'

'No,' they replied.

'Are you Jews? Are you Magians?'

'No,' they replied to these questions too.

When he asked them if they had a book or a prophet they stammered in reply and told him that they were unbelievers and the slaves of idols. When he asked them if they were willing to pay the poll tax exacted from non-Muslims, he told them that they had to accept Islam or adopt one of the other acceptable religions. According to the story, some changed their traditional dress and hairstyle, others became Christians, while still others accepted Islam. But a small number of them did not want to give up their traditions and religion, and after a consultation announced that they were Sabians.[8]

To qualify as Sabian 'people of the book' these Harranians needed to show both that they had holy books and that they were monotheists. They presented the Hermetica, the collection of writings attributed to the legendary Hermes Trismegistus, Hermes the Thrice-Great. A product of the very end of native Egyptian civilization, this blend of Platonism, syncretic paganism and practical mysticism is a distinctive product of the city of Alexandria. In its content and its origins, the Hermetica shares a certain overlap with Gnosticism, and is often counted as a cousin of ancient Gnosticism.

Thrice-Great Hermes

The core collection of Hermetic texts is full of references to deity in the singular: God, the One, the Father of all and there is even in Book 11 a statement that 'a plurality of gods would be absurd'.[9] The collection consists of several works with slightly varying points of view. This is, again, ideal as scripture. Works such as the Bible and the Quran are full of internal contradictions that require discussion and deliberation. Self-contradiction is an essential part of scripture. Without it a religion has no dynamic to carry itself forward via argumentation and reinterpretation. So the Hermetica was a suitable candidate for the qualification of the Harranians as Sabians and 'people of the book'.

Once the scriptures had been chosen the prophet was not difficult to find. In Muslim tradition Hermes is identified as Idris, who is mentioned in the Quran (19: 56–57), where he is described as 'a man of truth, a prophet'.[10] Idris is never associated with Hermes in the Quran but is traditionally understood as Enoch. Thus a useful identification of Hermes≈Idris≈Enoch could be made, one which stresses that Hermes Trismegistus of the Harranians was not really a pagan figure, despite his ultimate origins as a fusion of the Greek Hermes and the Egyptian Thoth.

The moon god Sin had been worshipped at Harran for millennia, along with the other Mesopotamian planetary gods. The planets were, of course, also forces in astrology. The planets are also important in Mandaean tradition, but their significance is a negative one. The names used by the Mandaeans are also Mesopotamian, and represent a continuation of Babylonian tradition. But the planets are associated with fate as limitation. This is a very Gnostic idea. *Heimarmene*, the Greek word for fate, is a force that limits and constricts people in this world. It is something to be escaped from. In some Gnostic traditions the use of astrology merely strengthens the negative influence of fate. We can see this in practical terms today. An incautious over-reliance on astrology can lead to an individual being trapped by the fear of the malign effects of cosmic cycles and influences: this is an astrology built on insecurity rather than understanding. However, it must be said that Mandaeans in all periods have practised astrology in general, although it is disapproved of in the official religion. (See Chapter 8, By the Rivers of Babylon.) It is not only the Mandaeans and the Harranians who preserved the importance of the planets: to this day, Yazidis and Alawites have similar elements that suggest the continuing influence of Harran.[11]

Harranians and Mandaeans

For a period the Harranians dominated any Muslim discussion of the Sabians. The term 'Sabians' became synonymous with pagans and it spread so widely in the Arabic-speaking world that even the Jewish philosopher Moses Maimonides referred to Sabian pagans. But with the destruction of their city, the Harranians faded from history. The quiet Mandaeans, surviving as best they could, were able to take the title of Sabians for themselves again. Today, with some of the least tolerant and least cultured forms of popular Islam active in Iraq, the Mandaeans emphasize their identity as 'Sabian Mandaeans' and hope any potential aggressors know the Quran well enough to leave them alone. Yet in Iran, Zoroastrians, who are mentioned separately in the Quran, have in recent years been granted a protected status as 'people of the book' at the expense of the Mandaeans, who no longer have a status as 'people of the book' and have lost many of their privileges that allowed them, for instance, to opt out of Muslim-specific education.

Perhaps those who argue that the Mandaeans have nothing whatsoever to do with the Sabians of Harran are protesting too much. The two traditions are certainly not the same, but in the Mandaeans' treatment of the planets as demonic figures we might be seeing an example of Gnostic inversion. Not only would the Mandaeans be distinguishing themselves from the pagans, but by overturning their gods and making them into demons we may be seeing in action the same attitude that converted the Jehovah of Genesis into the ignorant demiurge of the Sethians, or that turned Jesus into an apostate rather than a saviour.

However, Drower argues that the planetary spirits were seen as having both light and dark forms, and that the Mandaeans only honoured the light spirits because they were well aware of the malign influence that the planets and fate could offer. Even if there were no substantial connections between the Harranians and the Mandaeans, both religious communities were present in Baghdad during its golden era. It is difficult to believe that two groups that self-designated as Sabians could not have known of each other. The Mandaeans were arguably on a more secure footing with regards to their religion because it contained elements that derived from or interacted with Abrahamic tradition, whereas the Harranians were pagan. Although they acknowledged, via the Hermetica, the unity of God, in practice their temples were dedicated to various planetary deities and the ancient gods of Mesopotamia. We might expect the Mandaeans to have emphasized their abhorrence of the planets to distinguish themselves from the pagan Sabians.

There are, perhaps, memories of Harran preserved in the oral traditions. A folktale told to Lady Drower describes a community of dervishes in the north who 'till the ground, and harvest and pray. That is all'.[12] Dervishes are chiefly part of the Sufi tradition of Islam, but it appears that to the Mandaeans the name came to indicate any dedicated spiritual wanderer. These dervishes had no wives, and were probably vegetarian, had great knowledge of astrology and spoke Mandaic. A strange tribe meets them and the king of this tribe eventually gives everything up and travels to Jordan where he meets John the Baptist (Yahia in Mandaic). The tale then somewhat follows the story of John as told in Mandaean scripture. Lady Drower is tempted to identify these northern Mandaic-speaking dervishes with the Harranians. The point of the story would seem to involve some merging of the Harranian Sabian community into the Mandaean. When the Mongols destroyed Harran we know that there were refugees: some of them went to Damascus. It is not beyond the bounds of possibility that desperate Harranian Sabians, faced with the obliteration of their homeland, sought out those who were also called Sabians. Admittedly, this is a 20th-century version of a folktale, which in its telling combines several stories. But it is quite possible, as we have seen, that cultural memory can survive for centuries in myth and folktale. For historians the question is whether the claims can be corroborated. But it is at least suggestive of a link.

There is even an extant account by an 11th-century Muslim that distinguishes between the Harranians and other Sabians, who are very probably the Mandaeans:

> *Again, others maintain that the Harranians are not the real Sabians, but those who are called in the books* Heathens *and* Idolaters. *For the Sabians are the remnant of the Jewish tribes who remained in Babylonia, when the other tribes left it for Jerusalem in the days of Cyrus and Artaxerxes.*

> *Those remaining tribes felt themselves attracted to the rites of the Magians, and so they* inclined *(were* inclined, *i.e. Sabi) towards the religion of Nebukadnezzar, and adopted a system mixed up of Magianism and Judaism like that of the Samaritans in Syria.*

> *The greatest number of them are settled at Wasit, in Sawad-al'irak, in the districts of Jafar, Alja-mida, and the two Nahr-alsila. They pretend to be the descendants of Enos the son of Seth.*

> *They differ from the Harranians, blaming their doctrines and not agreeing with them except in few matters. In praying, even, they turn towards the north pole, whilst the Harranians turn towards the south pole.*[13]

There are other little connections. In the *Right Ginza* we are told that Noah's ark is constructed from cedars from Lebanon and ebony from Harran, showing that the Mandaeans knew of Harran probably before the coming of Islam.[14]

From Baalbek to Galilee

A 9th-century Muslim writer Abu Bakr[15] reported that the Harranians bewailed Tammuz, Sumerian god of food and male consort of Ishtar, goddess of love, fertility and war. The cult of Ishtar and Tammuz does not seem to have been central to their emphasis on planetary deities, although Ishtar is, of course, equated with the planet Venus. Some Mandaeans took part in Tammuz commemorations, to the protestations of Mandaean priests.[16] The cult of Ishtar and Tammuz was, it must be said, widespread in Babylon and probably survived into Muslim times.

Encounters between religions are not always defined by fear of authority and violence, or by enmity between communities. The Harranians had a temple at Baalbek in Lebanon, not too far from Druze settlements, offering the possibility of some transmission between the Harranians and the Druze.[17] If Muslims could tolerate the Harranians enough to allow some of them to live in Baghdad as scholars – some of them among the best of their period – then surely there were occasions when the Harranians and the Mandaeans could share their understanding of a transcendent God and His influence of the planets.

The intimations are that there were links between the Harranians and the Mandaeans. But they were not the same people and neither was one the origin of the other. Some scholars argue that Mandaeism only took on something like its present form after its encounter with Islam. The need to qualify as 'people of the book' made the Mandaeans adopt John the Baptist as a leading figure and make their religion look as if it might possibly derive from Judaism. It has even been argued that the Mandaeans did not exist before Islamic Arabs invaded Iraq, a claim which we will see has been disproved.

At least one scholar has rejected Harran as too arid a place for the baptismal Mandaeans. But if humans lived there – and they did – then there must have been adequate flowing water, and if there were adequate flowing water then the Mandaeans would have been able to perform baptisms. Today, Harran is desolate and what water there is comes from irrigation canals.

Furthermore, Harran referred not only to the city itself but to the whole region. There are several locations named Harran, Haran or Hauran. Edwin Yamauchi, a scholar, came to think that the Mandaeans originated not in Harran, but perhaps in Hauran, a mountainous area east of the Sea of Galilee and the Jordan. Both forms of name occur in Mandaean writings. The idea of this other Hauran might have legs, but the similarity between the names does not mean that it is either one or the other that has played a part in Mandaean history. A Mandaean sojourn near the Hauran range in Transjordania is not ruled out in the early part of the Mandaeans' story.

Chapter 6

'People of the Book'

No less controversial in Mandaean scripture than the depiction of Jesus as an apostate Mandaean are the few references to Muhammad. These are not specifically directed at Muhammad himself but at Islam. Different renderings produce 'son of the butcher', 'son of the Arab butcher' or 'son of slaughter'. Modern Mandaeans are of course not duty bound to accept all aspects of traditional religion any more than all modern Christians feel they should be anti-Semitic, anti-homosexual or should tolerate slavery, each of which may be justified by passages in the New Testament. The recent experiences of forced conversion and extremist violence in Iraq and the intolerance of post-revolutionary Iran may lead modern Mandaeans to secretly agree with their forebears.

Over the centuries the Mandaeans have got used to the arbitrary changes of local government and the occasional large-scale convulsions of empire and regime change. As a small, cohesive community they knew they had to ride the wave, no matter in which direction the tide was turning. Yet there was never such a major and irrevocable change to their conditions of life as the advent of Islam.

The Arab conquests were truly remarkable. The successors of Muhammad, Abu Bakr (632–634) and Umar (634–644), managed to unite the Arab tribes after the death of the Prophet. In the space of three decades they took Iraq and Iran, which had been under the Sasanian Empire, along with northern Mesopotamia, Syria and Egypt. When the Arab Islamic Empire added Mesopotamia to its conquests in 636 there must have been some violence and oppression against the Mandaeans – in potential at the very least – that caused their negative response. Although there was, of course, considerable pressure for the populations of newly conquered countries to convert to Islam, many ordinary people found that they were better off than they had been before the invasion, although it is not clear that this was true for the Mandaeans, who, given the little data we have on them in the pre-Islamic centuries, seem to have been fairly settled by that point. Many areas had been ruled by unresponsive and autocratic regimes, and many were already parts of other empires. The nature of Islam, particularly the majority Sunni Islam, which is based chiefly on the relationship between humankind and God, and which has no real priesthood, places each Muslim on a similar footing.

The Sasanians and the Christian Greek Byzantine Empire, or Eastern Roman Empire, had been warring for centuries. Syria and Egypt had typically been Byzantine during that time, but the Sasanians had had huge successes in besting the Byzantines in war in the decades immediately before the Arab conquests. Between 608 and 619 the Sasanians took the ancient cities of Antioch, Tarsus, Damascus and Jerusalem. In 619 the Sasanians conquered Egypt, only to see a Byzantine Empire (Eastern Roman Empire) resurgence. This ultimately saw the Byzantines regain Armenia, Mesopotamia, Syria and Palestine by 629. Both the Sasanians and the Byzantines would lose most of their empires to the Arabs in the following decades. By 649 the Sasanian Empire was at an end.

Subsequent to early Islam's massive territorial advances the Umayyad dynasty ruled the Muslim world from 661 to 750 from Damascus and then Harran. Baghdad was established in 763 near the ruins of Ctesiphon. Ctesiphon had been such an important city through so many different empires but it was in Baghdad that there would be initiated probably the greatest golden age of culture between classical antiquity and the European Renaissance.

Mingling scriptural traditions and tolerance

The Umayyad Mosque in Damascus is built on a pre-existing church that reputedly houses the tomb of St John the Baptist, containing his skull. After the Islamic conquest of Syria both Muslims and Christians worshipped side by side peacefully, using the building on their particular holy days: Friday for Muslims, Sunday for Christians. According to an informant of Lynn Picknett, Mandaeans made an annual pilgrimage to the shrine of John's skull in Damascus.[1]

The Mandaeans do not use the Quran, but it is important to understand that they do not use the Bible either – neither the New Testament nor the Hebrew Bible or Old Testament. Mandaean priests do not – or did not – mine the book of Genesis, the rest of the Torah and prophets in order to reinterpret them in the way that, say, Sethian Gnostics did. Neither did they read the gospels allegorically in the esoteric spirit of the Valentinians. They simply didn't read them at all. They read the *Ginza* and the *Book of John*, the *Qolasta* and the *Haran Gawaita* – scriptures that share many biblical characters and events such as Adam, Eve, Seth, Abel and Enoch, Noah and the Flood, or the crossing of the Sea of Reeds.[2]

In the Mandaean story of Nu (Noah), when the ark runs aground on the mountain (Kardun) he sends out a raven first of all. The raven finds a corpse to feed on and forgets its mission, which is reminiscent of the prince in the Gnostic writing called 'Hymn of the Pearl', who as soon as he is sent out into Egypt becomes involved in the material world and forgets his own mission to retrieve the pearl. Next, Nu sends a dove that brings back a spring of olive, although one might have expected the Mandaeans to prefer myrtle.[3] Muhammad (or the angel who dictated the Quran to him, or Allah himself) clearly knew some apocryphal traditions, quite probably from oral sources. The stories in the Quran in which Mary gives birth to Jesus beneath a palm tree, and in which Jesus makes birds out of clay, are also found in the earlier apocryphal infancy gospels. The Quranic view that Jesus was not actually crucified is also found in the Gnostic text, *The Second Treatise of the Great Seth*.

The literate, intellectually curious culture of the Islamic golden age has bequeathed to us some of our earliest accounts of the Mandaeans. A Mandaean colophon that may be dated to 639–640 sketches out how a Mandaean chief, Anush son of Danqa, led a delegation to the Muslim authorities, presumably to argue the case for the Mandaeans to be classified as Sabians, or at least to request their safety.[4] In 924 Abbasid caliph al-Qahir Billh asked a scholar, al-Istakari, about the Sabians in southeast Iraq. He was told that they paid a bribe of 50,000 dinars to be left alone. Somehow they have not been charged the poll tax for non-Muslim religious minorities, surely testimony to the diplomacy and negotiation skills of the Mandaeans. As ever, the only certainties are death and taxes.

The earliest account of the Mandaeans from an unambiguous outsider appears in the final chapter of the *Book of the Scholion* by Theodore bar Konai, a Syrian Christian who also wrote on the Manichaeans and other minority religions still existing at the time. He quotes from the *Ginza* but includes a thoroughly disreputable story of their origins, stating that they were founded by beggars, and claims that they belong to upper Mesopotamia, where they are still known as 'Nazarenes'.[5]

There are features of Mandaeism even today that were obviously necessitated by the fact that Islam was dominant in Mandaean regions. One is the wine substitute used in the weekly baptism. There may be other reasons for it too, but the unfermented faux wine produced by macerated dates soaked in water would be more acceptable to teetotal Muslims than real wine, whether made from grapes or dates. The other, and one that is crucial to the survival of Mandaeans today, is the refusal to accept converts. Any Muslim who converted to Mandaeism would have been apostate and therefore condemned to death, which would have endangered the Mandaean community. Parsi communities in India also refuse to accept converts.

But this difficult relationship with Islam extends into other areas of life too. Mandaeans should accept neither food nor drink from a Muslim, but Mandaeans do not have the same difficulty with accepting food from Christians. Partly this must have its origins in Islam being the dominant religion and cultural force for so long in Iraq and Iran. But it is surely significant that Islam has religious food laws, known in general as halal, whereas Christianity has none.[6] A Mandaean sheikh (the general term used for religious leaders in Arabic-speaking countries) had an audience with Pope John Paul II in 1990. Of the three major religions encountered by Mandaeans, Christianity is certainly seen as the most amenable.

It remains to be seen whether, outside of Muslim countries, Mandaeans may change their rules. There is already a certain amount of speculation that non-Mandaeans who have married Mandaeans may be admitted into the community. But Jorunn Buckley told me, 'The conversion issue is not something to be dealt with in public, at all, if you are an outsider'.[7]

The Quran, or the retelling of stories from the Quran, may have had an influence on episodes like that in the *Right Ginza* where the fire angels are instructed to bow down before Adam and Eve. In Sura 38: 71 Allah tells the angels that once he has created man from earth they will bow down and worship him.[8]

The invasions of the Mongols had a massive impact on Islam in the 13th century. The Mongols first upset the comfortable power of Arab Islam, which had enjoyed stability and wealth – and from that material success had produced a glorious high culture. The absorption of the Mongols into the Islamic world was a triumph of religion, but the influx of people with a different language and a radically different culture rocked the balance of power. Curiously, there is little evidence that the Mongols had much of an impact on the Mandaeans at all, excepting for the Harranian connection. Possibly the Mandaeans had by that time learned to stay out of the way, to hide behind their bland face as 'people of the book' and dissemble whenever their survival required it.

Mandaeans survived in the proximity of Islam, Christianity and Judaism for centuries. Although there are accounts of persecutions from time to time, these are people who all lived together with some degree of success for a long time. Until the 21st century Mandaeans lived in Iraq and Iran with varying degrees of comfort and ease. As scholar Nathaniel Deutsch has put it:

> *My view is that Mandaeism probably emerged out of a Jewish context at some point, and that over the centuries in Mesopotamia they had very close relations which were probably much more amicable than the texts would suggest. Not only Mandaean texts, but if you look at pretty much every religious tradition in the Middle East, if you look hard enough you will find negative things said*

about other people. But on the ground, particularly if you look at the so-called magical tradition, one example of which would be magic bowls, which we have a fair number of examples of, that survive, that archaeologists have discovered, where it becomes clear from the language that's used, from the different divine beings, angelic beings that are evoked, the names of the scribes, the names of the customers which are sometimes inscribed on them, that there was a lot of cross-cultural contact going on between these different peoples. Even if officially in their elite texts they were antagonistic, they were neighbours, in the case of the Jews, the script is different but the spoken dialect of Aramaic was very similar. Mandaean and the dialect of the Babylonian Talmud, for example, are quite similar. In some cases they were living in towns or areas that were overlapping one another, so it may be one of those cases of the anxiety of influence, where they generally get along with their neighbours, but when they fight it can take on a different connotation when you fight a neighbour versus a complete stranger.[9]

Nasuraiia, Nazarenes and Nizari

An unfortunate similarity of names may now bemuse the unwary reader. As we have seen, the Mandaeans' inner circle is known as *nasuraiia*. This group includes both the priesthood and learned laymen.[10] Similar-sounding names are applied to Christians throughout the Near East, Middle East and even in India, with English renderings coming out as Nazoreans or Nazarenes.

The Medieval Islamic sect established in Syria and known popularly as the Assassins was the Nizari, also called the Nizaris or Nosairs.[11] Although it would be more accurate to refer to them as Nizari Ismaili Shiites, the name Assassins is understandably more familiar to Western readers. This does not mean, however, that today's Nizaris are literally assassins in the modern sense of the word.

The Assassins were a warrior order that emerged in 11th-century Persia. Their first leader, Hasan-i-Sabah, established a mountain stronghold of Alamut, which acted as headquarters of the order. A mountain valley three miles wide and 30 miles long gave Alamut extraordinary defensive possibilities. Hasan-i-Sabah was said to have masterminded the strategies of the order for decades without leaving this sanctuary. Alamut was also characterized by technological marvels, such as an ingenious system of irrigation. The name Assassins derives from *hashishin*, a derogatory term that refers to a commonly held belief that hashish was used by the Nizari either to make their warriors fearless or to help initiate the assassins and briefly experience a visionary paradise to which they would return once the specified kill had been made (during the act of which it was expected that the assassin would himself be killed in retaliation).

Drugs may have been used in a kind of ascent vision. It is also possible that the experience of a vision like this might have inspired an assassin to disregard his own survival. But the suggestion that narcotics-induced visions would somehow hypnotize warriors to persuade them against their will to perform assassinations just seems off. Likewise, the idea that this would make them fearless seems naive. One imagines a stoned and paranoid Assassin with short-term memory problems forgetting where his dagger was or even whether he had killed his victim or not.

The placing of the Assassins in Muslim tradition requires a little explanation of the basic divisions of Islam. Sunni and Shia may be familiar terms from news bulletins on the Middle East but many non-Muslim Westerners are still uncertain about their meaning. After the death of Muhammad, Abu Bakr became leader of the rapidly expanding Muslim world as the first caliph. Abu Bakr was a senior adviser and close companion of Muhammad, and he represented what has become known as Sunni Islam (after *sunna*, meaning 'tradition', referring to the traditions that have developed). To this day around 80–90 percent of Muslims are Sunni. Abu Bakr united the community (*umma*) of Islam and initiated the military conquests of Arabia, but he ruled as caliph for only two years.

Umar ruled as the second caliph for ten years, from 634 to 644. The third caliph was Othman, of the Umayyad clan. However, Muhammad's own clan, the Hashim, felt that Othman was favouring the Umayyads and this led to his murder in 656 and a civil war between rival factions. Ali, Muhammad's cousin, became the fourth caliph, but in 661 he too was murdered. Ali's successor Muawiyah was politically astute, temporarily maintaining the support of Ali's faction. Having already been governor of Syria he moved the political capital from Medina to Damascus. He established the Umayyad caliphate, which would have a considerable influence on the Islamic world.

When Muawiyah died in 680 his successor, Yazid, would cause the permanent schism in Islam by massacring Ali's son Husein and his family. If the leadership of the caliphate was to be inherited then Ali's descendants argued they had the strongest claim. This is the basis of Shia Islam, which asserts that it is the descendants of Ali, and hence those who are blood relatives of Muhammad, who have the claim to spiritual and temporal authority in Islam. Ali became considered the first Imam, with subsequent Imams descended from him. There is a further split in Islam within Shia Islam itself. The majority of Shia, known as Twelvers, acknowledge 12 Imams and believe the twelfth will return as an apocalyptic figure known as the *mahdi*. An alternative view of Imamship is held by Ismailis, who are known as Seveners.

The Syrian Nizaris are considered a branch of Ismaili, or Sevener, Shia Islam. There are also theories that the Syrian Nizaris were *nasuraiia* – the Mandaeans. Some of these theories, including Conti and Norberg (see page 45), originate with enthusiastic amateur scholars in the early stages of modern Western encounters with the Mandaeans. Germano Conti of Aleppo in Syria published an inaccurate account of Nizaris.

The common ground between the Assassin Nizaris and the Mandaeans included the ritual use of myrtle, repeated handshakes, ritual use of surrogate wine made from rains and dried figs (dates for Mandaeans) macerated in water. These specific but partial resemblances between the Mandaeans and other obscure sects will become a running theme in our researches, suggesting linkages and relationships without any firm evidence to back them up. Additionally, some of these writers are held to considerably misrepresent the peoples they reported on.[12] Oddly, the

Nizaris take us back to our old friends the Templars. The Nizaris are the only religious minority for whom we have direct evidence of any contact with the Templars. The Templars were heavily involved in the defences of Outremer, the crusader kingdom. Manning the massive crusader castles dotted around its borders made the Templars neighbours of the Nizaris. After the murder of Count Raymond of Tripoli in 1152, the Templars attacked the Nizaris, who agreed to pay them a tribute of 2,000 besants a year. Twenty years later the Nizaris were enlisted to support King Amalric in lieu of their annual tribute. The Templars preferred to receive the money and, angered at what they saw as a betrayal by Amalric, they attacked the Nizaris' delegation as it returned from the parlez with Amalric. At another point the Templars had disagreed with a proposed conversion of the Nizaris to Christianity, again on the condition of ceasing to pay tribute. It is difficult to believe that the Nizaris were serious.[13] So here we finally have a link between the Templars and the Mandaeans, although an intensively speculative one. The Templars and the Nizaris undoubtedly knew each other, although their recorded interactions were hostile. Resemblances between the Nizaris and the Mandaeans allow us to argue that Mandaeans were in the vicinity of the Nizaris – thus perhaps the Templars also met the Mandaeans. It is a slim chance, but better than nothing.[14]

Muhammad and Mani

Mandaeism has been influenced by Islam but not in any religious beliefs or in the way that Mandaeans conduct their rituals. Apart from a few connections that might be attributed to the influence of the common culture of ancient Iraq, there are few similarities. There is little indication either that Islam was ever influenced by Mandaeism in any significant way, although local Muslim authorities were keen enough to receive payments to guarantee their ongoing safety. Islam was dominant and although during its Baghdad-centred golden age of Muslim scholarship there was a tremendous appetite for learning, the substantial foreign influence derived from the rediscovered Greek culture. But one unacknowledged religion may well have influenced Islam and was in turn influenced by the

Mandaeans. This was Manichaeism. As I asked scholar Nicholas Baker-Brian in an interview:

> APS: *I wanted to ask you about Manichaeism and Islam, because they were in similar regions of the world and Mani has sometimes been compared to Muhammad in intentionally founding a religion and including figures from previous religions, although Mani's range of figures was much broader. They have been compared sometimes, haven't they?*

> NB-B: *Certainly this idea that Mani is a seal, the seal of previous prophets, that is explicit in Quranic and* hadith *representations of Muhammad, so there are definite correspondences there. When you think about the time and the proximity of Manichaeism in relation to early Islam, it's unbelievable really that there's not going to be some sort of correspondence and influence between Manichaeans and early followers of Muhammad. Early Islamic writers are obviously very intrigued by the Manichaeans, because they see correspondences, although rather like Catholic Christians in the fourth and fifth centuries, the correspondences perhaps need to be exaggerated a little bit. So eventually the Manichaeans fall foul of Islamic writers and eventually of the Islamic authorities by being classified as heretics. There's certainly work that needs to be done on understanding how, for instance, Manichaean texts, particularly the very famous text that came to light in the late third century called the Kephalaia, which is a Greek word that literally means "Chapters", the representation of Mani in there as a great teacher, as a great authority, and the way that that authority is communicated by a chain of recognized teachers and authorities, is very similar to the way that* hadith *develops in Islam, and there are accepted, recognized authorities for passing on the teachings of the Prophet. So there are all sorts of correspondences that need to be teased out with more work.*[15]

The Mandaeans lived alongside Muslims for centuries, and continue to do so. It is impossible that they were not influenced by Islam, yet it is the secular side of Arabic-speaking Iraqi culture that is now a more obvious influence on the Mandaeans. Both Mandaeans and Manichaeans lived alongside each other before Islam even began. What are the relationships between these two religions, the one hanging on by the skin of its teeth, the other long since vanished?

Chapter 7

Mani and the Lost Religion

The prophet Mani is unique as the founder of an entirely new religion that incorporated Gnostic elements. The Manichaean religion inherited and absorbed Gnosticism, along with many other influences, and in turn Manichaean ideas flowed back upstream into the direction of earlier Gnostic groups. Manichaean influence can be seen in the syncretic Gnosticism (incorporating Sethian, Valentinian and other forms) found in late Gnostic writings such as the *Pistis Sophia* and the *Books of Jeu*. There are also similarities between Manichaeism and Mandaeism. Which was the chicken and which the egg?

Perhaps the earliest literary reference to the Mandaeans is in the 10th-century *Fihrist*, written by Ibn al-Nadim. Al-Nadim lists the various 'Sabian' sects that he knows of. It is a broad list, including Manichaeans and Marcionites. The Manichaeans did not make much of an impression in Muslim countries. It appears that the religion was already in decline in the Middle East, reliant for its survival on followers in Central Asia and China. Manichaeans did not explicitly shelter under the Sabian umbrella as 'people of the book'. Yet as a religion that was neither Muslim nor Jewish nor Christian, yet which appealed to Jesus and Moses as prophets, it received a certain amount of protection under the first caliphate. The Marcionites were followers of Marcion's semi-Gnostic version of

Christianity. Based in Syria, they were another surprising survival of an early heterodox Christian sect. In the 2nd century Marcion of Sinope had become massively influential with his brand of Christianity. He viewed the God of the Old Testament as a different figure to the God of Christianity. It is tempting to say 'the God of the New Testament', but the New Testament as we know it today didn't yet exist because the Christian canon was still in the process of being formalized. Marcion developed a canon based on a version of the Gospel of Luke and the epistles or letters of Paul. In doing this he established a formal canon for Marcionites whereas the texts that form the New Testament were still being recognized as authoritative by the Church Fathers who sought a consensus over what to include. That process was not to be concluded for some time. That the Marcionites were perceived as Sabians rather than Christians by Ibn al-Nadim shows that they were rejected by other forms of Christianity and perceived as sufficiently different. It is also possible that Syrian and Byzantine Christians had put pressure on Muslim authorities for themselves to be recognized as the only ones worthy of the 'Christian' category of the 'people of the book'.

'Those who wash themselves'

Another sect is the al-Mughtasila – 'those who wash themselves' – who inhabit the swamps of the Euphrates. Al-Nadim believes that they are breakaway Manichaeans who 'agreed with the Manichaeans about the two elemental [principles], but later their sect became separated. Until this our own day, some of them venerate the stars'. Thus he recognizes the dualist aspects of Mandaeism, although these certainly aren't as clear or as fundamental as they are in Manichaeism. He described the Mughtasila as follows:

> These people are very numerous in the regions of al-Bata'ih; they are (called) the Sabians of the marsh-lands. They observe ablution as a rite and wash everything which they eat. Their head is known as al-Hasih, and it is he who instituted their sect. They assert that the two existences are male and female and that the herbs are from the likeness of the male, whereas the parasite plants are from the likeness

of the female, the trees being veins (roots). They have seven sayings,
taking the form of fables. His disciple was named Sham'un. They
agreed with the Manichaeans about the two elemental (principles),
but later their sect became separate.[1]

Without naming the sect, a later passage adds: 'One group of philosophers and servants of the stars assert that they have talismans, based on [astronomical] observations.' This matches the practical magic side of Mandaean culture. There are several pages on the production of astrological talismans or amulets in the Mandaean scriptural text known as the *Book of the Zodiac.*[2] Successor to Abraham, Zoroaster and the Buddha Mani was very eclectic in his religion, incorporating not only the Abrahamic traditions (among which Gnosticism must be counted as an eccentric offspring) but elements from Zoroastrianism and Buddhism too. Mani's incorporation of other religions and his self-proclamation as the fulfilment of the line of prophets begs similarities with Muhammad. Since Muhammad lived centuries later we may wonder whether the founder of Islam was influenced by the widespread Manichaean religion. The Mandaeans, of course, did not agree that either Mani or Muhammad were the last word in religion. Despite their underdog status and the political exigencies of superficially respecting the powerful religions, they believed that their own beliefs and practices were the only real way to the Lightworld.

Mani's life is described in his own writings and in other Manichaean sacred writings, and it is reported indirectly in other sources, which rely on Manichaean writings and traditions. There are, of course, the usual difficulties in determining whether any particular aspect of his life is historical, or whether it has been put into that form in imitation of Jesus or other sacred heroes of the Manichaeans.

According to Jacques Waardenburg, there is no recognition in Islam of Mani's writings as scripture although other religions, which according to Islamic criteria were not strictly monotheistic, were recognized. Muslims did not consider Manichaeism a religion at all, but rather a philosophical system or a sect that resembled Islam; it was thus a caricature of religion as it should be. Muhammad himself may have heard

Manichaeans. Arabia had close commercial contacts with Egypt and Mesopotamia, where centres of Manichaeanism existed, and there was a Manichaean community in northeastern Arabia. Later, Muslim authors wrote that among the Quraysh, which was the leading tribe of Mecca, there had been some *zindiqs* (that is, Manichaeans) who had learned the doctrine of *zandaqa* (Manichaeism) from Christians in Hira in northeastern Arabia at the border of present-day Iraq. It has been hypothesized that Sura 6: 1–3 ('It is God who established darkness and light') implies a reference to the Manichaean doctrine that held that light and darkness are two independent principles.[3] That last point might as easily apply to the Mandaeans, for whom the Lightworld is so fundamental. But it may well be a reference to the creation in Genesis so little can be built on it as a reference either to Manichaeism or Mandaeism.

According to the *Shabuhragan* (a Manichaean sacred text written by Mani himself), Mani was born in AD 216 on the upper course of the 'Nahr Kuta River'. His birthplace had the Aramaic name of Mardinu. His father's name is rendered variously as Pattiq (Syriac/Aramaic), Pattig/ Patteg (Iranian) or Pattikios (Greek). Mani's father was given a noble, although not royal, lineage. His mother is given various names in Persian Manichaean tradition, traces her descent from a royal house, and was named Maryam after the mother of Jesus. This royal descent and other factors, such as an exile in childhood, resembling that of the Holy Family of Jesus in Egypt, mirrored events in the life of Jesus or other prophets considered to be precursors of Mani.

Mani's father was a pagan, possibly a worshipper of the traditional Babylonian gods, before he converted to follow a sect known as the 'Cleansers'. Pattiq heard a voice when he was in 'the house of the idols' telling him to 'eat no meat, drink no wine, abstain from all sexual relations,' which led him to approach the sect of Cleansers. They were named the Mughtasila ('those who wash themselves'), an equivalent to 'baptists'. The 'Cleansers' wore white clothing and used ritual ablutions in various contexts in their community. They had strict food laws, both to do with the ritual washing of vegetables before they could be eaten and with origins, regarding homegrown vegetables as 'male' and therefore pure (although they still had to go through the ablutions) and vegetables from outside the community as 'female' and forbidden. These kinds of relative values, such as male and female, are now well known to anthropologists through the work of Claude Levi-Strauss and his structural anthropology. Local flat bread was permitted and called 'Jewish' but foreign bread was forbidden and called 'Greek'.

Some of these details must be jumping out at the reader. A Babylonian baptist sect. White clothing and regular ablutions in 3rd-century Mesopotamia. Could Mani's father have joined the Mandaeans? Although they have not accepted converts for centuries, it is likely that prior to Islam they did so. It was for a long time believed that Mani had grown up among Mandaeans. I asked a Manichaean expert, Nicholas Baker-Brian, about this in an interview:

APS: *Although this group turned out not to be the Mandaeans, there do seem to be some overlaps between Mandaean texts and Manichaean scripture, don't there?*

NB-B: *Very much so. This was really before the appearance of the* Cologne Mani Codex *for the first time in the late 1960s but was published in the early 1970s in a series of articles. What we thought we knew about Mani's early period was very much aligned with existing ideas in Mandaean texts, for example the* Ginza. *Some key ideas there about God and about revelation seem to tie in very neatly with what Mani himself was saying. As I understand it, this literature and scholarship on the Mandaeans has really been picking up pace from the 1920s onwards and reached a point where there's a Swedish scholar called Geo Widingren, who wrote a very important book on Mani. He was first and foremost a Mandaean scholar and he was primarily the person who advanced this relationship or apparent relationship between the baptists that Mani seems to have grown up with and Mandaean ideas and practices. He was looking at correspondences in Mandaean texts, but he was also looking at what late Islamic sources, which prior to the arrival of the* Cologne Mani Codex *had been the principal sources of evidence really for Mani's early period. There's a very interesting text called the* Fihrist *by a character called al-Nadim, who's an Islamic writer in the 10th century. And this is effectively a kind of proto-wikipedia. It's an encyclopedia of all human knowledge and all human activity. Al-Nadim actually had an entry on Mani in there, so Widingren was looking at those entries in Arabic and making correspondences with what he was finding as he was editing the Mandaean texts, so certainly that idea that the baptists of Mani's early period were the Mandaeans has fallen out of favour really. Nevertheless, there still appears to be something in the water, the theological water. There are very strong correspondences between these baptists and the Mandaeans.*[4]

At the age of 12 and then again at 24 Mani had a vision of his double – his heavenly twin or light-self. I have already commented in *Secret History of the Gnostics* that this is unlikely to be a straightforward historical event. It recalls Luke's story of Jesus in the Temple at age 12, which is presented as an intimation of Jesus' future glory, as it does for Mani. But in Mani's case the specifics are more than a story about how great he was or how even as an adolescent his knowledge exceeded that of the Temple priests. Mani was experiencing his true self, which revealed the true nature of the universe. Potentially all Manichaeans would experience their light selves in this way and understand the nature of the world. In the greater scheme of Gnosticism we would call this simultaneous understanding of the self and the nature of the universe – *gnosis*.

In Mandaeism there exists the world of *mshunia kushta*, peopled by the secret or hidden Adam and Eve. This survived into the modern era, as a 20th-century priest told Lady Drower, 'of all things there are two, the actual and its *mabda* (ideal, or arche-type)'.[5] According to another modern Mandaean explanation, every living thing, including plants and animals, has an ethereal body in the other world which they will inhabit when the physical body dies. Thus the concept of the heavenly twin fits as easily into Mandaeism as it does into Manichaeism.

Mani tried to reform the Elkasite sect, the heterodox Christian baptismal sect, in which he grew up.[6] This led to a schism within the sect and he was expelled, with only his father and two others following him. He received his call to be the 'apostle of light' at the age of 24 on 19 April 240. The first Manichaean community was in Seleucia-Ctesiphon, on the eastern side of the Tigris. He taught and gathered converts in Iran, sent missionaries into the Eastern Roman Empire and further west, journeyed to India himself and converted the ruler of Turan. The geographical spread of Manichaeanism exceeded the early expansion of Christianity and came a respectable second to that of the later Islam, without using any military means. Typically, the Manichaeans were, like the Mandaeans, extreme pacifists. The Manichaean division into an inner circle of the elect and the hearers, who were lay people, will by now be a familiar pattern to the reader. In Manichaeism this was taken to an extreme. Not only were the Manichaean elect vegetarians, but they were not permitted to prepare any food for themselves and relied on ordinary Manichaeans to help them in all sorts of basic practical tasks which would otherwise have resulted in their hands becoming ritually unclean. The Mandaeans were never vegetarians, although the priests were subject to eating restrictions under certain conditions. This method of purifying food via washing and the preparation of unleavened bread or pitta are both Mandaean rites known to have been used by the Manichaeans.[7]

The perils of powerful ideas

When Mani returned to Babylonia, where Ardashir I's son had become king as Shapur I, two of the king's brothers became Manichaeans. Shapur continued the expansion of the Sasanian Empire begun by his father, expanding east into Bactria and north as far as Harran. Despite the otherworldly nature of Manichaeism, Mani was clearly not unaware of the advantages of political influence.

Mani's religion acknowledged Zoroaster as an earlier prophet and saviour. This may have had an element of political expediency, but Zoroastrian dualism fitted well with Mani's own light–darkness dualism and was undoubtedly an influence on Mani. But in absorbing key Zoroastrian ideas Manichaeism became a threat to the existing religion. Under the Sasanians Zoroastrianism had experienced a renewal and resurgence. Its magi priests had power of their own and were not going to take kindly to Mani's new religion, which could be perceived to be superseding or usurping Zoroastrianism.

After Shapur I died, Ohrmuzd I was briefly king of Babylon and also sympathetic to Mani. In addition to acquiring converts and establishing communities, Mani established a canon of seven scriptures, written by him in Aramaic. Their evocative titles were *The Living Gospel*, *The Treasure of Life*, *The Pragmateia*, *The Book of Mysteries*, *The Book of the Giants*, *The Letters* and *The Psalms and Prayers*. The title of the second work is particularly interesting. The central Mandaean collection of scripture is the *Ginza*, which means 'treasury', and the use of 'life' – the Great Life and the First Life, Second Life, Third Life and Fourth Life – will be familiar to the reader from Mandaean myth. Perhaps Mani adopted Mandaean teachings in the way that he did Zoroastrian ones?

In 274 Bahram I became king and this coincided with the powerful magi, the powerful priestly caste of the Zoroastrian religion, becoming more influential. Kerdir, the head of the magi, became a deadly opponent of Mani and his teaching. Bahram I imprisoned and then executed Mani. His corpse was flayed and the stuffed skin was displayed outside the city walls. The persecution of Manichaeans lasted for decades and many of Mani's pupils were martyred.

Although Manichaeanism had a hard time in Mesopotamia, it had spread through the Mediterranean world, to Syria and Palestine, Egypt, North Africa, and Rome. It also quickly expanded further into Asia, both through the missions of Mani during his own lifetime and of his disciples afterwards. India and Central Asia were somewhat receptive – Mani had acknowledged the Buddha as one of his predecessors and Manichaeism moulded itself around the local traditions. Manichaeism came without linguistic diktat, in sharp contrast to later Islam, which has been in the unusual situation of having its scriptures in the language of its originating empire, Arabic. The Manichaeans were happy to have their scriptures translated into the local languages.

Over the centuries Manichaeism reached China where Mani was remembered as a form of *buddha*, his image being preserved in a small temple in Fujian province as Buddha of Light. Despite its spread and influence it only became a state religion in one instance: it was adopted in the 8th and 9th centuries by the Uighurs (who would briefly resurface in the Western consciousness in the 21st century when they clashed with their Chinese overlords).

Manichaeism is hugely interesting in its own right. It was a minority religion but it was widely spread geographically and persisted for the better part of a millennium. Anyone who looks at Manichaeism cannot help but see similarities with Mandaeism, such as the Lightworld and the light–dark dualism. Although the evidence shows that Mandaeism was an early influence on Manichaeism, and not the other way round, it is unlikely that we are seeing only a one-way influence. Perhaps aspects of light–darkness dualism were strengthened by Mandaeism's encounter with Mani's religion of light. Mani's religion was successful in a way that Mandaeism never was, yet its popularity and appeal – despite the fact that it transcended barriers of language, ethnicity, and geography – would be dwarfed by the success of Islam.

A Coptic conundrum

Among a collection of Coptic texts found at Medinet Madi in Egypt in 1929 was the Manichaean *Psalm Book*.[8] One section of the Psalm Book is entitled 'Psalms of Thomas' and some of these psalms contain phrases or entire verses that strongly resemble passages in Mandaean liturgy. For example: Manichaean Psalm of Thomas:

> *My brethren, love me with your heart. Do not please me*
> *with your lips: the children of the lip are blotted*
> *out, the children of the heart abide. Do not*
> *be like the pomegranate. whose rind is gay*
> *outside; its rind is gay outside but its inside*
> *is full of ashes.*

Mandaean prayer:
> *My brothers,*
> *speak truthfully. not with lying lips*

prevaricate. Be not like a pomegranate;
which on its outer face is sound.
outwardly sound is its surface.
*but inside it is full of dry husks.*⁹

A Swedish academic called Torgny Säve-Söderburgh made a minute study of the 'Psalms of Thomas' and discovered almost verbatim reproduction of sections of not only the *Ginza* but the *Book of John* too. Linguistically, the only possibility is that the Manichaeans took parts of these psalms from an original in Mandaic. The 'Psalms of Thomas' are dated to the latter part of Mani's lifetime. The Thomas of the title is thought to be a disciple of Mani, not the Christian apostle Thomas, he of the eponymous Gospel of Thomas, although that apostle Thomas had strong legendary connections with Syria and India.¹⁰

Manichaeism may have been the world religion that we lost. It may have been the religion of light, but so is Mandaeism. The Mandaeans not only preceded the Manichaeans, they influenced them – and they survived them.

Chapter 8

By the Rivers of Babylon

Psalm 137

By the rivers of Babylon, there we sat down, yea, we wept, when we

remembered Zion. We hanged our harps upon the willows in the midst thereof.

For there they that carried us away captive required of us a song; and they that

wasted us required of us mirth, saying, Sing us one of the songs of Zion.

How shall we sing the LORD's song in a strange land?

If I forget thee, O Jerusalem, let my right hand forget her cunning.

If I do not remember thee, let my tongue cleave to the roof of my mouth; if I

prefer not Jerusalem above my chief joy.

Mandaean Canonical Prayerbook

From the home of the great community therein, I became the healer
for souls! I became a healer for souls who heals but takes no fee. I
set forth, came and reached the gates of Babylon. Of the children of
Babylon there were some who shut their doors on seeing me: There
were some who shut their doors. And there were those who opened
their doors. Those who shut their doors hated Life and loved death
and will be held back in the Abode of Darkness. Those who opened
their doors loved Life and hated Death, they hated Death and loved
Life. They will rise up in purity and will behold the Place of Light.[1]

By the 20th century the 'rivers of Babylon' were not to Mandaeans those
of a strange land but those of their ancient homeland. In the 21st century
the Tigris and the Euphrates of 'the land between two rivers' were not
part of a reminder of exile but the place from which many of them would
be exiled.

The Israelites had looked forward to the downfall of the
Babylonian Empire and its religion: 'And, behold, here cometh a chariot
of men, with a couple of horsemen. And he answered and said, "Babylon
is fallen, is fallen; and all the graven images of her gods he hath broken
unto the ground"' (Isaiah 21: 9). Yet Jewish communities remained in
Babylonia for centuries after the return of exiled Jews to Judaea. Like the
Mandaeans, these solid, established communities weathered the coming
and going of empires and endured the vicissitudes of being governed by
those who were neither of their ethnicity nor their religion. When Jews
were violently expelled from Judaea and from Alexandria they turned
to Galilee and to Babylonia. The Jewish Talmud, that hypertextual
collection of religious law, lore and commentary, has two recensions:
one from Galilee (misnamed as the Jerusalem Talmud), the other from
Babylonia. Two major Jewish academies, the Sura and the Pumbedita,
existed in Mesopotamia for over 800 years.

Mesopotamia is about as old as it gets in terms of human civilization.
The ancient empires of Sumeria, Akkadia, Babylonia and Assyria were,
along with Egypt, the dominant forces of the ancient world. It was the
Western whippersnappers, the Greek and Roman empires, which finally

dislodged them. Islam later came from the south and once again made the Middle East into the leading focus of civilization west of China.

Babylon the fallen

The great city of Babylon inspires a variety of responses. Located in the heart of one of the great early civilizations of the Middle East, it represents the success of an organized state, of technological and intellectual advances, of security and prosperity and longevity. It also represents the cruelties of empire, of class distinction and wealth accumulation, of slavery and oppression. To the Rastafarians 'Babylon' has come to represent modern imperialism, materialism and capitalism; or, alternatively, to many others it signifies the excesses of wealth and pleasure available to the rich, as in 'Hotel Babylon', 'Hollywood Babylon' and a multitude of other such Babylons.

For hundreds of years the city was a ruin, of little interest until Western archaeologists began to study it. In 1983 Saddam Hussein would, in an appropriately megalomaniac fashion, initiate the restoration and rebuilding of Babylon as a tribute to Arabic achievement and to himself. The resulting catastrophe was a Saddam-Hussein-themed Disneyland. A massive ziggurat palace, to be named Saddam Hill, was planned along with overhead cable cars. Nebuchadnezzar had stamped his names on the bricks of Babel, so Saddam did so too. A huge portrait of Nebuchadnezzar adorned the entrance, beside one of Saddam. The Western invasion prevented the completion. But anyone who enjoys seeing the desecration and destruction of ancient sites was not to be disappointed. The American military proved to be a worthy successor to Saddam as they turned parts of archaeological Babylon into Camp Alpha and reused the materials of ancient ruins for a helipad. They permanently damaged parts of the precious city. But they weren't the first to do so, and they probably won't be the last.

Shifting languages and empires

Throughout its history Mesopotamia has combined continuity with intermittent large-scale devastation and renewal. As one ethnic group after another gained then lost dominance, the languages changed from Sumerian to the Semitic languages: varieties of Aramaic, languages of various minorities including Hebrew, and then the persistence of Arabic. With Arabic came a massive change in religion. Prior to Islam gods and goddesses shuffled to and fro and foreign gods came and went. Most of the gods of the ancient world, the so-called pagan gods, could co-exist. Their temples were in the same cities; their myths inhabited the same imaginal spaces; and their rituals and symbols blended and shifted from one minor deity to another. But Islam swept all that away.

Yet beliefs and practices have a persistence that can always surprise. Ancient myths and folk culture can remain but go underground, resurfacing in transformed but recognizable forms. The Africanist Jan Vansina relates an account collected in 1954 from a caravan guide in southern Libya:

He said that west of the Teda (Libya/Chad) live people who do not know how to make fire. They are called the sun-fire-people. They live around a big well into which the sun sets every night. Then the water gets hot and they can cook their food. Thus they only eat once a day. Confirmation of this was given three weeks later by another guide. I cite this bit of gossip rather than another because it has already been told for the same general area by both Herodotus and Pliny. This fragment of information is 2,500 years old, and dispels the notion that gossip must be ephemeral.[2]

Similarly, ancient Mesopotamian religion and magic has survived through the Mandaeans, despite their official objections to planetary deities, astrology and sorcery.

The formative centuries of Mandaeism were between the 1st century and the Arab invasion in the 7th. The 3rd century, in particular ,was a turbulent and important period in the history of Mesopotamia and Persia, both in politics and religion. It is also an obscure period of history. In the West it seems that only specialists, with a few exceptions, are interested in the period between the fall of Babylon and the coming of Islam, but this was a period of around 1,000 years. Nor, it seems, are Muslim historians especially interested in much before the coming of Islam. For those who have only a knowledge of popular history, mention of names such as the Seleucids, Arsacids, Sasanians, Umayyads and Abbasids will be met with a blank stare.

Cyrus the Great (c.590–c.529 BC) and his successors in the Achaemenid dynasty maintained the Persian Empire from around 559 BC until its overthrow by Alexander of Macedon, who defeated Darius III in 330 BC. After Alexander's death, one of his generals, Seleucus, established a new Hellenistic kingdom that lasted from 305 to 225, when it was eclipsed by the Arsacid dynasty's Parthian Empire, which in turn was replaced several centuries later by the Sasanian dynasty in AD 224. The Sasanian dynasty lasted until the Arab invasion. We will meet its predecessors when we delve further back in time and discuss the migration of the Mandaeans.

Jewish or Babylonian?

Mandaean scriptures suggest to the researcher that it is to Judaea that we should look for their origins. But attentive study of their practices may suggest a different tack. In *Heirs to Forgotten Kingdoms* Gerard Russell emphasizes the Babylonian elements of the Mandaeans:

> *I discussed it with one or two scholars before writing the book, just to see, not necessarily that they would agree with me in stressing the Babylonian heritage. Some of them would put Judaism as a more important influence. But it's debatable... It is a valid interpretation. But also one that, as you say, appeals more if you look at the practices of the people. So much scholarship, especially these days, is done in a sort of protestant context in which one looks at the scriptures and says the essence of a religion lies in its scriptures and its origin lies in when those scriptures were written. But if you look at, particularly, a group like the Yazidis, it doesn't make much sense to say that, in my view. I think it makes more sense to say, let's look at their customs and its practices and ask where do those come from, and how long have those existed? It's a different way of reading the history of these people. Of course, both are valid, but they come from different traditions.[3]*

According to at least one scholar, the particular Mandaean use of the Mesopotamian gods shows the influence of specific time periods:

'Analyzing the Mandaean texts, one can find that the demonized Mesopotamian deities, which are also mentioned in the later Mandaic text corpus, prove without doubt that they were borrowed from a Late Parthian cultural setting of Central Babylonia.'[4]

What exactly are the Babylonian elements in Mandaeism? The Mandaean and Babylonian stories of creation share some minor but suggestive details, such as 'the creation of the saviour and his fight against the forces of evil' who appears in Mandaic literature as Manda d-Hayyi or Hibil Ziwa.[5] The source of baptism Mesopotamia is famously located 'between two rivers', the Tigris and Euphrates, and the myths of this most ancient land are rich in tales of primeval waters and associated deities. It would not be surprising if baptismal practices had evolved there independently of Judaic ones. As Lady Drower writes:

> Ritual immersion was ancient indeed in Babylonia, and during Iranian domination shrines had been built on the Tigris and Euphrates to the water-goddess Anahita, who under her Semitic name Nanai or Nanaia is still invoked in Mandaean exorcism books. Did these Nasoreans from Harran and Media find on the rivers of southern Mesopotamia and Khuzestan a baptising sect so similar to their own that they incorporated and dominated it?[6]

Cult huts were known in Babylonian times, such as the *bit rimki*, which were somewhat similar to the *mandi* and the other huts required for Mandaean ritual.[7] But repeated baptism was a common feature among the different Gnostic sects of Babylonia such as the Elkasites who were attacked by Mani for their daily baths.[8] As far as Drower was concerned, the Mandaeans had adopted existing Babylonian baptismal rites and attached an esoteric interpretation to them.[9]

The care with which the Mandaean baptism and other rituals are exercised is comparable to ancient Babylonian rituals. If a minor mistake is made the section of the ritual must be repeated again correctly. Certain events, like a drop of blood falling into the river water, can make the baptism impossible to complete. Having found evidence of baptismal practices that somewhat resemble those of the Mandaeans in ancient Babylonia, the only land apart from a contiguous region of Iran where we have hard evidence that the Mandaeans lived before modern times, should we stop looking elsewhere? Shouldn't we apply the principle of 'Occam's razor', which prevents us from multiplying hypothetical entities – that is, finding additional explanations and reasons when it seems that the simplest may suffice? If the Mandaeans could have got their baptismal practices from Iraq, why would we need to propose that they were ever near the Jordan or that they have any connection with 1st-century Judaean baptisers like John?

If the Mandaeans were a baptismal sect before they even reached Mesopotamia, they might have wanted to settle in an area that was felt to be best suited for such practices. The baptisms that John gave in the Jordan must have been quite improvisatory affairs at times. The early Mandaeans could have had baptismal practices that were either undeveloped or were difficult to execute in their new environment. It would have been natural to adopt the existing technologies and usages of the region. As the decades turned into centuries it would have been almost unavoidable for Mandaean practice not to have been influenced by existing local practice. We should expect to see Babylonian features in Mandaean practices, whether the Mandaeans are indigenous to Mesopotamia or are migrants from the region around the Jordan.

During a Mandaean baptism the name Bihram is invoked (see Chapter 1, note 9). He may be understood as a version of Abraham, but he may also have Zoroastrian links. Lady Drower suggested: 'His name is Iranian ... and the Mandaean Bihram may be the Persian genius of victory (New Persian Bahram ... Middle Persian Varhran) ... The presence of the banner at Mandaean baptism may be connected with Bihram's banner of victory.'[10]

The home of astrology

The Babylonian sexagesimal system of timekeeping has, along with its astrology, become universal in the West. Having settled in the home of astrology, it is not surprising that it has a large, if ambiguous, part in Mandaean beliefs. Astrology is generally frowned upon in the official Mandaean religion. This disapproval is typically Gnostic. The ancient Gnostics did not deny the power of the planets, but they felt that their influence was malign and imprisoning. Fate was something that trapped you. The planetary spheres surrounded the material world. The soul, either at death or via a visionary ascent that could prepare the Gnostic beforehand, would ascend upwards through these spheres. The soul of the Gnostic would be armed with passwords to be given to the rulers of each sphere and which would enable it to pass ever upwards. The 3rd-century Syrian Bardesanes, a heterodox Christian who doesn't quite fit into any category, believed that the stars, zodiac and planets (which he called 'the seven') were hostile powers.

However, such was the popular appeal of astrology that ordinary Mandaeans would consult natal charts and appeal to the planetary gods and goddesses even while the attitude towards these in the official religion was much more antipathetic. Astrology is even today used to give each Mandaean their true name. Each Mandaean has four names. A common Arabic name is used in everyday life (or presumably Farsi in Iran) that does not mark the person out as a Mandaean. There is also a family name and a tribal name. But the 'true name', known as the *malwasa*, is used in all religious observances and, traditionally, during medical treatment. The *malwasa* is constructed astrologically using a scripture known as the *Book of the Zodiac*.

Beginning with the sun sign in which the baby is born, the priest counts through the zodiac as many signs as there were hours in that sun sign before the birth. The sign that is arrived at has a number from 1 to 12. This number is then subtracted from the numerical value (also 1 to 12) of the mother's name. The final number is consulted in the *Book of the Zodiac*, where each corresponds with a list of male and female names.[11] In the lists given in Drower's translation of the *Book of the Zodiac*,[12] and in the more up-to-date list given by Buckley,[13] there are surprisingly few of these: no number has more than eight names associated with it, and some have as few as two. Astrological names are usually given with the mother's name following it: eg, Yahia son of Yasmin. This allows for reverse-engineering: the numerical category of the name may be added to that of the mother's name to obtain the number, mode 12, that indicates, if not uniquely, the hour and sign of birth.

The cultural importance of the *Book of the Zodiac* is revealing about the status of astrology in Mandaeism. The *malwasa* astrological name is used by the priests in ritual but the *Book of the Zodiac* not considered canonical. At the time of Lady Drower's sojourns with the Mandaeans it was common practice to have astrological amulets made and to produce annual horoscopes for each individual. The Mandaeans also practised mundane astrology, making predictions for large-scale events that affected nature, entire countries and leaders. This kind of astrology is thought to be similar to that practised during the Sasanian Empire, which means it is unlikely to have originated elsewhere.

So, the actual practice of the Mandaeans has been to consult horoscopes regularly for all the usual reasons. Astrology is ingrained into traditional Mandaean culture. But the view of the more Gnostic, inner religion is that the stars and planets are not benign. As Lady Drower put it:

> *The stars and the signs of the zodiac are the enemies of the soul. This we may, I think, look upon as refutation of the idea that man is the helpless victim of* heimarmene, *the plaything of the planets under the influence of which he was born.* Nasiruta *is an urgent denial of fate, it is a call to the soul of man to hearken to its own* mana *which is at once an image and part of the Great* Mana. *If man listens to this call from within, he is proof against fate and the planets.*[14]

The cycle of time

The Mandaean months have Babylonian names, but may also be referred to according to the signs of the zodiac. New Year was set at the time of entry of the sun into Aries. Each year is named after the first weekday in the year. Each day is governed by a particular planet, and the 24 hours of the day are similarly governed by the planets. Thus any particular time of day is governed by a complex set of overlapping astrological factors. The Mandaean calendar and method of keeping time follow ancient Persian methods but with Semitic names.

> *The Mandaeans count the 24 hours of a day and night as beginning at dawn, i.e. Tuesday is followed by Tuesday night: 'the night of Tuesday' to an Arab, on the contrary, means the night preceding*

Tuesday. The Mandaean calendar has the additional incongruity of beginning the year with the winter season, whereas the Persian-Zoroastrian New Year is normally associated with the spring. The Persian-Zoroastrian New Year coincided with early winter in the 1st century B.C.E., so the essential names of Mandaean months may have been instituted in this period. The Mandaeans are the only non-Iranian people who adopted the old Iranian calendar, along with quite a number of other beliefs, of the later Sasanian period i.e., the time of Khosrau the Great (6th century) without the slightest change. But the Mandaeans did not use the Persian names of the months and kept the Semitic ones, as mentioned above.[15]

The Mandaeans also had their own astrological epochs. From the creation of Adam until the end of the world is estimated as 480,000 years. Each epoch is governed by a sign of the zodiac, beginning with Aries or, to give it the Mandaean (Babylonian) name, Umbara. The age of Umbara lasted 12,000 years, of Taura 11,000 years and so on. Although the names of the zodiac are different to the Western versions, many of the symbols are the same – although the equivalent of Gemini is symbolized by the scales not the twins, Virgo (Shumbulta) by the ear of corn, Libra (Qaina) by a reed, Sagittarius (Hatia) by a mare and Aquarius (Daula) by a camel.[16]

Mandaean astrology has a house system, with the aspects of life governed by each house being roughly similar to those of Greek and Arabic astrology, although the way of calculating the houses is simpler than the Hellenistic models.[17] The Mandaeans also used decans, the astrological division of each sign into three 10-degree sections, which originated in Egypt, although these weren't generally associated with the vivid images which accompanied the decans in other astrological systems.

Aside from the zodiac cycles, the Mandaeans had four great ages. The first age began with Adam and Eve and ended under the power of the sword. The second began with Ram and Rud and ended by fire. The third began with Surbai and Sarhabil and ended via water. The fourth age is ours, begun by Shem, son of Noah, and Nuraita. Our age will end through the power of air.[18]

The system of ages immediately brings to mind the classical ages of gold, silver, bronze and iron, as described by Hesiod (who also has a heroic age) and Ovid. The Indian yugas offer an even closer approximation, because the Mandaean ages decrease in length as the world progresses from one to the next. However, the total of 480,000 years is considerably shorter than the truly vast periods of the *yugas* – furthermore, the Mandaean system is not cyclical, whereas the *yugas* repeat endlessly. After our age the world comes to an end.

Mesopotamian antecedents

Just when we seem to be swimming about in speculation, or living in an atmosphere of reasoned arguments but with little proof, we find a bit of archaeological evidence that points towards the presence of Mandaeans in Mesopotamia at the very beginning of the Sasanian Empire.

The 3rd-century AD Sasanian priest Kerdir, who is likely to be the head of the magi responsible for the martyrdom of Mani, left us an inscription at Naqsh-e Rustam proclaiming the violent triumph of his religion over others in the area:

> *In kingdom after kingdom and place after place throughout the whole empire, the services of Ahura Mazda and the yazds became preeminent, and great dignity came to the Mazda-worshipping religion and the magi in the empire, and the yazds and water and fire and small cattle in the empire attained great satisfaction, while Ahriman and the demons were punished and rebuked, and the teachings of Ahriman and the demons departed from the empire and were abandoned. And the Jews, Buddhists, Brahmins, 'Nazarenes', Christians, 'Baptists' and Manichaeans in the empire were smitten, and destruction of idols and scattering of the stores of the demons and god-seats and nests was abandoned.*[19]

There are two possibilities for the Mandaeans in that early 3rd-century list: Nazarenes and Baptists. There is a Mandaean tradition that in the early period all Mandaeans were Nazarenes; the term was not restricted to the priestly class (*nasuraiia*) as it is now. This may mean that as the religion developed the usage of the word 'Nazarenes' was no longer applied to the Mandaean population as a whole but to the esoteric priestly circle only. Mythically, it may mean that in ancient times all Mandaeans were believed to operate at the level of priests; thus it was a kind of golden age. 'Baptists' may refer to any of the baptismal sects that existed, including not only the Mandaeans but also perhaps the Elkasites. Either way, there is plenty of scope to claim that the Mandaeans are on this list.

There are further reasons to believe that the Mandaeans had been in Mesopotamia for centuries prior to the Muslim conquest. The *Left Ginza* describes a purification rite necessary for someone who has gone into the House of Tammuz, the god of vegetation who was mourned by Ishtar after he had descended to the underworld.[20] The text addresses those who 'sit there twenty-eight days, slaughter sheep, mix bowls, offer cakes, and sit mourning in the house of Libat'.[21] Clearly this Mandaean rite must refer to the pre-Islamic period and was a priestly attempt to fence in a community that could see the value of the pagan gods. Drower saw similarities between the Mandaean figures of Ur and Krum and the Mesopotamian Tiamat, along with possible links to Vedic dragons or serpents.[22]

Ruha was credited with introducing demonic chants to the Mandaeans. These were rejected by the priests and play no part in the official religion. They are identified by some scholars with the songs of lamentation used at festivals dedicated to Tammuz's death. However, vowel chants were practised by various Gnostic groups in late antiquity and it is not out of the question that similar chants were used by the Mandaeans. Babylonian lamentations may have been adopted, which were then objected to by the priests at a time when it became important to distinguish the Mandaeans from Babylonian pagans. Gnostic chants, which were similar to the Babylonian ones, may have been preserved, or elements of them may have been absorbed, and then forbidden to the community for similar reasons. We simply don't know.

So could the trail end here? Are the Mandaeans essentially a Babylonian remnant that preserves ancient Mesopotamian baptismal rituals? Are references to John the Baptist merely a late development, intended to ingratiate the Mandaean community with the Islamic authorities and secure some degree of security in their lives? To exhibit

Babylonian influence is not the same as having an ultimately Babylonian origin. Jews in Iraq also had rituals that were probably derived from post-biblical Babylonian influence, including vegetarian ritual meals.

Marsh Arabs and Marsh Mandaeans

Scholar Edwin Yamauchi came to think that the western (Jewish and Palestinian) elements of Mandaeism had been emphasized too much because of the comparative wealth of materials and information available. His suggestion was that the Mandaeans may have been 'an indigenous Aramaean group living in the Marshes of lower Iraq and of southwestern Iran'. By the time of the Sasanian Empire they had spread upcountry as far as Baghdad. After Islam came to Iraq they were largely displaced from their original territory by the Shia Muslim Marsh Arabs. But the Mandaeans persisted in the marshes for centuries, using the reeds to build their cult huts.

The Iraq marshes, created by the historical flooding of the Euphrates, were known as the 'blessing of Iraq' – rich in wildlife and home to water buffalo and a stopping-off place for many species of migrating birds, such as cormorants, kingfishers, teal and flamingos. Approximately the size of Wales, the area was drained by Saddam Hussein in the 1980s. This was an engineering project on a vast scale with a network of canals and embankments 45 miles long and more than 20ft high. The canals diverted water away into the Persian Gulf, 150 miles away. After 12,000 sq km were drained, what had been endless wetlands was now a desert. The marshlands were reduced to 10 percent of their former size, and 250,000 Marsh Arabs who had once lived in the area had been reduced to just a few thousand.

After the fall of Saddam Hussein a variety of efforts have been partially successful in restoring the marshes, breaching sections of the embankment and once again flooding parts of the area. Some of the Marsh Arabs began to return and reeds are regrowing in what had become dried-out, drought-blighted remains of the former marshes.

Chapter 9

Alphabets and Incantations

Although condemned by Mandaean religion, astrology was a common feature of Mandaean life. Likewise, other magical practices received official disapproval from priests and in scripture but they remained an important part of everyday life. The Mandaeans have a varied magical tradition – and, as might be expected, this magic has a strong native Mesopotamian element.

The Mandaean alphabet is another of the most inarguably ancient features of Mandaean culture. It is a distinct alphabet but one that has close resemblances to another obscure ancient alphabet, that of the Nabataeans, an Arabic people who in the ancient world and late antiquity inhabited a wide area east of the Jordan. The Mandaean alphabet was itself subject to esoteric interpretation and used for divinatory and magical practices.

Magic undermines authoritarian structures. On the other hand, magic can often survive and even thrive in the shadow of religion. For instance, folk magic was part of the fabric of peasant society in the medieval south of France even though it lacked the approval of the Cathar heretics who were popular with the peasantry nor with the dominant Roman Catholic Church. Similarly, both the Catholic and the new Protestant churches condemned magic in the Renaissance and early modern period – yet the European magical grimoire-based tradition (such as the *Lesser*

Key of Solomon, The Book of Abramelin and a host of others) is set within a Christian or Jewish framework.

Lady Drower was interested in certain customs that seemed to be universal among Mandaeans in Iraq during the first half of the 20th century; activities that the priests described as irreligious. When a new house was built a sheep was killed and its head buried beneath the threshold – a widespread practice throughout the world in various forms, which have included human skulls in Britain. The threshold of a Mandaean's house was also protected by charms such as inlaid blue beads or pottery (curious, since blue was forbidden to be worn by Mandaeans) or by a rag doll covered in blue buttons, beads and other decorations. Metal dishes or plaques inscribed with spells were also buried beneath the threshold, particularly when a member of the household was sick. When a newlywed bride entered the house a cock or dove was killed and the blood rubbed onto the bride's bare foot. This was popular culture rather than part of the official Mandaean religion and the bird's throat was slit by a layman. The possibility exists that these were aspects of Mandaean religion that were excluded from official practice when the religion was reformed by priests but had survived among ordinary people.[1]

The influence of Ishtar

One form of Mandaean divination closely resembled the modern ouija board. Two people place their fingers on an inverted tea glass placed on a marble slab, which has letters arranged in a circle. When a question is put the glass moves from letter to letter to spell out the answer. It might be tempting to ascribe this to contemporary European influence, but the name of the practice is *'ilm Liwet*. Liwet, or Libat, is the goddess of the planet Venus and associated with the ancient Mesopotamian goddess Ishtar. Ruha, like Ishtar, was also considered to be very beautiful, and because of her role as an adversary priests would use a blue cord as a bookmark in Mandaean scripture to appease her.[2] According to at least one scholar, the particular Mandaean use of the Mesopotamian gods shows the influence of a specific time period: 'Analyzing the Mandaean texts, one can find that the demonized Mesopotamian deities, which are also mentioned in the later Mandaic text corpus, prove without doubt that they were borrowed from a Late Parthian cultural setting of Central Babylonia.' He concludes, 'Therefore, Mandaean incantations are essential to the study of the origin of this people.'3

In earlier times a child was put outside the town on a Sunday so that Liwet would descend into him or her. The possessed child would then give answers to divination questions. The practice of using children as seers goes back to the ancient world and there are many surviving Hellenistic examples of the practice. In a Mandaean folktale a *ganzibra* takes his daughter into a secret sanctuary of Liwet and puts a bowl of water before her. He read incantations constantly until the glass of the bowl became red, then white, then green, then blue, then, finally, like a globe of light. The girl fell into a sleep and Liwet then entered her thoughts and spoke through her mouth. The *ganzibra* pleaded with Liwet for her to help the Mandaeans evade the Turkish soldiers who were coming. She offers to blind them or surround them with water, but the *ganzibra*, as a good pacifist, is concerned that ordinary soldiers will be harmed. He settles for help from another spirit who ensures that the arms of the soldiers are nudged when they fire their guns so that their shots go astray. Later on in the story an astrologer who accompanies the Turkish army has come into the possession of a magical bowl with Mandaean inscriptions on it. This should not be in his possession so the *ganzibra* arranges for it to magically disappear. We are told that the bowl had been buried in the mountains of the north.4 The presence of a bowl in the spirit-inspired divination of the folktale is notable. Around 2,000 magical bowls, also known as incantation bowls, have been found in Iraq, discovered chiefly through 19th-century archaeological digs. They were typically buried beneath the entryway to houses or underneath rooms. Most have a round base, similar in shape and size to a cereal bowl, although some are as small as an ashtray and others are shaped more like jugs. They are inscribed with spells and scriptural passages, the text typically beginning at the bottom of the concave side of the bowl and spiralling out clockwise towards the rim, although there are many variations on this theme. Jewish Aramaic bowls are the most common, with Mandaic bowls second. Most of the bowls date to the 6th–8th centuries AD. Sometimes they have figures of dogs, or of demons familiar from Mandaean or Jewish folklore, at the centre of the bowl. Many of the magic incantation bowls have spells that are concerned with warding off Lilith, the demoness who was responsible for miscarriages and child mortality.[5] The bowls were in general used either for protection or for cursing. Those buried beneath houses or their thresholds would have protected the occupants from malign influences.[6]

In many cultures magic is considered illicit, bypassing priesthoods and official religion and, as we have seen, that attitude is no different with the Mandaeans.[7] Some Mandaean priests would even deny that there is any magical practice in Mandaeism. It is unlikely that much of this has transferred to the Mandaean diaspora, and perhaps they are not very current in Iraq or Iran nowadays, either. Nevertheless, they are part of the overall historical tradition and deserve consideration. Magical practice plays a part in Gnosticism in general, as is becoming widely realized, and my own position on this has shifted too.

The magical Mandaean alphabet

Although the Mandaeans have an alphabet that is distinct to them, from it philologists are able to determine the origins of Mandaic. The *Haran Gawaita* describes how John the Baptist learned the Mandaic alphabet: 'When he was seven years old, Anush Uthra came and wrote the ABC (*abaga*) for him, until when he was twenty-two years old, he had learnt all the priestly-craft.'[8] This little incident shows that the Mandaic alphabet was considered of sacred origin, and that it was the foundation of the priestly and esoteric knowledge of the Mandaeans. Furthermore, the episode itself almost certainly comes from Christian apocryphal tradition. In the pseudepigraphal *Infancy Gospel of Thomas* the young Jesus is taught the Greek alphabet, from alpha to omega, by a man named Zacchaeus. But he looked at Zacchaeus the teacher and said to him: 'How do you, who do not know the Alpha according to its nature, teach others the Beta? Hypocrite, first if you know it, teach the Alpha, and then we shall believe you concerning the Beta.'[9] Jesus then goes on to teach Zacchaeus the esoteric meanings of the letters of the alphabet.

The 24 letters of the Mandaic alphabet are considered sacred and represent the powers of life and light.[10] Mandaic writing occurs almost entirely in either scripture or in magical artefacts and had no secular function. Both scripture and magical inscriptions are considered to be protected by Nbu (Babylonian Nabu), the god of writing and wisdom, identified with the planet Mercury, as he was in his Roman, Greek and Egyptian equivalents. Here we see the ambivalent and inconsistent approach to the old Babylonian gods: as protector of the alphabet Nbu is sacred and benign; elsewhere he is allied with deceptive forces, and is identified as the spirit who empowers Jesus.

The sacred letters were also used for divination. The technique was to place the 24 letters, inscribed on scraps of silver or gold (the Mandaeans were often silversmiths and goldsmiths), under the pillow of the person who needed divine guidance. Each night one of the letters was removed randomly from the pillow until the querent had a dream that related to the desired topic. The letter that was then removed was one that referred to the spirit that had aided the dream revelation and was worn as a charm around the neck. The earliest known surviving writing in Mandaic is a lead amulet from the first half of the 3rd century AD.

The Mandaic alphabet is known as the *abaga* – a word that also indicates the incantation of a spell. Magical scrolls begin with the entire alphabet in order (also a handy way for the scribe to practise his letters). The circular letters that begin and end the alphabet have solar implications, as do the signs used for vowels. Each letter has words or phrases associated with it, perhaps similar to the kennings used with Norse runes. For instance, the letter *ta* means *tab* ('good') or *tayr* ('bird'), the bird that represents the soul leaving the body to return to the world of light. *Ka* refers to the myrtle wreath or crown (*klila*) or the Rightness or right-dealing (*kushta*, the term also used for the ritual handshake).

This kind of mystical and esoteric use of the alphabet was not confined to the Mandaeans. In both Hebrew and Greek (Latin had the well-known Roman numeral system instead), numbers were represented using letters. Thus any word could represent a number, a feature that is well known today in kabbalah and occultism. The Hebrew alphabet is essential to all forms of Jewish mysticism. There was at least one Gnostic who used alphabet mysticism – a Valentinian named Marcus, whose number and letter systems were many and complex.[11] Marcus saw in a vision the 24 letters of the alphabet placed in pairs on various parts of Truth as a personified being. The alphabet may be followed in sequence down one side of the body and back up the other. Thus Marcus's 'vision of truth' may have been used for techniques of body meditation, which is particularly interesting because a similar approach existed in Mandaeism. In the Mandaean text 'The Great "First World"' a stylized human body is inscribed with alphabetic sequences running up and down the left and right halves of the body.[12]

In Mandaean myth the alphabet is the creation of a pair of divine entities: the feminine of these is the primordial Wellspring, the masculine is the Date-palm. The *abaga* precedes the creation of humanity and the universe, just as the Hebrew alphabet or the texts of the Torah and Quran are considered fundamental to the universe in esoteric Judaism and Islam. In one legend an *uthra* named Melka d-Anhura proclaimed (in the manner of a jealous demiurge), 'There is none mightier than I'. When he saw the alphabet spanning the face of the waters like a bridge, he conceded that the one that made the alphabet was mightier than he was.[13]

According to another version of the origin of the Mandaic alphabet, B emanates from A. B then praises A, and as a result G (the third letter of the alphabet, as in Hebrew) emanates from B. G turns towards B and the process continues. One by one each letter is emanated from the previous one. The process is thoroughly Gnostic and it has a counterpart in descriptions of the formation of the pleroma, the divine world, in which each level emanates from the previous one. In a weird, complex and also very Gnostic development of the story, the alphabet becomes swollen with pride and thus falls, collapses, and 'is abortive'. The alphabet splits into two and one half begins to war on the other. Eventually, the letters realize that disaster will follow and so they take each others' hands, symbolizing the formation of words. Three letters (H, *ayin* and D̲) represent spirit, body and soul. The complexity of this system resembles kabbalah but on somewhat different principles.[14]

Literacy in Mandaic is itself a defining quality of the status of a Mandaean. A *shganda* traditionally began to learn the alphabet at the age of four (younger even than John the Baptist who at seven learned it comparatively late). Once literate he was considered a *yalufa*, a non-priestly educated layman who may consult the *Book of the Zodiac*, say prayers and make Mandaic amulets.[15]

World mythology is full of fabulous hybrid beasts made out of cockerels, lizards and lions; gods with human bodies and the heads of falcons, elephants, jackals or ibises; talking snakes and blue goddesses with many arms, the scope is almost infinite. Mandaean myth has a figure associated with the alphabet who is more peculiar than any of these: Dinanukht is a being who is half-man half-book and able to read himself.[16] In a strange story in the *Right Ginza*, Dinanukht encounters a smaller book named Disai, and he tries without success to drown and burn Disai. Dinanukht falls asleep and has a vision given by Ewat (a form of Ruha) in which she proclaims:

> *I am the Life that was from the beginning. I am the truth ... which existed even earlier in the beginning. I am radiance; I am light. I am death; I am life. I am darkness; I am light. I am error; I am truth. I am destruction; I am construction. I am light; I am error. I am blow; I am healing ...*[17]

Dinanukht then makes an ascent of the soul, rising through a realm in which Ruha herself acts as a seductress, on to a level characterized by the dichotomies Ewat proclaimed in the dream vision. Dinanukht then finds he can ascend no further and must return to the Earth and communicate to others what he saw without being allowed to experience the Lightworld itself. His wife (we are not told if she is half-book too) thinks him mad. The meaning of the story is probably connected to the relationship between written scripture and visionary experience. There is surely no other story in the whole of mythology about a half-man half-book who makes an incomplete ascent of the soul!

Chapter 10

Among the Gnostics

Mandaeism is often considered a form of Gnosticism. But what does Gnosticism even signify? Gnosticism as a scholarly category is very much disputed by academics currently, to the extent that some have rejected it as a useless construct. To clarify what I, and others, mean when we say that the Mandaeans are Gnostics, I will have to provide some background. Over the years I have honed and sharpened my own definition of Gnosticism until I have come up with the perfect summary: 'Stuff like what the ancient Gnostics used to do.'

Gnosticism is criticized both as an unclear term of definition and as a label that derives from their enemies, rather than being a self-designation by Gnostics themselves. Our evidence for the Gnostics comes from two sources: from their own writings and scriptures, and from the polemical writings of the Church Fathers. For Church Fathers like Irenaeus (later a saint) in the 2nd century – and those who followed him, such as Tertullian, Hippolytus and Epiphanius – Christian sects that didn't agree with them on what they thought were essential points of doctrine, or sects to which they were antagonistic, were heretical.

These heresiologists listed and attempted to refute a great many individuals, groups and scriptures. Among the groups that Irenaeus attacked were the Gnostics. The name derives from the Greek word gnosis, which denoted spiritual knowledge – a more mystical, experiential form of knowledge than that derived from books. It may be considered as both a combination of a direct knowledge of the divine and the lore and scripture that accompanies it.

These Gnostics had a certain approach that combined in a revolutionary way elements of Platonic philosophy with Christian or Judaic – biblical – tradition. The cosmology of Plato, laid out primarily in the *Timaeus*, involved a figure known as the demiurge. The demiurge (meaning craftsman rather than half-god, or even half-crafter as often mistakenly believed) was a lower kind of god than the absolute transcendent God. It was the demiurge who formed or crafted the world, using the world of forms or images as his template. This move by Plato would be very influential down the centuries (his academy continued until AD 529, when it was closed by command of the Christian emperor Justinian). The notion of the demiurge as an intermediary figure in creation set the transcendent God free from the responsibility of all the imperfections and troubles of the physical world.

After the conquests of Alexander the Great, Greek culture spread throughout the Mediterranean world and beyond, interacting with existing local traditions. The chief city of intellectual and spiritual ferment was Alexandria on the coast of Egypt, its design marked out on the ground with barley flour according to the instruction of Alexander himself but not built until after his death. There the millennia-old Egyptian culture combined with the learning of the Greeks and other ethnic and religious traditions. One of these other traditions was Judaism. By the 1st century Hellenized Jewish intellectuals had syncretized the Platonic approach with that of the Old Testament or Hebrew Bible, suggesting that the creation of the world was affected by a demiurgic figure rather than directly by Jehovah.

The stroke of genius on behalf of the Gnostics was to understand the demiurge as a malign or ignorant figure rather than the benevolent craftsman depicted by Plato. The demiurge was the creator of the material world. The material world was (and is) full of pain, suffering, disease, war and brutishness. In contrast with the material world, the spiritual world was pure and unsullied. The world of God was that of the spirit.

But what of Jehovah, the God of Christians and Jews? According to the Gnostics, that God behaved throughout the Bible like a petty despot – like the tribal God that he once was. That jealous God could not be the transcendent, loving God of spirit. Therefore the God of the Bible must have been the ignorant, malevolent demiurge. Yet if humans could come to understand and experience something of the spirit, this must mean that they had a spark of spirit in themselves. Out of these musings, and perhaps revelations, the Gnostics developed a myth that explained the situation of humanity and the world.

The Gnostic creation...

In the beginning there had only been the true God, the One. He had sought self-knowledge and as a natural result of this process – of seeing himself as if in a mirror or a pool of water – a second divine being had emanated from him. From that being more divine emanations appeared (the details are many and varied) until there was a heavenly realm of divine emanations known as the pleroma, the fullness of God. The last of these emanations, often called Sophia ('wisdom'), had sought to explore outside the pleroma (again, the options are many) and as a result had fallen. In the course of this she gave birth to the demiurge, often known as Ialdabaoth, who sought to create the physical world, and subsequently humanity, in a kind of witless imitation of the heavenly pleroma that he had never seen directly. As a result of the fall of Sophia a portion of the pleroma is trapped in the material world. Ialdabaoth tried to create Adam, as did Jehovah in the book of Genesis, but Adam was unable to stand upright until the demiurge had been tricked into including a spark of pleromic spirit within each human.

Spirit was trapped in matter. Yet there was a way out. Throughout history entities have descended from the pleroma at crucial times to reveal the truth to humankind; the best known of these was Jesus. The spark within each human may be recognized, recovered and restored eventually, at death, to the pleroma. This is achieved through knowledge of the situation that humans are in and knowledge of the divine spark in humans, through *gnosis*.

Such is the rough outline of a typical Gnostic myth. No two versions of this myth are identical – not in the dozens of Gnostic scriptures found in Egypt at Nag Hammadi in 1945 or in the accounts left by the Church Fathers. And from this last fact stems the thorny issue of Gnosticism.

Since the mid-1990s academics began to feel that their peers and predecessors had concocted a synthetic religion from these scriptures and the polemical patristic accounts and called it Gnosticism. It was possible to isolate a number of characteristics of this religion – an ignorant or evil demiurge, emanations, Sophia, demonic archons who assisted the false God, and so on. Yet on closer examination not a single text had every single one of these features. In none of these scriptures did the authors refer to themselves or their communities as Gnostic.

Sethians and Valentinians

In older scholarship much was made of the differences between Eastern and Western Gnosticism. The former was of an 'Iranian' type, and had clear Zoroastrian influence in its absolute dualism. The latter was the Alexandrian Gnosticism we know from the Church Fathers.

The two main groups of Gnostics were known as Sethians and Valentinians. The central saviour figure of the Sethians was Seth, the mysterious third son of Adam and Eve, born after Cain and Abel. They believed that Jesus was a manifestation of Seth. The Sethians were the more revolutionary of the two groups, having a more antagonistic attitude towards Jewish scriptures and noticeably different from proto-Catholic Christianity.

The Valentinians, on the other hand, were more reconciled to their fellow Christians. They read the Bible allegorically in preference to inverting the received meaning of certain passages, as the Sethians did. The Valentinians were named after their founder Valentinus, an educated, Greek-speaking Alexandrian who is reputed to have stood for the position of bishop of Rome, the post that is now better known as that of the pope.

It is chiefly the Sethians who will be our concern with respect to the Mandaeans, but we shall discover a single, odd, Valentinian connection. Other figures and groups who may be associated with Gnosticism, such as Simon Magus and Dositheos, will be discussed in connection with the 1st-century baptismal setting of the Mandaeans.

It seems unlikely that the Valentinians ever referred to themselves as Gnostics specifically, while the Sethians may well have used that label (although not in any of their writings that we possess: it is still very much the term used by their enemies). In the aftermath of all this deconstruction of scholarly categories there is a growing tendency to use Gnostic only for the Sethians. However, many scholars still find the terms Gnostics and Gnosticism as meaningful. I am not an academic and I don't feel quite the same need to neatly categorize. Thus for me Gnosticism is 'stuff that the ancient Gnostics used to do'. I don't require an exact equivalence of identity between different Gnostic groups, nor do I have a checklist of features that are required for membership in the Gnostic communion of churches. My idea of Gnosticism is characterized by a similarity of pattern to the ancient Gnostics, plus the possibility of a historical transmission, but above all by a certain taste, a certain attitude to religion and spirituality.

Is Mandaeism Gnostic?

I see Gnosticism not so much as something that is rigidly organized into categories but rather as a network of interrelated nodes, each node sharing common features with its neighbours but not necessarily having to tick a required number of boxes to qualify for the identification label of Gnostic. However, there are so many overlaps between the Mandaeans and other Gnostic groups, both in the general orientation and in specifics, that it is neither anachronistic nor inaccurate to call Mandaeans Gnostic and to say that the Mandaean religion is a form of Gnosticism. I should add that one of the leading experts in Mandaeism has no trouble in calling the Mandaeans Gnostics. When I conducted an email interview with Jorunn Buckley, I asked her, 'Does the contemporary academic deconstruction of the category of Gnosticism have any impact on how you perceive and classify Mandaean religion?' Her reply was simply, 'None at all.'

Although Mandaeism has the hierarchy of *uthri* who were involved in the creation, there is no single figure who mirrors the kind of ignorant demiurge found in Sethian writings. The Second Life, Third Life and Fourth Life combine features of the Gnostic aeons with those of the demiurge. Ruha is the most notable 'evil' character, but she belongs to the darkness and isn't truly involved in fashioning the world. Perhaps the attribution to Adam of this quality shows a kind of slippage in accommodating Sethian or other ideas that the Mandaeans encountered and accommodated to their own mythic scheme. Malka Dhshuka is the king of darkness who self-generates and emerges from water then creates demons and other evil creatures. His lion head suggests a common origin with the leonine Ialdabaoth, yet he really has no such demiurgic role. There can be no systematic explanation for each of these occasional details but they add up to family resemblances.

A greater similarity is seen in the account of the creation of man by Ptahil in the *Ginza*. Ptahil creates Adam but Adam cannot stand up and instead wriggles on the ground like a worm. This precise image is found in a number of Gnostic writings, and it was also used by the medieval Bogomils and Cathars.

The Gnostic aspects of Mandaeism are understood to have been there from early on. With the exception of Manichaeism, which we have covered, Gnostic influence was not widespread after the 2nd and 3rd centuries, and it was considerably diminishing in the 4th century, around the middle of which were buried at Nag Hammadi in Egypt the dozen jars containing Gnostic codices. Apart from the Mandaeans themselves, no other Gnostic survivals are known about after that period, except for a few isolated freak examples.

Moreover, there is little that currently suggests an arrow of dependency between the Sethians and Mandaeans. Any similarities are likely to be due to common origins. Or so it seems. Perhaps if Mandaean studies advance considerably we might discover that they are at the root of ancient Gnosticism. Who can tell? The history of Gnostic sects is poorly known and much of it is conjectural. Those involved were more concerned with seeking an understanding of the inner meaning of scripture (Valentinians) or understanding the salvation history of humankind (Sethians) than recording their own historical development. Gnostic writings typically give us a great deal of information about what they thought was the importance of the creation of man and the Garden of Eden, a little on the patriarchs and a good chunk on the esoteric teachings of Jesus between his resurrection and the ascension.

Sidestepping history

The national myth of the Mandaeans is recorded in the *Haran Gawaita*, which gives a linear, if eccentric, history of the development of the Mandaean people. It is not history in the modern sense of the word (nor would Livy, Tacitus or Suetonius have accorded it that status either). In the case of the Sethians, Valentinians and others we do have external testimonies in the pages of the Church Fathers, but these heresy-hunters were hardly impartial witnesses; their main purpose in writing works like *Against All Heresies* (Irenaeus) was to thoroughly discredit the Gnostics.

Mainstream, emerging Christianity on the other hand was quite determined to establish the history of its origins. Of the books of the New Testament the genuine Pauline epistles are most likely the oldest of all the writings, and Mark is the oldest gospel, with Matthew, Luke, Acts and John following. However, they are presented in the order: Matthew, Mark, Luke, John, Acts, Pauline epistles, other epistles, Revelation. Thus the Christian canon paints a clear picture of the development of Christianity – one that is at odds with the canon's own history of development! As we shall see later, attempts to establish the historical identity of Jesus and problems of Christian origins have resulted in wildly varied theories, although this is not to suggest that the gospels' own stories – of the journey from cradle to grave, manger to empty tomb, or from pre-existent *logos* to ascended Son of God – can be taken literally, unless you are an evangelical Christian.

So any attempt to trace the history of a Gnostic sect back from 4th-century copies of its scriptures and the rantings of Church Fathers dated to the 2nd and 3rd centuries may or may not be helped by subsequent scholarship or, better still, by the discovery of lost Gnostic writings and other documentary evidence. Yet, as with the Mandaeans, that is not to say that a reconstruction of the history of the Gnostics shouldn't be attempted.

Sethian mystery

Seth is a curious figure. Most Christians today probably barely know that Seth existed. If my own early religious education is anything to go by, if asked who the children of Adam and Eve were, most people would answer 'Cain and Abel'. Seth, despite only the briefest of mentions in the Bible, inspired an extensive speculative and spiritual tradition in Judaism, Christianity and other religions such as Gnosticism, Manichaeism and our very own Mandaeism. He was an important figure in heterodox Jewish literature around the same period (the early centuries AD) and his life story and significance is amplified and expanded in Jewish apocryphal and rabbinical literature. Sethian texts contain phrases in which reference is made to the 'race' or 'generation' of Seth. The Sethians referred to themselves as 'the immovable race', 'the seed of Seth' or 'the children of Seth'.

In Sethian mythology the first emanation of the father God is the mother figure of Barbelo. Then follows a son called Autogenes, the 'self-generated', who is illuminated by four angels – Harmozel, Oroiael, Daueithai and Eleleth. In Sethian writings the demiurge is often named Ialdabaoth, Saklas or Nebruel and is usually identified with the Jewish God.[1] In Mandaeism there is no comparable divine feminine figure: the *uthri* may have been male and female, but each of the named powers is masculine. The most prominent female figure in Mandaean mythology is Ruha, and the popular presence of pagan figures like Ishtar and the liliths (female demons) perhaps indicates that a hunger for the divine or mythic feminine had to be met elsewhere, through folk memories of Babylonian religion.

The Sethians held baptisms and their sacraments were known as the five seals. John Turner, an academic who is the leading expert on the Sethians, has suggested that they may have originated, like the Mandaeans, as a 'non-Christian baptismal sect of the first centuries BCE and CE' along the lines of John the Baptist's disciples, or the Essenes. The Dead Sea Scrolls contains evidence of a Jewish sect (possibly but not necessarily the Essenes) with dualistic qualities (dark versus light) that withdrew its support from the Temple of Jerusalem. It is possible that the inversionary element of Sethianism originates from a similar process of Jews who rejected not only the centralized Jewish faith, but saw Judaism itself as a tool of the demiurge.

These early Sethians would have seen Adam and Seth as divine revealer figures and looked forward to an apocalyptic return of Seth in the near future. The Sethian text *Apocalypse of Adam*, dating from the 2nd century or earlier, has no definite Christian features at all. In a second stage of development, Seth was identified with Christ in the early decades of Christianity as Christian and Sethian groups came into contact with each other.

Thus the Sethians developed into a form of Christian Gnosticism and attached themselves to the quite variegated Christian movements of the time, and it is at this time that they were attacked by Irenaeus. But as the proto-apostolic Church and its norms became more powerful, heterodox groups like the Sethians were forced out, and the Sethians themselves may then have rejected the Christian elements in their systems. Turner sees a further stage in which the Sethians, having become estranged from the community of mainstream Christianity, then turned towards a more Platonic emphasis and identified themselves with the classical philosophical current, which eventually led to them being rejected once again – but this time by mainstream Platonists such as the Neoplatonist Plotinus. Turner proposes that this further rejection led to a fragmentation of Sethianism into various groups such as the Audians, Borborites, Archontics and Phibionites, some of which survived into the early Middle Ages. In Turner's words:

> But it's clear in Sethianism that Barbelo was almost an entirely transcendental mother figure and acts more or less as the consort of the high deity, the Invisible Spirit. Then to complete the Trinity you have the figure of the self-generated Child, who is a very interesting figure because this is the one in which essentially a heterodox Jewish form of speculation becomes gradually identified with Christ as the Sethian tradition becomes Christianized, that is, it essentially enters into some relationship with the Christians.

In any case, I try to suggest this may have happened in roughly five or six stages, so that you begin then with this group, who – I'm not sure whether they were very aware of a distinctive Jewish identity – but I think that they certainly arose from that general milieu of worship in the heavenly Temple, which then accounts for the very heavy occurrence of acts of vision and acts of liturgical praise which occurs in the various Sethian documents.[2]

The stages Turner refers to may be summarized as follows:

1. The Sethians originated as a 2nd-century AD fusion of two distinct groups identified as Barbeloites and Sethites, each of which might be called a proto-Gnostic Jewish group.

2. The Barbeloites come to see Christ as the divine son, the Autogenes, and thus in the mid-2nd century AD they enter the fold of Christianity, although in the broadest way.

3. The Barbeloites and Sethites amalgamate in the later 2nd century. Now both Seth and Christ are seen as 'alternative bearers of the true image of God who had recently appeared in the world as the Logos to rescue Jesus from the cross'.3

4. This Christian Sethian movement gradually became estranged from Christianity, indicated by the polemics against other Christians that may be found in Sethian works.

5. By the 3rd century Sethianism was rejected by the heresiologists and the so-called apostolic or Catholic Church. The rejected Sethians latch onto Platonism, which had already contributed to their myth-building.

6. Late 3rd-century Sethianism became estranged from Platonism in turn as Plotinus attacked them. The Sethian movement fragments into several groups, which may have survived for centuries in small numbers in a variety of areas.

While Palestine is an obvious location for the origin of the Sethians, Egypt is a possibility too. Seth or Set was an Egyptian god, who was sometimes associated with the Jewish people. However, the Gnostic Seth is primarily derived from Jewish tradition.

The Sethians saw themselves as a 'race' set apart. But unlike the Jewish or Hebrew people, whose scripture they interpreted in such a different way, 'the seed of Seth' or 'the immovable race' was not a group that self-identified on the basis of ethnicity. Like so-called mainstream Christianity, particularly in the late 1st and early 2nd centuries, it had recruited members from a variety of backgrounds. Some scholars, such as April DeConick, have proposed that the Sethians probably organized themselves as lodges rather than as churches – something more like the activities of Freemasons or Theosophists rather than a full-blown

Church with its hierarchy and its greater involvement in family life and daily affairs.

John Turner sees the Barbeloites as the originators of the five seals of baptism. The ultimate origin he suggests is the priestly lustrations of the Jerusalem Temple. Perhaps, like the Dead Sea Scrolls group and Jewish Wisdom groups, the Barbeloites withdrew from the Temple in the 2nd or 1st century BC. Could these decentralizing independent movements have anything in common with the Mandaeans? There are indeed a number of connections between the Mandaeans and the Sethians.

Sethian–Mandaean connections

Turner notes the similarity between the sequence of actions in the Mandaean baptism and the five seals in the Nag Hammadi text *Trimorphic Protennoia*. These consist of 'the entrance into the "Jordan," triple self-immersion, triple immersion by the priest, triple sign with water, triple drink, crowning, invocation of divine names, ritual handshake, and ascent from the "Jordan").'[4] According to the 13th-century Muslim geographer Yaqut, writing in c.1223, there were Sabians in Tib who spoke Nabataean and revered Seth, who was said to have lived in the city in ancient times. They regarded themselves as his descendants. These Sabians had converted to Islam. Tib is also associated with two Mandaean scribes, Ramuia in the 7th century and Sganda in the 6th century, who are known from the colophons of Mandaean scrolls, thus testifying to a continuing Mandaean presence in the city. Tib is mentioned in the *Haran Gawaita*.[5]

In the *Gospel of Judas* and other Sethian texts entities are often described as being within a cloud, a form of description that has an echo in the Mandaean *Haran Gawaita* when the *uthra* Anush goes to Jerusalem clothed in clouds. The *Gospel of Judas* demonstrates a mocking tone towards the Temple, which has its counterpart in the Dead Sea Scrolls and in Mandaean scriptures the Temple is reported to have been destroyed as a result of the influence of Ruha and Adonai.

A demiurge who boasts of his creation occurs several times in surviving Gnostic writing. The *Apocryphon of John* is a prime example, in which Samael speaks a perverted version of the words in Genesis and says,

'I am a jealous God' (Isaiah 56: 5–6 and other places). This also occurs in a Mandaean book, *Alma Rishaia Rba*, but the speaker is Adam, who is initially unaware of the existence of any being prior to or superior to him:

> And then he arose and sat at the wellspring of Vain-Imaginings and said 'I am a King without peer; I am lord of all the world' ... Then he prostrated himself and cast himself down upon his face and said '(If) there is none loftier or mightier than I, whence comes this stream of living water, white waters coming without limit or count?'[6]

Adam is, however, redeemed by his recognition that the living water comes from beyond him. He recognizes that the one who sends the water is greater than he and begs to behold the likeness of him.

Other Gnostic connections

There are fewer similarities between the Valentinians and Mandaeans, although the Valentinian formula 'I am a precious vessel' is seen by some scholars as having a strong link to the Mandaean formula 'I am a mana of great life', which has the same meaning and is used to open several hymns.[7] Although it may seem a chance resemblance, it is the kind of formula that impresses scholars. There was a Valentinian church in Callinicum near the Euphrates, which confirms that there were Valentinians operating in Mesopotamia.[8]

The *Book of John* contains in several places the phrase 'Out of thousands I found one; out of generations two at most', which may be familiar to some readers from the Gospel of Thomas: 'I choose you 1 out of a 1000 and 2 out of 10,000.'[9] In this case it seems more likely that the author of the *Book of John* knew of the saying from oral tradition or from the Gospel of Thomas itself than that the Mandaeans bequeathed the phrase to the author of the Gospel of Thomas. The Gospel of Thomas is unlikely to be Gnostic per se, but it was certainly appreciated by Gnostics, as its presence in Codex II of the Nag Hammadi library, along with Sethian and Valentinian writing, testifies. The minority Mandaeans could easily have felt that they were barely two from 10,000.

There are other family resemblances to Gnostic writings outside of the Sethian world. The 'Hymn of the Pearl' tells the story of a young prince's mission to retrieve a pearl guarded by a serpent in a far-off land. He leaves his father's palace in Parthia and removes his robe of light and travels down to Egypt. The prince forgets his mission and becomes immersed in the life of the strange country, and has to be sent a letter to remind him of his purpose. He then successfully defeats the serpent, recaptures the pearl, returns to his own land and is reclothed in his wondrous robe. As the story ends – it is all told in the first person – he is about to meet the king of kings. Because Parthia is the prince's homeland and Egypt is the fallen world, it seems that the author's sympathies lie in the east, perhaps before the rise to power of the Sasanians after the fall of the Parthian Empire. Yet there is nothing explicitly Zoroastrian about it, thus suggesting that the 'Hymn of the Pearl' was written within the context of another religion. We know the 'Hymn of the Pearl' because of its inclusion in the *Acts of Thomas*, a 2nd-century apocryphal work with strong Syrian Christian connections: while the apostle Thomas is in prison he sings the 'Hymn of the Pearl'. Yet there is nothing specifically Christian about it whatsoever.[10] It has been suggested that it might be Manichaean, yet there isn't anything to imply that either. Nor, to our chagrin, does it have any features that are Mandaean, Sethian or Valentinian. Regardless of its origins, the 'Hymn of the Pearl' functions as a general purpose Gnostic myth. For a long time the focus on the 'Hymn of the Pearl' was Western, after its discovery in the apocryphal *Acts of Thomas*, but the Islamic scholar Carl Ernst has shown that it was well known in Islam, and has survived in several languages, including Arabic, Persian, Turkish and Urdu. There are also echoes of the hymn's theme in Muslim Sufi literature. Elements such as the letter from the higher world that summons the hero to remembrance (known as the 'call' in Gnosticism), 'the robe of glory' and 'the pearl' occur widely in Mandaean literature.

What has made Mandaeism?

There are a number of factors that have contributed to the overall religious make-up of Mandaeism. Some are easy to explain. The presence of Babylonian planetary deities and astrology in Mandaeism is due directly to the influence of Babylonian paganism on the Mandaeans during their centuries in Mesopotamia prior to the Muslim conquest. Similarly, any Zoroastrian elements are due to the Mandaeans proximity to the resurgent and renewed Zoroastrianism that was the official Sasanian religion.

Controversy arises with the presence of the baptismal and Jewish elements on the one hand, and the Gnostic on the other. Baptism, as we have seen, has two possible sources: one is the Babylonian practice and the other is the 1st-century Jewish baptismal sects, to which the Mandaeans claim to belong, albeit often in an antagonistic way. In Mandaean legend and history it was John the Baptist who reformed and renewed these baptismal practices, but their existence goes back to Adam.

Curiously, it is therefore the Gnostic element that, although widely accepted, is the most mysterious aspect. We have seen that there are resemblances between the beliefs of the Mandaeans and those of the Gnostics, as given in the texts from the Nag Hammadi library and the Church Fathers, but what is the nature of those resemblances? John the Baptist does not feature widely in the Nag Hammadi library, with just a couple of exceptions. What could be the link between the Gnostics and John the Baptist?

Chapter 11

Sects, Sects, Sects

The trail of scribes represented in the lists of copyists at the end of Mandaean manuscripts runs cold in the late 2nd century. Neither are there any hostile accounts of the Mandaeans as ancient as the 2nd century, although we cannot rule out the possibility of new discoveries awaiting us. Surprisingly, the Church Fathers, who picked up on any sect or movement declared heretical, did not mention the Mandaeans. It may have been an oversight, but perhaps it indicates that by that point they had become invisible to the Western Church Fathers.

Yet we have seen that the mythological schemes and speculations of the Mandaeans fit easily into the milieu of the Gnostics. So too does their emphasis on baptism as a sacrament. Although the evidence for Gnosticism proper begins in the early 2nd century, we have also seen that it is very possible, and even likely, that there were Gnostic groups in the 1st century. So can we push the history of the Mandaeans further back into the 1st century? The answer is yes. Mandaean baptismal practices are quite typical of 1st-century Jewish baptismal sects.

From Ququites to Elkasites

The Mandaeans can be seen to be part of a disparate Jewish religious world that included many heterodox sects, not least of which were the Essenes. In 554 a Mandaean named Qiqel committed heresy – instigated by Ruha, according to the story. The heresy was characterized by returning to, or taking on, Jewish traditions.[1] Buckley believes the heresies attributed to Qiqel are a memory of Ququite influence. The Ququites were an exceedingly obscure Jewish-Christian sect. Like others of their ilk they kept Jewish Law but believed in Christ as the Messiah with a low Christology – that is, understanding Jesus more as a prophet than as the Son of God in any divine sense. The name of their supposed 2nd-century founder was Quq, which means a 'jug' or 'pitcher'. The Quqites preferred the Old Testament to the New Testament and put a lot of stress on the 12 disciples, each of whom were associated with one of 12 prophets and a specific gospel. Evidence suggests that they were still going in Syria in the 6th century.

We have come across the Elkasites before, when we looked at the Mandaean influence on the Manichaean religion. We saw that scholars initially believed that their founder Mani was raised among Mandaeans (and this may still be true, because there is certainly evidence of Mandaean influence on the Manichaeans, and perhaps on Mani too) but Mani was raised among Elkasites.

The Elkasites owe their name to their founder Elkasai, who began to teach towards the end of the 1st century. According to the Church Father Hippolytus of Rome, a 3rd-century heresiologist, Elkasai proclaimed himself a prophet in AD 101, the third year of the reign of the emperor Trajan. A later Church Father, Epiphanius, explained that Elkasai's name (also spelled Elchasai and Elxai) comes from the Aramaic *hail kesai*, which means 'hidden power'. This suggests some sort of connection to Simon Magus who, according to Acts, was called the 'Great Power of God' (Acts 8: 10). (We will come across Simon again soon as he may provide a missing link between John the Baptist and Gnostic sects.) The term 'hidden power' may suggest that Elkasai saw himself as an incarnation or manifestation of God or the highest divine power.

Epiphanius wrote that Elkasai joined the Ebionites[2] and that during the reign of Trajan he joined the 'Ossenians' or 'Ossens'. According to Epiphanius these were an early Jewish baptismal sect, and it seems reasonable to identify them with the Essenes. Epiphanius is not only biased and unreliable but is also writing a couple of centuries after the life of Elkasai. But it is notable that these late traditions about 1st-century Jewish baptismal sects keep slipping into these familiar grooves, like the strange attractors of chaos theory.

Epiphanius also tells us that Elkasai came from the Transjordania region surrounding the River Jordan, the very area from which the Mandaeans believe they migrated. Hippolytus places the Elkasites further east in Parthia (modern Iran plus extensive regions to the west), all of which may simply indicate that, like the Mandaeans, some Elkasites migrated eastwards.

Elkasai wrote an apocalyptic work, known simply as the *Book of Elkasai*, which has vanished. Our only references to it come from the Church Fathers; it was apparently written in Syriac.[3] The book prophesied that there would be an apocalyptic or eschatological war in AD 116, which would break out three years after Trajan had conquered the Parthians. Trajan did so in AD 113, so scholars – ever reluctant to acknowledge the possibility even of accidentally fulfilled prophecy – believe that at least that portion of the *Book of Elkasai* was written after AD 113, not in AD 101, the date given by Hippolytus. The book was revealed or dictated to Elkasai by a massive male angel called the Son of God, who was 96 miles high and 24 miles wide. Elkasai was said to have been accompanied by a similarly huge angel called the Holy Spirit. Or, according to Hippolytus, the male angel was called Christ, the Great King. These two figures have some similarities to two angels, the Lord and the Angel of the Spirit, described in the *Ascension of Isaiah*, a Jewish-Christian text that is part of the so-called Pseudepigrapha ('false writings', which are Jewish and Christian scriptures written under the names of biblical figures). The Pseudepigrapha are apocryphal or non-canonical writings from the centuries around the turn of the common era. The Pseudepigrapha encompass a wide range of material, from the beautiful Gnostic *Odes of Solomon* (distinct from the *Psalms of Solomon*), which, as we shall see, have some relation to Mandaean writings, to the Jewish *Book of Jubilees*, which develops the stories from Genesis. Little else is known of the *Book of Elkasai*, but it was central to the religion of the Elkasites.

Elkasai rejected sacrifice. According to Hippolytus, the Elkasites practised magic and astrology, and claimed knowledge of the future. They were an esoteric sect and did not reveal the contents of their sacred book to outsiders. If the Elkasites were faced with persecution they were permitted to deny their beliefs and their membership of the sect. This is somewhat similar to the Mandaeans who have been content to see their beliefs and origins misrepresented if it helps their survival.

Dositheos the Samaritan baptiser-Gnostic

Although Samaritans had a common ancestry with Jews, and used a slightly different version of the Pentateuch, they were not considered Jewish and were thought to be of mixed blood. In the 1st century, being Jewish was synonymous with being a Judaean or of Judaean descent.

The Samaritans survive by the skin of their teeth in modern-day Israel, but their population of around 750 places them right at the gates of extinction. The Samaritans show that tiny minority communities can cling on tenaciously against all odds. There are the seemingly ubiquitous strange links between the Samaritans and the Mandaeans: both use 'Life' as a name for God, and the phrases 'the word of Life' and 'the treasure of Life' are common to both.[4] Although these are tiny details, it is through such unlikely similarities that connections are made.

Dositheos was from Samaria, although both Epiphanius and a later, 14th-century, Samaritan historian both describe him as Jewish. Origen and Eusebius wrote that Dositheos was considered to be Christ (the Messiah) to the Samaritans. According to Origen he claimed to be the Son of God and the Saviour. He was also said to still be alive at that time, perhaps indicating some belief in his resurrection, because he is dated to the first century and Origen was writing in the third century. Baptism was an important part of the practice of the followers of Dositheos – the Dositheans – and they kept the Sabbath strictly. According to the Samaritan historian, Dositheos was also thought to be the founder of the Ebionites, although this is very unlikely.

In Acts 8: 20 and John 4: 10, the phrase 'gift of God', which is the literal meaning of Dositheos, is associated with Samaria. Dosithean beliefs have also been linked to Jewish-Christian Ebionite beliefs. The Ebionites were Jewish Christians. The name Ebionite comes from a word for 'poor', satirized by Eusebius as referring to their impoverished notion of Jesus, who was a man and not divine in their Jewish-Christian worldview. Tertullian, another patristic polemicist, claimed instead that Ebion was the name of their founder, thus distancing them from Jesus. Sometimes their name is connected with Paul's reference to the 'poor of Jerusalem'.[5]

The Ebionites were vegetarians and would have disapproved of John the Baptist eating locusts. The Gospel of the Ebionites, preserved only in quotations, has John eating pancakes and honey – a much more attractive proposition than the locust. The two Greek words for 'pancakes' and 'honey' have just one letter difference, so this Ebionite gospel reference shows us not only a clever adaptation of existing material but also that the Ebionites used Greek despite being ethnically Jews.[6] The Ebionites were believed to have escaped to the east of the Jordan after the destruction of Jerusalem, broadly the area to which the Mandaeans must have belonged in their infancy.

It is quite possible that the Dositheans were originally Mandaeans. Or vice versa. Or at least that they have common roots. Like the Mandaeans, the Dositheans were also known as Nazarenes – this is stated by Theodore bar Konai, the Syrian Christian monk who was the first to write unambiguously about the Mandaeans. He equates the Dositheans with both the Mandaeans and the *nasuraiia* (the Mandaean inner circle). His unflattering account of their origins says that they were founded by Ado (Adam), a lazy beggar who moved with his family from Adiabene in northern Mesopotamia to Mesene on the banks of the Karun River. He begged from a roadside shack given to him by someone called Papa. Pupils gathered around him and hence the Mandaeans came into being.[7] Mandaeans do indeed live by the Karun in Iraq.[8]

From this first, albeit virulent, account of the Mandaeans some truth can be discerned. Ado is obviously Adam, the first Mandaean. The roadside shack must be making fun of the cult hut. The move from Adiabene to Mesene is obviously also a garbled account of the Mandaeans' traditions of their peregrinations. Theodore bar Konai also compared them with the Marcionites, named after Marcion, a 2nd-century Christian, who believed that the God of the Old Testament was a different figure to that of the New Testament and that there was a kind of dualistic mutual opposition between them. But Marcion didn't go as far as truly Gnostic groups did, and he seems not to have created his own myths, but rather to have used for his scripture a narrow selection of the Gospel of Luke and the Pauline epistles. Marcionite groups survived for centuries.

Simon Magus

Simon Magus was believed by many of the Church Fathers to be the arch-heretic and heresiarch (founder of heresy), and one of the first Gnostics. Although there were apparently Gnostic groups in the 2nd and 3rd centuries who claimed descent from Simon – and were named Simonians after him – none of the texts in the Nag Hammadi library is actually Simonian and we do not possess any complete account of Simonian teachings.

Simon first appears in Acts, which is conventionally dated to the late 1st century, although it may be even a decade or two later, and is generally considered much less historically reliable than the letters of Paul. 'Simon the sorcerer' is said to have already had a wide following in Samaria, but is so impressed ('startled' or 'driven out of his wits') by the 'wonders and great miracles' demonstrated by the apostle Philip that he followed Philip after being baptised a Christian. The second, more historically dubious, reference in Acts has Peter and John coming from Jerusalem to pray for the people of Samaria to receive the Holy Spirit, which had not yet descended on them. When Simon sees that this is achieved by the laying on of hands he offers Peter money to enable him to do the same. Peter utters a diatribe against Simon, telling him to pray for himself, to which Simon Magus asks Peter to teach them to pray. It is unlikely that Peter and John would travel all the way from Jerusalem to bolster Philip: it is simply another attempt at demonstrating that the early Church was unified and that Peter was, with James and John, at its head. Of course, the letters of Paul show that there were disputes and personality clashes within the early Church.

Further traditions about Simon crop up in the work of the Church Fathers. Justin Martyr, who is also from Samaria, writing around AD 150 specifies the village of Gitta in Samaria as Simon's hometown.

Irenaeus, writing in about AD 180, tells a strange story about Simon. Visiting a brothel in the city of Tyre in Phoenicia (modern Lebanon), Simon recognized that a prostitute named Helen was an embodiment of Ennoia, the First Thought, a Gnostic form of the highest divine feminine principle. Simon himself was an incarnation of the very highest power who was 'father over all'. Helen had been imprisoned in a body in which she suffered many afflictions and was then transmigrated from one body to another through the ages until she found herself incarnated as Helen of Troy. Centuries later she had been reborn as the prostitute Helen. Simon, in turn, had descended into the material world to take on a mortal life in order to rescue her. This story encapsulates a version of the Gnostic myth in which the soul descends into matter and is subsequently liberated. It suggests that there are genuine connections between the figure of Simon Magus and Gnosticism, rather than the story being mere slander from the Church Fathers.

In a later tradition, the *Recognitions of Clement* adds the important detail that both Simon and Helen were disciples of John the Baptist, as was Dositheos who supplanted Simon as John's successor.[9] If there is anything reliable in the connection between John the Baptist and Simon Magus, we may have our link between the Mandaeans and other Gnostics. The links between Simon Magus and Dositheos and John the Baptist give an association between John the Baptist and Gnosticism that parallels that of the Mandaeans, yet is independent. Mandaeism is a Gnostic religion that is associated with John the Baptist. Simonianism is a form of Gnosticism that is associated with John the Baptist.

The Magharians and Essenes
This quasi-Jewish sect mentioned by Arab writers of the 10th and 11th centuries was said to have interpreted the Bible allegorically, reading any passages in which God was referred to anthropomorphically as referring to a creator angel rather than God himself. This practice put it somewhat in the tradition of Gnosticism. The sect's name comes from the Arab word for 'cave', *magar*, because – in an echo of the Dead Sea Scrolls – their writings were discovered in a cave.

It is difficult to make a patchwork of all these little scraps of information. The Mandaeans are never named. John the Baptist is not identified as a Gnostic, but it has to be said that he is associated with Gnosticism via his followers such as Simon and Menander. Nothing is certain, but we might expect that the ancient Mandaeans might have felt quite at home in this maelstrom of Gnostic and baptismal sects.

The Essenes were a breakaway Jewish sect active from the 2nd century BC to the 1st century AD. The discovery of the Dead Sea Scrolls has made them famous throughout the world, although there is still controversy among scholars over the extent to which the Qumran Dead Sea Scrolls community may be considered Essene. In addition to the books of the Hebrew Bible that were discovered (going back as early as 300 BC and representing the oldest known manuscripts of any part of the Bible), there are documents detailing the disciplines of a community (the *Community Rule*), which may be that of the Qumran sect, apocalyptic books such as *The War of the Sons of Light and the Sons of Darkness*, and oddities such as the Copper Scroll, which may describe the location of buried treasure.

The Essenes practised water purification rituals, and there is a possible, although unverified, relationship between the Qumran community or the Essenes and John the Baptist. It is feasible that John was connected with Qumran or a similar community in his youth. Conventional scholars deny any direct relationship between Jesus and Qumran or the Essenes, but some believe they can see coded references to Jesus in the texts. Thus the questions concerning the identity and relationship of the Essenes, Qumran and the authors of the scrolls are complex ones. For the purpose of my discussion I will simply assume that the Dead Sea sect was a variety of an Essene community, without placing any particular burden of proof on it.

John the Baptist may represent a middle term between the Essenes and the Mandaeans. There are certainly parallels between the two groups. The phrase 'Lord of Greatness' occurs in Mandaean writings and it has also been found in the pseudepigraphal Qumran *Genesis Apocryphon*. In the *Haran Gawaita* John 'took the Jordan and the medicinal water (of life) and he cleansed lepers, opened (the eyes of) the blind and lifted the broken (maimed) to walk on their feet by the strength of the lofty King of Light – praised be his name – and gave speech and hearing to all who sought (him)'.[10] The passage immediately recalls Matthew 11: 2–5 (and Luke 7: 22) – 'the blind have regained their sight, the lame walk, lepers are cleansed, the deaf hear, the dead are raised, and the poor have the good news preached to them'. Qumran fragment 4Q521 has a quite similar passage, 'He will honour the pious setting prisoners free, opening the eyes of the blind, raising up those who are bowed down.... For He shall heal the critically wounded, He shall revive the dead, He shall send good news to the afflicted ...'.[11]

Does the speech in the *Haran Gawaita* indicate knowledge of the gospels? Or does it suggest a link with Qumran, at however many removes? Or do all three versions have a common source? Perhaps it is significant that Jesus directs his reply to John, and that the passage is shared by Matthew and Luke but not Mark. According to the most widely held view about the relationship between the three synoptic (from a Greek word meaning 'seen together') gospels, the material shared by all three originated with Mark and has been reworked by Matthew and Luke. The material shared only by Matthew and Luke is from a hypothetical common source known as Q (from the German *quelle*, or 'source'). This proto-gospel Q document must have been written before Matthew and Luke, and perhaps before Mark, thus pushing it back to an earlier strata of Christianity. Was this a teaching of John that Jesus was actually quoting back to him, presenting himself as the fulfiller of this particular prophecy known at Qumran, and establishing himself as superior to John? If John the Baptist is the immediate source, perhaps the Mandaean use of it derives from that channel rather than a later encounter with Christians.

Drower saw a resemblance between the *mshunia kushta* of the Mandaeans and the paradise of the Essenes as reported by Josephus: 'Good souls have their habitations beyond the ocean, in a region that is neither oppressed with storms of rain or snow, nor with intense heat, but refreshed by the gentle breathing of the west wind which perpetually blows from the ocean.'[12]

While this is certainly not identical to the ideal world of the Mandaeans, which is often placed in the north, both the Essene and Mandaean afterworlds belong to a type that is common to many cultures but not in Christianity or Judaism: it has a physical location and is characterized by temperate weather. The Mandaean version may easily be considered to extend back to native Mesopotamian or Iranian myth, such as the cave-afterworld in *The Epic of Gilgamesh.*[13]

The Essenes had withdrawn their support from the Temple in Jerusalem and created an alternative in the harsh environment of the Dead Sea. Whereas the Temple at times resembled a giant abattoir, its gutters filled with the blood of animals – doves and sheep – sacrificed to Yahweh, the Essenes had centred their religion on water and substituted water in the place of blood. Immersions and lustrations, ablutions and cleansings and baptisms were essential to the ritual life of the inhabitants of Qumran.

Other Essene–Mandaean similarities include the use of white vestments (by no means universal), the concept of the soul trapped in the body, the confession of sins at baptism, the belief in the fundamental conflict between the light and the darkness, and the phrases 'living water' and 'the fountain of life' are common to both.[14]

According to Philo of Alexandria an Essene-like sect called the Therapeutae chanted in separate groups of men and women, then in unison. Mandaean chanting is also antiphonal and is known as *nianas* ('responses').

The north–south orientation of the Mandaean cult huts, the *mandi*, is shared with the Essenes. Barbara Thiering, a scholar who believed that early Christian conflicts were codified in the Dead Sea Scrolls, notes:

> *The burials in the huge graveyard at Qumran are remarkable for being placed in a north-south direction, with the head on the south, and Mandaean shrines are built north-south, with the washing pool on the south and the building on the north. Both differ from normal Jewish practice, which preferred the east, with the temple placed east-west, its entrance on the east.*

At Qumran there is a long north-south courtyard, which has the same dimensions and shape as the wilderness tabernacle of the Hebrews, with a row of stones across its northern third. It has been argued in my books that this was the substitute sanctuary of the Essenes, built when they were expelled from the Jerusalem temple. It had the dimensions of the tabernacle, and was placed north-south, in order to make it clear that it was not a true temple, which could only be in Jerusalem. As time went on they did not regain the temple, the north-south direction was thought of as the one expressing the idea of a spiritual temple, found in the Manual of Discipline. Moreover, at the related building at Khirbet Mird (Hyrcania), some six miles inland from Qumran, there is an arrangement at the wady (winter stream) north of the building which indicated a baptismal rite. Two long underground tunnels have been constructed, one in the south bank of the wady, another in the north. Some form of dramatisation of a 'birth' is to be suspected, with washings in the waters of the stream. My suggestion, based on the grades of membership, is that a lower grade baptism was performed on the south bank, and was followed by a higher one on the north bank, and after this the baptised could proceed down the wady, which led straight to Qumran, in order to advance to the higher kind of initiation.[15]

There are suggestions of similarities between a Mandaean practice of prognosticating via the day of the week and day of the lunar month and an Essene calendar found in Qumran Cave 4. The two are not identical, due to the use of the weekdays by the Mandaeans, but there are similarities. Also The *Treatise of Shem*, a work that may date back to the 1st century BC and is categorized under the Old Testament Pseudepigrapha. Shem is, according to some Mandaean traditions, the first male ancestor of the Mandaeans after Adam.[16]

Yet it is easy to overemphasize these details. At Qumran the Essenes had constructed a complex of cisterns and feeding canals that enabled their water rituals to be conducted in the punishing dry heat of the Dead Sea area. The Mandaeans also set up pools to facilitate their baptisms but there is a crucial difference in the methods. Whereas the Essenes stored their water in cisterns, the Mandaeans required running water, either directly in a river or by using a system in which the water is flowing in and out and remains a part of the flow of the river. To Mandaeans, cisterns would be holding dead water rather than living water.

River baptisms such as those of John the Baptist or the Mandaeans may even be seen as a reaction to the sectarianism of the Essenes. The Dead Sea community had withdrawn from life. In their caves and hewn chambers they lived apart from the world. Their cisterns and canals gave them water that did not depend on the natural resources of great rivers, nor on the massive and elaborate aqueducts and water supplies of the Romans. Anyone who used Essene water was locked into the rigid, limited and celibate communal life of the sect – the water of Qumran was a closed and artificial system. The Jordan was open to all.

Chapter 12

At Last, John the Baptist

Occasionally, scholars have asked why, if John the Baptist is not a late addition to the beliefs of the Mandaeans, do they have no historical knowledge of John outside of what may be found in the New Testament? For instance, Lupieri asks:

> If the Mandaeans are actually the direct descendants of John's disciples, why do they not have any traditions of their own concerning their founder but derive everything they have to say about him from Christian tradition, sometimes even dating from some centuries after the New Testament? However, if the Mandaeans have always been where they are now and are not related directly to John the Baptist, why did they go and 'recycle' a saint (and only that one!) from a rival and hostile religion?[1]

In Mandaean tradition John the Baptist had a wife and children. His family is never mentioned in the New Testament. However, his family are seen as unhistorical because they occur only in Mandaean texts, while John living off locusts and wild honey is somehow considered historical by those scholars who have a bias towards the canonical gospels.

Bring forth children

The question of John's historical authenticity does raise the issue of John's descendants. Is there a bloodline of John the Baptist waiting to be discovered? The Mandaean John the Baptist was married and had children. The Mandaeans have quite strict guidelines on sexual conduct but celibacy is anathema to them. There are certain ritual situations during which priests must be celibate, but permanent celibacy is seen as an abomination. One passage in the Mandaean *Book of John* is worth quoting in full to give a taste of the marked difference between the Mandaean style of scripture and the familiar passages on John from the New Testament:

> *And he said, "John, you are like a scorched mountain which does not bring forth into this world any blossoms. You are like a dried-up stream on which plants are not planted. You are like a desolate house, before which all who see it are afraid. A land which has no lord have you become; a house in which there is no strength. An evil prophet have you become, who has not left after you one who remembers you, who will equip you and will provide for you, John, who will come after you to the grave.'*

> *When John heard this, in his eye formed a tear, and he said, 'Pleasant would it be to take a wife, and precious to have sons. But if I were to take a wife, when sleep comes perhaps desire would inflame me, and I would neglect my nocturnal devotions. Perhaps desire would enflame me and I would forget my Lord from my mind. Perhaps desire would inflame me and I would neglect my devotions every time.'*

> *When John said this, a letter came from the House of Abathur, 'John, take a wife and establish a family, and see that the world does not come to an end. On the dawn of the second day and on the dawn of the third day observe your marriage bed. On the dawn of the fourth day and the dawn of the fifth day betake yourself to your sublime devotions.'*[2]

John goes on to explain that he dearly wants a family but he is worried that desire will swallow him up and he will have no time for his devotions. A letter is sent to him from the house of Abathur, the Third Life. He is given a pattern of days on which to have sex and on which to abstain, with accompanying rituals.

John goes on to get a wife, named Anhar, and to have as many as eight children: Handan and Sharrath, then Birham and R'himath-Hiia, and finally Nsab, Sam, Anhar Ziwa and perhaps a second Sharrath. Many of these names are associated with entities from the Lightworld. It is extraordinary that with all the speculation over whether Jesus was married and if he had children, that with John the Baptist we have the name of his wife and a list of all his children. Perhaps there is nothing reliable in this, but one can search high and low through all the apocryphal traditions of Christianity for the name of Jesus' wife and children only to find nothing. Yet the fact that John is concerned that having a family might mean that he will be unable to fulfil his religious obligations suggests that at some point in the distant past celibacy had been a spiritual requirement but was no longer necessary.

Mandaean priests are married and the denial of sex found in Christianity is abhorrent to Mandaeans. Yet sexual practice is very much bound up with both ritual observance and family life. Lifetime celibacy has no part in Mandaeaism, and would be a recipe for extinction in a religion that does not admit converts.

The murky Jordan

In both Mandaeism and Christianity John is closely associated with the River Jordan. How feasible is it that baptism could have been conducted there? As one scholar put it:

> *A long tradition of Christian art depicts John the Baptist standing waist-deep in the clear waters of the Jordan pouring water over the heads of converts (or perhaps immersing them), watched by crowds of onlookers. However, no such scene can be found in the gospels, or in Josephus for that matter. Nothing is said about how John baptised. A little reflection indicates that such a scene is a pious fiction unconsciously modelled on centuries of Christian practice.*[3]

Ritual purification was widely practised and took various forms, but the use of the Jordan for such purposes is odd and virtually unprecedented. Ritual baths dating from the Second Temple period have been discovered at numerous places including Qumran, Jericho, Masada, Sepphoris, and the Ophel and Essene quarters of Jerusalem,[4] but never at rivers. Also, individuals generally bathed and ritually purified themselves without the involvement of a third party. But John's ritual 'of repentance for the forgiveness of sins', whatever its form, was administered by 'John the Baptist' himself (Mark 1: 4).

We are so used to hearing or reading about the Jordan as a place of baptism that we might not question its suitability. Colin Brown has written:

> If one fell into the southern part of the Jordan where John is traditionally believed to have baptised, the first thing that one would want would be a shower to rinse off the dirt from the sediment. Apart from times when swollen by the winter rains, those southern stretches of the Jordan that are accessible are often shallow and sluggish. While religious bathing in unclean water is not unknown and intention counts more than the quality of the water (as is evident from bathing in the Ganges), insistence on purity of the water is well attested in Jewish literature. If ritual purification were the prime consideration in John's baptism, the lower Jordan would seem to be precluded. The Damascus Document appears to rule it out on two counts: 'Concerning one who purifies himself in water: Let no man bathe in water which is dirty or insufficient to cover a man.'[5]

The river may not have been suitable all year round. In the fourth gospel, John baptises in Aenon near Salim in Samaria 'because there was plenty of water' (John 3: 23). Sometimes this is seen as a brief sojourn by John in Samaritan territory towards the end of his life, perhaps when things were hotting up for him in Judaea due to his fractious relationship with Herod Antipas. Yet it may have been a seasonal requirement, avoiding the intense heat of the Jordan valley in summertime.[6]

John is associated with water and desert, both liminal zones, where the laws and habits of cities and farmland may not apply.

Colin Brown therefore suggests that the significance of baptism in the Jordan was not ritual purification but a symbolic exit from the current Israel, with all its sins and imperfections, into a renewed Holy Land. If so, perhaps the disciples of John chose to make their symbolic exit and never returned again.

Despite his baptismal associations, John is only ever referred to in Mandaean scripture by his name Yuhana,[7] without the title 'the Baptist' or 'the Baptiser', sometimes specifying his parentage, which is the same as given in the Gospel of Luke. Perhaps the point was too obvious to be remarked on: John was a Mandaean priest and every priest was a baptiser. In the gospels he is frequently given his title, perhaps providing further evidence that Mandaean traditions were not all dependent on Christianity.

John the Gnostic

Although there is nothing essentially Gnostic about the New Testament figure of John the Baptist, nor does he appear extensively in surviving Gnostic texts, the question should be asked, was John a Gnostic? The medieval Cathars contrasted the baptism of John – which was of water and as far as the Cathars were concerned was the false baptism of the Catholic Church – with their own baptism of fire and spirit received during the *consolamentum* rite.[8]

If, as seems likely, the Mandaeans had a connection with John, then the answer to this question might be yes. The Church Fathers were all keen to emphasize that early Gnostics such as Simon Magus and Menander and Dositheos were pupils of John, yet they do not seem to be able to go the extra mile and say that John was a Gnostic. Their motives for refraining are clear: John is a somewhat admirable figure in the gospels. And if John was a Gnostic, might not Jesus have been a Gnostic too?

Both John the Baptist and Jesus are mentioned in Josephus's *Antiquities of the Jews*. Although both accounts occur in book 18 of the Antiquities, the two figures are not linked with each other in any way. Moreover, although most scholars believe the section on John the Baptist to be the authentic work of Josephus and integral to the text, this cannot be said of the passage on Jesus. Many critical scholars have argued that phrases like 'He was the Christ' are later interpolations added by Christian scribes.

> *Now about this time there lived Jesus a wise man, if one ought to call him a man, for he was a doer of wonderful works, a teacher of such men as receive the truth with pleasure. He won over many Jews and*

> *many of the Greeks. He was the Messiah. When Pilate, upon hearing*
> *him accused by men of the highest standing [lit., 'the principal men']*
> *among us, had condemned him to be crucified, those who in the first*
> *place had come to love him did not forsake him. For he appeared to*
> *them alive again on the third day, as the holy prophets had predicted*
> *these and many other wonderful things about him. And the tribe of*
> *the Christians, so called after him, continues to the present day.*[9]

Any proposed reconstruction of Josephus's original, without Christian interpolations, makes it into something that would have been historically acceptable for an aristocratic Jew like Josephus to come up with, cutting out anything that sounds like it might have been interpolated by a Christian. Any historically acceptable testimony is hypothetical and there is no evidence anywhere for this simpler, supposedly more authentic version. Recent work has shown that the passage is unlikely to be genuine at all.[10]

We cannot assume that Josephus is giving us anything like an encyclopedic knowledge of 1st-century Judaea. In fact, this is clearly not the case: many 1st-century rabbinical figures whose names – accompanied by teachings, biographical details and legends – survive in the Mishnah, the Talmud and other rabbinical writings, are not mentioned in Josephus. Others are. Josephus is a notoriously partisan writer, making little attempt at a neutral position. He was a Jewish turncoat, having backed the Roman general Titus who would become emperor.

John and the gospels

Most scholars agree that the gospels were written in the order Mark, Matthew, Luke and John. Matthew and Luke are generally considered to have used Mark as the basis of their own account; John, may have had some knowledge of Mark too. In any case, the four gospels may be read in chronological order as documenting a movement that was fast moving beyond its Jewish roots in Judaea. That Mark, Matthew and Luke are known as the synoptic ('seen together') gospels refers to the fact that when the texts of each gospel are placed next to each other all three usually follow the same sequence of events and show close verbatim similarities. This is not true of the Gospel of John.

In Mark (1: 7), Matthew (3: 11), Luke (3: 16) and John (1: 27), John the Baptist is already stating that he is unworthy to unstrap the sandals of the one who is to come. Later in the Gospel of John (3: 27–36), John the Baptist is given a long speech in which he diminishes his own importance and praises Jesus in the highest terms possible, stating that it is exclusively through the Son (Jesus) that eternal life will be given.

In the Gospel of John, Jesus has accepted disciples of John the Baptist (Andrew and Philip) into the Twelve (John 1: 40–45), further emphasizing that the future belongs to Jesus not John. In the Acts of the Apostles (18: 24–19: 7), generally believed to be written by the author of Luke, we are told that an Alexandrian Jew named Apollos was knowledgeable about the way of the Lord, preached with spiritual strength, had accurate information about Jesus and yet had only received the baptism of John, as had other disciples that the apostle Paul discovers in Ephesus. It is only when Paul lays hands on them that they receive the Holy Spirit, of which they previously had known nothing. The message is clear: John was only important as the forerunner of Jesus. Few Christians would disagree with this, or even question whether John should be seen in any other way.

All this adds up to show that the New Testament, and Christianity in general, is rather dismissive of John the Baptist as a figure in his own right. This will all have relevance to the discussion of John and Jesus, but for the moment I would like to highlight how offensive this view of John the Baptist might be to any religion that descends from him. This is worth bearing in mind. Of what worth is it to tiptoe around the beliefs of Christians, Muslims and Jews while stomping all over those of minority religions?

I believe that we have to maintain a balance between respecting the beliefs of others and being critical. But anyone who finds the Mandaean view of Jesus offensive might want to consider whether the Christian view of John the Baptist is equally offensive to a Mandaean. Modern Mandaeans have a variety of opinions about Jesus. He is usually seen as a Mandaean who became apostate because he was lax with the Mandaean traditions, which is not all that different to the way Jesus is viewed by many Jews.

It may seem surprising that such an important aspect of John's life as his being killed by Herod is absent in Mandaeism, but this is not without parallel – in Islam it is usually understood that Jesus was not crucified.

Witness to the light but not the light

'There was a man sent from God, whose name was John. He came for testimony, to bear witness to the light, that all might believe through him. He was not the light, but came to bear witness to the light' (John 1: 6–8).

There are few Mandaeans of any time period who could disagree with this at face value, although their reading of this would differ from Christians. To Christians, John was not the light because Jesus was the light. To Mandaeans, John was not the light because the Lightworld existed long before John – as did their entire religion.

In Josephus the passage that mentions John the Baptist is, unlike the one concerning Jesus, widely considered to be authentic, although there are some dissenting voices. Let us for a moment consider this as an option: what are the repercussions if Josephus never mentioned John the Baptist? It would mean that aside from the Mandaean accounts of John the Baptist, our only knowledge of him would come from the New Testament and the later Apocrypha. As we have already seen, the gospel accounts are interdependent – Matthew and Luke used Mark as a basis – and progressively put more and more spin on their account of John until in the Gospel of John he is reluctant even to baptise Jesus. It is difficult, or even impossible, to show any real literary relationship between the Gospel of Mark and the Gospel of John, but it is entirely feasible that the author of John had heard the Gospel of Mark read out aloud. There seems to be little clear consensus on the relationship of the Gospel of John to the synoptics or about the origin of the material in the Gospel of John. The long discourses of Jesus in the fourth gospel, so different to the brief parables and pithy sayings of the other three gospels, may not derive from memories of Jesus' own speech. But the author of the fourth gospel was surely not making it all up on the fly either. He may have had written sources that he reworked, or he may have elaborated on oral tradition. At the very least he had some idea of the sort of things that Jesus *should* say. Thus the New Testament is not exactly a disinterested account.

If the passage about John in Josephus is another interpolation, is it possible that John was not actually beheaded? Could he have led the Mandaeans east of the Jordan? For this to be possible it would necessitate that neither Matthew nor Luke nor John had any independent knowledge of John the Baptist. In that case it is a possibility that Mark invented the story about the beheading of John the Baptist.

Why would Mark do this? Well, some scholars believe that many aspects of Mark's narrative were constructed in order to contextualize the sayings of Jesus. The sayings tradition is often thought to be more reliable than the narrative tradition. That is, Mark was faced with the problem of writing a coherent narrative of the life of Jesus and needed to insert sayings into that narrative. Mark then deduced what kind of setting a saying must have originated in (and he may have been convinced that he was acting through inspiration, or the influence of the Holy Spirit, rather than just making stuff up) and then he wove the saying into his narrative.

Mark contains a fragment (6: 14–16) that, although not a saying of Jesus, may have another meaning. If Jesus is John the Baptist risen from the dead this may not mean literally dead but spiritually dead, as in Paul.

Deconstructing the death of John

In the synoptic gospels Matthew (11: 7–11) and Luke (7: 24–28), and the Gospel of Thomas (78), Jesus asks, 'What did you go out to the wilderness to behold? A reed shaken by the wind?' John the Baptist is not connected with this saying in the Gospel of Mark, the Gospel of Thomas or in the reconstructed Q. The death of John the Baptist is not found in Q nor is it in the Gospel of Thomas. The tradition of sayings ascribed to Jesus is often believed to be more historically reliable than the stories attached to them.[11] It is quite possible that this saying had no connection with John the Baptist originally but that it became associated with his death later. This illustrates that few aspects of the gospels are unassailable.

However, if John the Baptist really was beheaded by Herod, as the gospels and an authentic Josephus would indicate, why does

Mandaean scripture not refer to this? All sorts of calumnies are brought against the Jews of Jerusalem and all manner of divine events conspire to help the Mandaeans. If the Mandaeans were merely taking their knowledge of John the Baptist from the gospels and seizing on him as a prophet through whom they could link their religion to the Abrahamic faiths and secure a preferred status as 'people of the book', why did they not seize upon the beheading of John the Baptist as a central event? It would be a perfect fit for their very justified persecution complex. The mystery of the unmartyred John is difficult to understand from either perspective. However, as G.R.S. Mead notes:

> This omission of all reference to the death of John would be incomprehensible, did we not reflect in the first place that no attempt is made in the existing Mandaean documents to give anything that could be called a 'Life' of John, and conjecture in the second that in all probability nothing of doctrinal importance was attached to the way of his ending as it was in the case of Jesus.[12]

We have become so used to the life of Jesus dominating the Christian religion (including the Christian year, with its central festivals of Easter and Christmas) that it is easy to forget that this is not the case with every religion. Judaism is the religion of the Jewish people rather than primarily the religion founded by Abraham or by Moses. The Quran is absolutely foundational and central to Islam, but very little of the life of Muhammad can be extracted from the Quran alone. Even the *hadith*, the traditions of the prophet passed on orally and eventually collected, do not give a full picture of Muhammad's life. It was only centuries after the death of Muhammad that a traditional life was published. John the Baptist is not considered the founder of Mandaeism. Put in this context it is perhaps unsurprising that the Mandaeans have no tradition of John's death. Yet still odd.

From the head of John to the *Book of John*

Despite the inferior status of John the Baptist in the New Testament, later Christianity considered him a saint and he enjoyed extensive popularity in the Christian world. According to tradition, John the Baptist is believed to have been buried at Sebaste in Samaria. By the 4th century there was a shrine there. The tomb was desecrated by Julian the Apostate as part of his grand, yet futile, attempt to oust Christianity from its dominant status and restore the ancient pagan religions in a new version. (Julian might have achieved better results with a more generous choice of tactic.) John's official birthday is 24 June, a date produced by subtracting six months from Christmas because John was said to have been conceived six months before Jesus. John was patron of the Knights Hospitaller, officially known as the Order of the Knights of Saint John of Jerusalem. In England 496 churches were dedicated to him. As a church name his was sixth in popularity, with Mary, Peter, Michael, Andrew and All Saints higher on the list.[13]

Throughout Christendom there are places that claim to own the bodily relics of John the Baptist, including Rome, Amiens, Munich, Getinje in Montenegro, Istanbul, Damascus, Wadi Natrum in Egypt, Sozopol in Bulgaria and Sveti Ivan (St John's Island) on the southwestern coast of the Black Sea.

The *Secret Book of James* has an intriguing section in which Jesus tells the disciples, 'The head of prophecy was cut off with John'.[14] When James protests that it is impossible to cut off the head of prophecy, Jesus tells him that if he understood what 'head' meant he would know that prophecy comes from the head. It is a mysterious statement that I do not claim to understand.

John the Baptist doesn't play a very large part at all in surviving Gnostic writings.[15] In the Nag Hammadi text the *Testimony of Truth*, John the Baptist recognized the power of Jesus on the Jordan, meaning that 'the dominion of carnal procreation had come to an end'.[16] The Jordan is explained as 'the function of the body, its sensual pleasures. The water of the Jordan is the desire for sexual intercourse. By "John" [the Baptist] is meant the ruler of the womb.'[17]

The *Testimony of Truth* gives an ascetic, anti-sexual interpretation of the significance of John's baptism of Jesus. It is also clearly at odds with the Mandaeans' understanding of the Jordan as the living water, the representative of the Lightworld in our own physical world. In the Nag

Hammadi text known as the Valentinian Exposition, the Jordan seems to cohere with the Mandaean view: 'The meaning of John [the Baptist] is the aeon, the meaning of the Jordan is the descent that is the ascent, our exodus from the world into the aeon.'[18] Given that other Gnostics don't attribute John with this kind of transcendent meaning, I wonder whether the author of the *Valentinian Exposition* had some contact with the Mandaeans?

Perhaps the notable lack of reference to John in Gnostic writings, despite the Mandaeans being both Gnostic and followers of John, is due to the absence of the Mandaeans from the Mediterranean coastal locations in which much of the Nag Hammadi material was composed.

The Mandaean John the Baptist

The Mandaeans' own traditions about John are quite disparate. The Mandaean *Book of John* is far from being a systematic account of the life and work of the Baptiser, nor does it contain much in the way of teachings by John. The 'Instructions of Yuhana' section of the *Right Ginza* contains what are probably the only teachings attributed to John the Baptist outside of the New Testament.[19] Many of them are variations on a theme: 'The believer is a successful farmer', 'The prudent person is a masterful artist', 'The steadfast person is like a mountain' and so on. Some are intriguing, such as 'Wisdom for the ignorant is like a mirror for a blind person', which is suggestive of Gnostic teachings; another is, 'The apex of gnosis is not to be controlled by your temptations'. One, in particular, stands out because it is atypical of the general sayings and proverbs of this short collection as well as in line with the words attributed to John in the New Testament: 'You, the chosen and righteous ones: keep yourselves away from deceit, sins, falsehood, lying, falsity, and from evil. Keep away from temptation, cruelty, and ignorance. Do not blaspheme and do not engage in adultery. Avoid envy and hatred, resentment and malice, and shamelessness.' These teachings are unremarkable in themselves but they are in line with the uncompromising teachings attributed to John in the gospels. Could this last one be a saying of John that has come down through the centuries?

Mandaean baptisms were used for ritual purification and as the standard regular community religious practice to ensure an ongoing connection with the Lightworld. John's baptism was for the remission of sins, a specific purpose that in the eyes of scholars sets it apart from other forms of baptism. However, in the *Right Ginza* (11.20–24) there is a baptism for the remission of sins.[20] This provides a link to the baptismal practices of John as described in the New Testament. Is this an indication of subsequent Christian influence on the Mandaeans, which does not seem to have been substantial anyway, or is it a fossilized fragment from the 1st century embedded in Mandaean scripture?

Lupieri argues that most scholars are now convinced that Mandaean knowledge of John the Baptist derives neither from their own traditions nor from the New Testament but from the apocryphal gospels. He also suggests that the Mandaeans believed that John taught for 42 years,[21] but doesn't state which apocryphal gospel this information comes from. We might also ask why most of the Church Fathers know nothing reliable about Jesus apart from what is found in the canonical gospels? This is still commonplace among scholars of Christianity. Few of them like to ask why so little of Jesus' life and teaching is known.

The *Haran Gawaita* tells how John the Baptist is hunted by Herod and is sheltered on a white mountain. Something remarkably similar is described in the pseudepigraphal *Protoevangelium of James* when John the Baptist is taken by his mother Elizabeth and protected by a magic mountain.[22] The link between the two stories is approximate but suggestive, somewhat like that of the Apocrypha and the Quran, as described in Chapter 6 'People of the Book'. For example, Muhammad (or the angel who dictated the Quran to him, or Allah himself) clearly knew some apocryphal traditions, quite probably from oral sources. The stories in the Quran in which Mary gives birth to Jesus beneath a palm tree, and in which Jesus makes birds out of clay, are also found in the apocryphal infancy gospels. The Quranic view that Jesus was not actually crucified is also found in the Gnostic text, *The Second Treatise of The Great Seth*. Both suggest oral retellings that made their way back into written texts.

Just as Jesus is seen as an apostate and false Messiah to the Mandaeans, John the Baptist was perceived as a false prophet in Jewish Christianity.

Much later on we have the *Recognitions of Clement*. The Pseudo-Clementine literature is written in the name of the early Church Father Pope Clement I. The *Recognitions* is understood by scholars to be in the form of a Hellenistic romance, as were some other examples of apocryphal literature such as the works known collectively as the Apocryphal Acts. *Recognitions* is particularly concerned with the influence of Simon Magus and St Peter's triumph over him. Simon Magus is commonly seen as a cipher for Paul and Pauline Christianity. Although written in the 3rd/4th century (and late enough to get excluded even from many discussions of apocryphal Christian literature), and clearly fictitious in many respects (in a way that is more obvious to us than the canonical gospels and Acts, to whose extravagances we have been culturally inured through centuries of familiarity), they have interesting aspects. *Recognitions* has an episode in which John's followers claim that John the Baptist was the Messiah rather than Jesus. Some commentators have interpreted this as an encounter between the community responsible for *Recognitions* and a contemporary (3rd/4th century) group of followers of John. The only group at that time known to have followed John are the Mandaeans. Perhaps we have another tantalising early glimpse of the Mandaeans preserved in the *Recognitions*?

Petra and the Nabataeans

We have seen that the Mandaic script has close resemblances to Nabataean (see Chapter 9). There is one curious link to John the Baptist that could open up all sorts of possibilities. To quote Eusebius, the 3rd-century official historian of the Church:

> *Not long after this John the Baptist was beheaded by the younger Herod, as is stated in the Gospels. Josephus also records the same fact, making mention of Herodias by name, and stating that, although she was the wife of his brother, Herod made her his own wife after divorcing his former lawful wife, who was the daughter of Aretas,*

*king of Petra, and separating Herodias from her husband while he
was still alive.*

*It was on her account also that he slew John, and waged war with
Aretas, because of the disgrace inflicted on the daughter of the latter.
Josephus relates that in this war, when they came to battle, Herod's
entire army was destroyed, and that he suffered this calamity on
account of his crime against John.*[23]

Thus, the Mandaeans use an alphabet that quite possibly derives from the
kingdom of Nabataea. Herod Antipas's first wife was the daughter of the
Nabataean king of Petra. John went on to criticize Herod for marrying
Herodias, his brother's wife. Herod then went to war against Aretas and
the Nabataean kingdom of Petra, in the process of which Herod lost most
of his army.

Could the Mandaic alphabet be evidence of the Mandaeans'
connection with John the Baptist? John's objection to Herod's marriage
is usually understood as being on moral grounds, which may well have
been a factor. But if John was in some way allied with Nabataea, or at least
in sympathy with the area, there may have been a more personal element.
And if Nabataea was sympathetic to John, perhaps it would have been
a natural location for his disciples to retreat to as conditions in Judaea
became more and more difficult as the century progressed.

The Herodians were Idumean in origin, an area south of Judaea
whose people legendarily were descended from Esau, brother of Jacob.
Herod's own mother was Nabataean and he may have lived for a period
in Petra as a child. Nabataea was east and south of the Dead Sea. Qumran
is on the northwestern shore of the Dead Sea. Trajan would eventually
conquer Nabataea and add it to the Roman Empire. Perhaps such an event
might have motivated the Mandaeans to move further away to the east.
As we have seen, there is evidence that disciples of John were known as
far away as Alexandria and Ephesus, so southeast of the Dead Sea, which
is so much closer to the Jordan, would present no problem of feasibility.
As Drower remarks:

Was John the Baptist connected with these [Nasoraeans of Epiphanius]? He left no book behind him, but there are traces of grave differences between his disciples and those of Jesus. It is certain that Simon the Magian was never a Nasoraean although the Divine Man was the centrepiece of his system, and he himself claimed to be a Messiah. Had he been, we might have found his name, like that of John the Baptist, in the Nasoraean Commemoration prayer. ... John is never the mouthpiece of Nasoraean doctrine as it appears in the secret scrolls, and John's figure may have been inserted at a later date, for the name Yuhiu is Arabic not Aramaic.[24]

For there to be a genuine connection it would not be necessary for all of the early Mandaeans to be associated with John the Baptist. A small number of them may have been connected to John, and John's influence perhaps became definitive only when the community was put under stress and had to migrate. If they were an ethnic group from a particular area they might have had a form of local Semitic, slightly Hellenistic-influenced religion. If they had had to migrate in response to Jewish pressure as a result of the Jewish War against the Romans, an entire community might have found itself on the move. Communities under pressure need distinctive elements to hold themselves together. They can also develop a combination of stubbornly conservative elements that give them identity, combined with the kinds of innovation that emerge when a culture is under pressure. Thus their language remained Aramaic and their alphabet Nabataean, but John the Baptist emerged as a figure who came to represent a revival of Mandaeism, which was now seen as stretching back in time to the first human.

Chapter 13

The Apostate Jesus

'Guard me, my brother, from the god fashioned by a carpenter!

If a carpenter made a god, then who made the carpenter?'

FROM THE *Book of John*, TRANSLATION BY JAMES MCGRATH

There is still a great deal of squeamishness, even taboo, about criticizing Jesus, even outside of the circle of churchgoing Christians. Many readers may be able to swallow with few problems the notion that the Mandaeans go back to John the Baptist, but will then choke at the idea that Jesus was an apostate Mandaean, and especially that he was a somewhat disreputable figure. Of course, in the gospels he consorts with prostitutes and sinners and tax collectors, winebibbers and gluttons, breaks the Sabbath and performs magical deeds like exorcism, healing, multiplying loaves and fishes, and so on. But few people like to consider the fact that these were genuinely disreputable acts for a 1st-century Jew. This is understandable. For most Christians, John the Baptist is merely a man. He may have been considered a saint by the Catholic Church, he may be acknowledged as the forerunner of Jesus, even a prophet, but he was merely a man – not the Son of God, and not even a Christian.

Everyone likes Jesus. To Christians he is the Messiah and Son of God. To Muslims he is the final prophet before Muhammad. Many Jews now see him as a variety of 1st-century rabbi. Hindus, Buddhists and Taoists find much that is admirable in the teachings of Jesus. John Lennon gave a homespun opinion that still resonates with post-religious Westerners: 'The way I see it, Jesus was alright but his disciples were thick and ordinary.' The ancient Gnostics who are represented in the Nag Hammadi Library and the heresiological writings of the Church Fathers believed that it was not the true God in the Garden of Eden but Ialdabaoth, the lion-headed evil or ignorant demiurge; to them, Moses was not a true prophet, he was a tool of the demiurge. So many of our traditional assumptions about the Bible stories are turned upside down by the Gnostics. But they never said a word against Jesus.[1]

Everyone likes Jesus – apart from the Mandaeans. Here I should once again interject that modern Mandaeans aren't anti-Christian. Iraqi and Iranian Mandaeans have long felt a greater degree of commonality with Christians in their regions than with Muslims or Jews. And yet enmity with Jesus is at the root of their story of how they came to leave Palestine for Iraq and Iran, and hence how they came to be the Mandaeans.

The Mandaean interpretation of the story of Jesus is a radical one. It is also filled with clearly mythic and legendary elements: Jesus is identified with Nbu, the Babylonian planetary god Mercury. Jesus' mother is Ruha, the evil female spirit. Jesus is not greeted by John the Baptist as the long-awaited Messiah; instead, Jesus tricks John into baptising him. John is given divine knowledge of Jesus' motives and intention, and is advised to go along with it.

Surely these are made up by the Mandaeans to justify some later events? Perhaps at some point in their history the Mandaeans were in danger of being absorbed into Christianity. The story of Jesus being a false Messiah served to emphasize the differences between Mandaeans and Christians. While it is certainly possible that these stories were made up by later Mandaean priests, it is also possible (if not likely) that they preserve some historical memory of Jesus and John the Baptist. If this is so, then perhaps we are seeing Jesus from a different perspective.

We are used to assuming the basic historical truth of the gospels. The quest for the historical Jesus has been going on since the 19th century. The Jesus of history is the person who will be revealed by applying the usual historical-critical techniques to the gospels in the same way that one might to any documentary sources. The outcome of the quest for the historical Jesus seems to depend on what the investigator puts into it. Protestant evangelicals and hardline Catholics find Jesuses who match their existing expectations. More liberal Christians of whatever domination get liberal Jesuses. On the other hand, the few scholars who investigate the New Testament and Church Fathers because of intellectual curiosity (they are a small but growing band) come out of the quest with little treasure. Like radiocarbon dating, genuinely historical-critical Jesus research is a destructive technique. It seems that the alternatives are either to confirm one's own prejudices or to find oneself unable to say much about Jesus at all.

The disappearing man

The search for the historical Jesus has been summarized succinctly by Professor Stevan Davies:

> From ... our earliest surviving Christian texts, the New Testament epistles, show almost no interest in the life or teachings of Jesus. Except for his last week on earth, there is almost no such interest shown in the Acts of the Apostles. Interest in Jesus' life story was surprisingly late to develop, and when it developed it did so almost entirely through the reworking and creation of ahistorical legends and miracle stories and, in the case of the Gospel of John, accounts of a divinity come to earth. Indeed, there really are only two accounts, that of Mark and that of John, and the latter may be dependent on the former for its basic narrative. ...

> Faith that there was a historical Jesus begins with the fact that we have several biographical narratives about his life: the narrative gospels of Matthew, Mark, Luke, John and James, at least two long lists of his sayings, the Gospel of Thomas and Q, and letters by foundational Christians, especially those of Paul and the pseudo-Pauls. Scholars today tend to presume that these materials, while certainly not accurate by the historical standards of the 21st century,

are good enough for religion work, and as good as you have any reason to expect from people writing so very long ago. But they are not good sources at all for an historical Jesus. In fact, for well over a century now, scholars of the New Testament have found evidence that what appear to be biographical narratives about the life of Jesus are, with one possible exception, works of fiction.

A moment's thought will reveal that you, gentle reader, know more of the life of Jesus than Matthew or James or Luke or John ever did. You have read all their works and the Gospel of Thomas besides, and the Gospel of Mark, and the reconstructed Q. None of the sacred authors had as many written sources as you have. An appeal to their knowledge of unwritten sources is meaningless for, if any of them had a significant store of information that they did not incorporate in their writing, we know nothing whatsoever about it because they did not think it significant enough to use.

The biography of Jesus is really only transmitted by one narrative gospel, not five. The Gospels of John and James are fictitious, the revised versions of Mark, i.e. Gospels of Luke and Matthew, are fictitious narratives except insofar as they are following the Gospel of Mark if indeed Mark is a valid historical source. If a Gospel gives reliable information regarding the biography of Jesus it is only Mark's. But Mark's Gospel is far from reliable.[2]

Another approach to the historical Jesus is that proposed by N.T. Wright who advocates a method of testing hypotheses. He uses that method to conclude something along the lines of 'He truly was the Son of God'. But one does not have to be, like Wright, a committed evangelical to play this game. Let us try a hypothesis of the Mandaean approach: Jesus perverted the teachings of John the Baptist.

John the Baptist is baptising and preaching forgiveness of sins. His movement is Jewish but, like the Essenes and other groups, it places no trust in the centralized and compromised system of the Jerusalem Temple. He probably has some relationship to the Essenes, but whereas their communities are inward-looking and restrictive – typified by the stone cisterns used to collect water for ritual use – John's baptisms are out in the open, on the banks of the majestic Jordan. Like the Essenes, John sees the world as a battleground between the forces of light and darkness. The Judaism of the time was a rich stew of cultural influences and folk traditions, mixed in with the Bible and established religious traditions. Apocalyptic apocryphal writings looked forward to the end of days, to a final battle between good and evil, light and darkness. Heterodox Jewish literature made much of obscure biblical characters like Seth and Enoch. Complex cosmologies came into being, with angels who perhaps abused their positions as deputies of the Lord, and if there were semi-divine entities around abrogating the will of the one God, perhaps some people were tricked into worshipping them instead of the real God. Perhaps the moneygrabbing and power-hungry priests, royals and collaborators were worshipping the wrong God?

What if the Lord, Adonai, who stalked through the books of the Hebrew Bible was not the true, transcendent God, but a god of darkness – of matter rather than of spirit? Was the true God experienced amidst the moneychangers of a Temple that functioned as a massive slaughterhouse, or in the direct spiritual experience that was engendered by a voluntary immersive baptism conducted by someone who looked as if he lived the life? It is but a little step from the milieu of the Essenes and biblical apocrypha to Gnosticism. Perhaps John the Baptist took that step? Perhaps Simon Magus, Menander, Dositheos and the Mandaeans all followed him. Admittedly, it is speculation – but then so much of the study of Christian origins is.

What if Jesus only took half a step – and in doing so he found he could neither go forwards into the developing proto-Mandaeism, nor backwards into any kind of mainstream Judaism? There is no role for Judas in Mandaean tales, as far as I have been able to see. Perhaps this is because Jesus has the negative role himself. It might be tempting to see the Mandaeans as having adapted the relationship of Jesus and Judas to correspond with John the Baptist and Jesus respectively, but there are not enough parallels for this to hold up. Jesus is not a trusted disciple who betrays John, nor is Jesus responsible for John's death in any way, whereas it is the betrayal by Judas that leads directly to the crucifixion of Jesus.

Lax with the Torah

In the rabbinical tradition of the early centuries AD, Galilee had a reputation for being lax in upholding Jewish Law, although an influx of Judaean rabbis eventually put paid to this. In the gospels Jesus is portrayed as flouting Torah law for a higher cause, when he plucks corn on the Sabbath, heals on the Sabbath or rubs shoulders with a tax collector and prostitutes. When, after Jesus' death, gentiles join the early Christian movement Paul allows those most definitive of Jewish religious practices – male circumcision and kosher food practices – to be superseded. Although many Jewish Christians, well into the 2nd century, kept kosher law and were ethnically and culturally Jewish, most Jews must have seen Christianity as a weird form of Judaism that allowed unclean practices.

The reputation of Christians was no different among Mandaeans. Christians did not keep to Mandaean practices, as they saw it, because Jesus had been too lazy. As Mandaeans put it, 'Our religion is very difficult'.[3]

It is not often that we acquire access to any hostile view of Jesus. Morton Smith argues that Jesus was a *goes*, a 'magician', as evidenced by several of his actions in the gospels, such as the healings and the interaction with demons. These were among the accusations made by the Roman pagan Celsus, who infamously reported that Jesus was the illegitimate son of the Roman soldier Pantera, and by the Jewish anti-gospel spoof *Sefer Teledot Yeshu* (*The Book of the Life of Jesus*), which relates how Jesus broke into the Temple to learn the secret name of God so that he could use it for magical purposes, and he has it tattooed on his thigh because he knows that it will be erased from his memory once he exits the Temple. The Mandaean view of Jesus provides us with another example in this vein.[4]

The Johannine problem

Although earlier scholars toyed with the possibility that a Mandaean-style Gnosticism may have underpinned the community associated with the fourth gospel and John the Evangelist (the Johannine community), it is not an influential idea nowadays. Apart from the Mandaeans themselves – and, apparently, Lady Drower in her final, unpublished book – no one has seriously considered that Jesus could have been a proto-Mandaean. There is widespread hostility even to the notion that there might have been proto-Gnostic elements in Jesus' teaching, or even tiny hints of similarity. Maybe there aren't. But unless the idea is taken seriously and someone takes the ball and runs with it, we shall never know.

There is plenty in Mandaean texts about Jesus, but early Christianity did not reciprocate. Unless we count each and every reference to John the Baptist as a potential reference to Mandaeism (which, arguably, may be valid) we have nothing to discuss when we look in the opposite direction, from Christianity towards Mandaeism. Even so, there are potential linkages in some of the themes shared between Mandaeism and the Gospel of John. John the Baptist is the first person to appear in the Gospel of John, yet it is emphasized that although he came to 'bear witness to the light' ... 'He was not that light' (John 1: 7–8).

Immediately the image of light gives us some common ground with the Mandaeans, for whom their equivalent of heaven is a world of light. The distinguished scholar Raymond E. Brown believed that the Gospel of John goes out of its way to diminish the importance of the Baptist because the Johannine community was at that time in dispute with the remaining followers of John the Baptist.[5]

The apostle John himself is not explicitly an important character in the Gospel of John.[6] John the Baptist actually occupies considerably more space, although his importance and stature is intentionally diminished by the author of the gospel. None of the canonical gospels contain any internal references that give the supposed author any special importance within the text.[7] It is even possible that the gospel was named John because of the presence of John the Baptist right at the beginning.

It was German theologian Rudolf Bultmann, a giant among scholars, who argued that similarities existed between the Gospel of John, the *Odes of Solomon* and Mandaean and Manichaean literature. Rather than seeing a direct influence from the Gospel of John to these other writings he believed that a pre-Christian Gnosticism underlay all of them. His views became so influential and defining for decades, particularly in German scholarship, that there was a backlash. It is true that much of his work is speculative, but the contradictions and paradoxes that are in the New Testament and exposed by critical scholarship necessitate a degree of speculation.

Although Bultmann's views are now discredited, perhaps the new wave of scholarly work on the Mandaeans will result in a renewed discussion of the mutual influences between the Johannine community and the Mandaeans. It is entirely possible that the Gospel of John stresses belief in Jesus as the only way to salvation as a reaction against competing groups like the followers of John the Baptist or early Gnostics. Whether those particular followers of John the Baptist were proto-Mandaeans is another issue. Perhaps the Mandaeans were no longer around in Palestine. Either way, the more I think about it, the more the Mandaean vilifications of Jesus and the complex of dismissals of John the Baptist found in the fourth gospel, the Johannine epistles and the Revelation of John look like mirror images of each other.

Chapter 14

Home of the Baptisers

If the indications of their myths are anything to go by, the Mandaeans must have been experienced migrants at important periods in their history. They were certainly not unique in this. Jews were expelled first from Jerusalem following the First Jewish War and then from Judaea itself following bar Kochba's revolt and the Second Jewish War. These events must have been on a similar scale to modern refugee crises, although we might imagine that ancient peoples were in some ways better adapted to the loss of home and livelihood than we are.

We must admit that we do not have even a broad outline of the movements of the Mandaeans. It is all speculation, but some hypotheses cohere better with our incomplete knowledge of the ancient world than others. A single, large migration suits the demands of myth and storytelling for narrative and meaning, but it is more likely that any movement occurred in stages; Kurt Rudolph posited successive migrations in the 1st century, and possibly before.

Edwin Yamauchi observed that any ancestors of the Mandaeans must have been non-Jewish but acquainted with the Hebrew Bible, or Old Testament. According to his reasoning – an attempt to profile a cultural footprint for a proto-Mandaean people – they would have been antagonistic to Jews, spoken a form of Aramaic, used the Nabataean alphabet, worshipped the god of the Hauran mountains and some of them may have followed John the Baptist.

Yamauchi envisages the cataclysmic motivating event as the need to escape from Jewish attacks in the area east of the Jordan on the eve of the war waged against Rome by Jewish rebels. Antioch seemed to him to have been a likely stepping stone on their journey, where they might have picked up Gnostic elements from Menander's groups. Further pressures might then have seen them head east into Mesopotamia, with sojourns at Harran and then the Median hills of Adiabene. A final trek down towards the marshes of the south, where they found a degree of stability and security, and then some territorial expansion (on the typically modest scale of the Mandaeans) up as far as Baghdad before Islam intervened and changed the nature of Iraq forever.

Such are the speculations of scholars. But there is much to be said for a theory that provides plausible answers to many of the known issues.

However, it is Jorunn Buckley, the leading living expert on Mandaeism and a friend to Mandaeans, who has come up with the most convincing proposal for the locality and early origin of the Mandaeans. The most notable early scribe who is datable from the colophons (although not the very earliest) is Zazai, from around AD 270. This was during the early Sasanian period. However, it would not be accurate to believe that Zazai suddenly composed all these texts off the top of his own head. Mandaean scriptures, like almost all others, are only meaningful to a religious community. Nor are the earliest Mandaean writings merely the products of an inspired individual composing quirky variations within a Christian or Jewish community. If the Mandaeans were ever a heterodox Jewish or Christian group that stage was long past. Thus Zazai must have been writing as a culmination of a long oral tradition, writing for her community and for her own religion.

It would not be necessary for them to have practised for the Mandaeans to be ethnically Jewish (whatever that might be considered to mean in the 1st century). There were some notable Jewish converts at that point in Queen Helena of Adiabene and her sons in the north of Mesopotamia. Her son and successor Izates may have had a direct involvement with the migration of the Mandaeans.

Because the Mandaeans do not practise circumcision, and consider it a form of mutilation that bars any male from the priesthood, does this mean that they are descended from non-Jews? Or that at some point they abandoned circumcision? If the latter, it may have been a way to distinguish themselves from a nearby community that did practise male circumcision, although not necessarily a Jewish one because many ethnic groups in the larger region practised it.

There is certainly enough vilification of Jews in Mandaean scripture, and Christianity offered an example of how quickly a movement could transform from a radical Jewish sect into a trans-ethnic movement that had abandoned basic Jewish precepts like circumcision and kosher food laws. Jews blamed Jesus for being a Jewish apostate; Mandaeans blamed Jesus for non-observance of their own purifications and ritual practices. If the early Mandaeans numbered among their population Nabataeans or other peoples who had converted to Judaism (and, according to the geographer Strabo, Nabataea – particularly Petra – was home to a variety of ethnic groups), their Jewish religious identity might only have been skin deep. Ethnic Jews, when confronted with the warring Herod Antipas or the rising political unrest of 1st-century Judaea, could easily have rejected them, resulting in a community that had some knowledge with and sympathy for Jewish religion but wanting to put the metaphorical clear blue water of the Jordan between them.

On the other hand, Jews would have reciprocated the antipathy, treating the Mandaeans as heretics. Or they may even have initiated it. Mandaean communities were establishing themselves and solidifying the form of their religion at the same time that Jews were discovering how their own religion could adapt and evolve after the destruction of the Temple. The Jewish academies in Mesopotamia that were involved in the codification of Jewish oral law, which became the Talmuds, were fairly close in location to Mandaean communities. The Jewish presence in Babylonia was an ancient one, extending back without interruption to the exile to Babylon in the sixth century BC.

Ancient Nabataea

The Nabataeans were an interesting people, mainly ethnic Arabs who by the 1st century spoke a dialect of Aramaic. Their country covered a vast area that gave them control of the lucrative trade routes along which passed the incense in demand among the religions of the Middle East and beyond.

The Mandaeans had women priests and scribes in the past. Nabataean women had a relatively high status and were able to own and inherit property. Nabataean queens appeared on the coinage alongside their husbands. Is it possible that this is the source of the high regard for women in ancient Mandaeism? And is the reputed Nabataean dislike of military matters reflected in the pacifism of the Mandaeans? Perhaps – although the Nabataeans were able to repel the attacks of Herod Antipas with great success, which doesn't suggest they were pacifists. About the Nabataeans, Strabo reported: 'A great part of the country is fertile and produces everything except oil of olives. Instead of it they use the oil of sesame.' Interestingly, the Mandaeans use sesame oil for anointings rather than the olive oil used by Jews and Christians.[1]

Damascus had been in Nabataean hands on and off since the 1st century BC. The Nabataean leader Aretas IV ruled Damascus briefly around the time that the apostle Paul had to escape the city for fear of his life: '... the governor under King Aretas guarded the city ... in order to seize me, but I was let down in a basket through a window in the wall and escaped his hands' (2 Corinthians 11: 32–33).

Curiously, Nabataean has been used as a synonym for Sabian by Muslim writers. The term Sabian was used by Moses Maimonides for surviving pagans, and over time both terms have come to mean pagan. Even the 20th-century writer Wilfred Thesiger, whose book *The Marsh Arabs* is a travel classic, believed the Mandaeans to be some sort of pagans – a very fuzzy term, which in its broadest form refers to every religion that isn't Jewish, Christian or Muslim. Thus the Sabian Mandaeans could have been known as Nabataeans in the medieval period. Or is this a mere trick of nomenclature?[2] If the proto-Mandaeans left the Jordan area early in the 1st century, in the 30s, perhaps they do not refer to the beheading of John by Herod Antipas because reliable news had not yet spread before they began their migration.

Inner Harran

The key to understanding the migration of the Mandaeans is their own scripture, the *Haran Gawaita*:

Haran Gawaita (The Inner Haran) received him and that city in which there were Nasoraeans, because there was no road for the Jewish rulers. Over them was King Ardban (Artabanus). And sixty thousand Nasoraeans abandoned the Sign of the Seven and entered the Median hills (fura dMidai), a place where they were free from domination by all other races. And they built cult-huts (bim andia) and abode in the Call came to their end.[3]

As discussed in Chapter 5, there are several locations in the Middle East with variations on the name Harran, including an area east of Damascus and west of the Jebel Hauran mountains (also known as the Jebel Druze, from its being an ancestral homeland of the Druze).[4] There is also the Wadi Hauran on the Jordan/Saudi Arabia/Iraq border, which itself goes under the alternative spelling of Wadi Hauran and Wadi Hawran.[5] Wadi Hauran has a seasonal river that flows into the Euphrates between Jadida and Khan Baghdadi.

Buckley argues that the 'inner' Haran refers to a mythologized and spiritualized Wadi Hauran. In a hymn in the *Canonical Prayerbook*, reference is made to 'Hauran-Hauraran, the Radiance' where souls that descended to the Jordan were baptised. We are again encountering a mode of thinking that is quite foreign to modern Western thought: a place that has been transformed into a mythic entity. Buckley points out that the peculiar stuttering repetition of syllables was sometimes used in the names of beings from the Lightworld. The implication is that Hauran-Hauraran is mythically personified as a Lightbeing. A second reference to Hauraran is coupled with Karkawan, which may refer to a Lightworld image of the Karka River in Khuzestan, the Mandaean region in Iran. In a prayer in the *Canonical Prayerbook* a blessing is said 'in the Jordan and in the land of Hauraran'. If Buckley is right, the original homeland of the Mandaeans is embedded in prayers and hymns used even today.

'Over them was King Ardban'

This precious reference to a king who was ruling at the time of the migration of the Mandaeans is contained in the *Haran Gawaita*: 'Over them was King Ardban.'

There were four Arsacid dynasty kings named Ardban, or Artabanus (down from a previous estimate of five after a scholarly reassessment of coins bearing the name Ardban). Arsaces, the founder of the dynasty, was a king of the Scythians, a people who originated from the steppes of Turkestan and the Caspian Sea. By the 2nd century BC they had gained power over southern Mesopotamia and would hold on to it in the form of the Parthian Empire, with brief problems with the Romans, until the coming of the Sasanians in the 3rd century.[6]

It is not known which Ardban is referred to in the *Haran Gawaita*. Ardban I ruled from 128 to 124 BC, Ardban II/III ruled from AD 11 to 38, Ardban III/IV AD 79–81 and Ardban IV/V died in 226. The final Ardban has been a popular choice, but that displaces the migration of the Mandaeans to the 3rd century. Arban I is too early to have any meaningful application to the presence of Mandaeans in Mesopotamia. Ardban III/IV might be a reasonable fit, and his reign began at the end of the decade in which the Temple was destroyed in Jerusalem, but it is unlikely that the Mandaeans' move to Mesopotamia could have been accomplished in barely two years (the brief reign of Ardban III/IV). This leaves Ardban II/III. He ruled over a Babylonia that had a Greek upper class but a largely Semitic population, who were mainly Aramaic-speakers but there were also Jews. Ardban II/III aided Izates, king of Adiabene, who was a Jewish convert, against his enemies.

The *Haran Gawaita* tells us that the Mandaeans went to Media where they were 'free of domination by all other races'. Buckley sees the Mandaeans as having been aided by King Ardban II/III in the late 30s, and given support to cross the Tigris en route to Media (the 'mountains of Medes' are referred to in Mandaean scripture). Ardban II/III seems to have had sympathies with Semitic peoples. For instance, he backed Jewish rebels in Neerda on the Euphrates. Ardban was surrounded by enemies, with the Romans to the west and the empires of India to the east, where King Gundaphor is associated with Thomasine Christianity and appears in the Acts of Thomas.

A notable line in the *Haran Gawaita* describes how the Mandaeans 'abandoned the sign of the seven'. The seven is usually understood to refer to the classical planets, which the Mandaeans did not abandon in their religion and culture, but perhaps it could be understood to mean that they abandoned Jewish influence with 'the sign of the seven' perhaps being a reference to the seven-branched candleholder, the menorah, which is a symbol of Judaism.

Buckley feels that the migration to Medea also explains why Josephus never mentions the Mandaeans as a presence in Judaea around AD 70. Personally, I don't see why an absence of a mention in Josephus should have any meaning whatsoever. Josephus wasn't an encyclopedic writer: he reports on people, sects and events that suit his interests and his bias. Apart from the almost certainly interpolated mention of Jesus, there is no mention whatsoever of Christians, nor of Simon Magus or of any number of 1st-century rabbinical figures.

According to the *Haran Gawaita*, the Mandaeans stayed in Medes (Media) until 'they came to their end'. This sounds like the population died out, but it might as easily mean that their time in that area came to an end – and that, for whatever reason, they found themselves on the road again. Astonishingly, given all these vague and perhaps even suspect references, Characene coins, from southern Iraq, with inscriptions resembling the Mandaean alphabet have been found close to the Karka River and near a major trade route. They date to around AD 180. The action then switches back to Mesopotamia.

Seven Mandaean leaders

We are told that after the time of John the Baptist, seven leaders were installed by the *uthra* Anush by command of Hibil Ziwa. Thus we find ourselves in mythological territory again, with the Mandaeans guided by the *uthri* of the Lightworld. Yet we are given a very specific list of names and locations:

– Zazai in Baghdad. The *uthra* Hibil is her father.

– Papa, son of Guda, on the Tigris and at the mouth of the Karun, the major Iranian river in Khuzestan. This is the region of Iran in which Mandaeans still live today. Theodore bar Konai mentioned a Papa as the leader of the Kantaeans, the religious group that have clear connections to the Mandaeans and may even have been an early heretical offshoot.

– Anush, son of Natar.

– Anush Saiar, son of Nsabon on the Euphrates.

– Brik Yawar, son of Bihdad at Pumbedit on the Euphrates, which had a Jewish academy, near the modern town of Fallujah.

–Brik Yawar, teacher of Bayan Hibil, who is mentioned in lots of colophons.

– Nsab, son of Bahram, from the mountains of Glazlak. This location is unknown, but is obviously in a mountainous region.

– Ska Manda, at waters near the mountain range of Parwan.

– Bhira, son of Shitil, is 'a descendant of Ardban king of the Nasoreans'. We can see that, by this point, Ardban's assistance to the Mandaeans has become legendary and he is considered a king of the Mandaeans himself.

These leaders may have spread out after the sojourn in Medes/Media, or they may be identified with other Mandaean leaders at different time periods because these are among the oldest Mandaean names preserved to us. Perhaps the earliest of them is another name from the colophons. Intriguingly, the very earliest scribe who can be dated by this method is female.

The female copyist Zazai can be dated to the last quarter of the 3rd century. But the colophon evidence can take us back even further. Slama, a female priest-copyist from around AD 200, was the daughter of Qidra, who may be the earliest reliably attested Mandaean. Buckley writes that Slama is 'several generations' (presumably generations of textual copying from manuscript to manuscript rather than parent-child generations). It seems likely that Slama could be pushed back into the 2nd century and her mother Qidra a little further. At a conservative estimate – allowing for pregnancy at an arbitrary age of 20 (although Qidra may well have been older because she was a scribe and an early pregnancy might have interfered with her professional functions) and allowing that Slama may have been 30 or older when she copied so many manuscripts – Qidra could have been born around AD 150 or earlier. Her grandparents or great-grandparents might have taken part in the migration of the Mandaeans. Perhaps they even knew John the Baptist. Beyond the chain of human copyists, many texts are attributed to scribes who are uthri in the Lightworld, reaching back beyond time itself.

Their hidden origins

Gradually, a picture of Mandaean origins has emerged. It seems entirely feasible that they had a link to John the Baptist. Either at their inception or somewhere along the way, but early on, their religion became a form of Gnosticism. It seems most likely that they were there at the beginning, among the earliest Gnostics. Whether they were in contact with Sethians – or with a sect connected with alleged disciples of John, like Simon Magus, Menander and Dositheos – is unknown. Perhaps the time was right for Gnosticism and theirs was one of a number of similar reactions to existing religion that sprouted up somewhat independently. Perhaps some Lightworld entity inspired and guided them.

From their homeland in Nabataea they made their peregrinations along routes that are largely lost to us: Wadi Hauran, Damascus, Harran, the 'mountains of Medes', the Tigris and Euphrates, and the marshes of Mesopotamia. They lived their lives and had families and passed on their religion down the generations. They lived and died and went into the Lightworld, away from the material world of Tibil and the dangers of the forces of darkness.

Chapter 15

Survival:
The Last Gnostics

The Mandaeans never claimed to have originated with John the Baptist, however much it may be our conviction that this is where their story truly begins. The first Mandaean was not John but Adam. But aren't we all descended from Adam?

Egypt and the Flood

The Mandaeans side with the Egyptians in their version of the Exodus story of the Jews. Could they really be descended from the ancient Egyptians? This is likely to be a reimagining of Jewish tradition. But, as so often, there are little details that might suggest otherwise. The Mandaean astrological system uses the 36 decans of ten degrees each, which originated in Egypt and some think precedes the development of the zodiac. Could the Mandaean calendar of 360 days plus five intercalary days be remnants of Egyptian influence handed down over the centuries? Or do both of these common features come from Babylonian intermediaries?

The Jews were not the only people to hold a memory of the Flood, which occurs in the story of Gilgamesh and was a Middle Eastern tradition. The Mandaeans also have their own traditions about the Flood and Noah, which they may have known about from the Bible narrative.

Promised lands

And what of Ceylon? Could the ultimate origin of the Mandaeans really be on the far side of India? At first glance the prospect is an enticing one. The unlikeliest events can be preserved in myth, despite the distortions and exaggerations in such a process. Did the Mandaeans emerge somewhere in the Indian subcontinent, make the trek to Palestine/Judaea, become absorbed into Jewish tradition yet separate from it, only to then migrate again to Mesopotamia? Even today, Mandaeans speculate on the relationship between their religion and those in India. It is surely unlikely. Here we see mythmaking in action. When the Portuguese planned to relocate the Mandaeans to Ceylon as soldiers, the Mandaeans saw an opportunity to establish themselves in a country where they would not be persecuted so readily as they were in Iraq. Ceylon became a potential promised land. This migration was never to happen but the idea of Ceylon maintained a hold on Mandaean consciousness. In a mythic transformation Ceylon became the location not of a potential Mandaean utopia but was reimagined as their original homeland. The southern marshes of Iraq, or other locations down to the Gulf, are arguably the Garden of Eden. If the Mandaeans were already living in that Garden of Eden, to where could they desire to return? If it was Ceylon, the return to an earthly paradise was once again in the East, over the horizon, somewhere other than in the difficult present. And the present has been difficult indeed for the Mandaeans.

The plight of the Mandaeans

Although Mandaeans have become a presence in the wider world, the information on Mandaeans in the Western world is very confidential and sensitive. Yet Jorunn Buckley emphasizes, 'You can be in touch with Mandaeans directly, if they trust you.' It took her 20 years to track down Mandaeans in the United States. They don't have a public profile, are pacifist, and have no national or political ambitions beyond the desire to avoid persecution and maintain their traditions. Buckley's status as a scholar and a friend of Mandaeans has led to her being considered among Mandaeans, in certain circumstances, an honorary male.[1] In the Middle

East, the persecution of Mandaeans came to a head in the aftermath of the 2003 Western invasion of Iraq. Under Saddam Hussein's regime the Mandaeans had an official status as 'people of the book' – but 'of course they were "tolerated" only to a very limited extent under Saddam Hussein only for complex reasons,' said Buckley.

Despite this status, Mandaeans growing up in Iraq in recent decades were often told little about their religion so that they would not draw attention to themselves. Mandaeans in Iraq are often perceived as being unclean, which has limited their ability to take part in public life. Sam, a Mandaean now in Australia, described what it was like to grow up in the Iraq of Saddam Hussein:

> *Living in Iraq as a Mandaean boy, you first grow up feeling normal. And then somewhere in your classes you'd find that a religion class, the Islamic religion class, would come up. And you would be asked to stand up, and then they'd either make you stand in the corner where all the students will look at you, as you being different. But at that age you don't understand the difference – but you feel it. Or you get told that you are a sinner and an infidel, and you must leave this class, because you are making this class 'religiously dirty'. Also, then you would go back home, and you would find that your grandmother had gone to the vegetable shop, or to buy some fruit, where they were not allowed to touch the basket or the selection of vegetables, because you have made the whole thing religiously dirty – therefore all of it has to be destroyed. And usually you get told off in front of the whole market, or the street, or the supermarket, and that would be done on the spot, the destroying of the vegetables. It gives you the psychology that you have something wrong with you, a kind of religious leprosy.*[2]

Mandaeans in Iran have not had an easy time either, particularly since the 1979 Islamic revolution – 'but the situation there is entirely different, politically. Nobody dares to reveal much public information on this,' commented Buckley. When Ayatollah Khomeini came to power, he removed the officially protected status that Mandaeans had as Sabians and extended it instead to the Zoroastrians. Attempts by the Mandaeans to have protected status restored have so far proved fruitless. In Iran the Mandaeans are concentrated in the southwest, far from Tehran, and are little known to the Islamic theological authorities. Mandaeans in Iran have to give their children legally approved Muslim or Persian names, they cannot opt out of Quran lessons (unlike Jews, who can), and they have no representation in parliament (unlike Zoroastrians, Jews and Christians).[3] The scholar Mehrdad Arabestani summarized it as follows:

> *The Islamic revitalisation in Iran following the Islamic Revolution of 1979 paradoxically led to religious revitalisation among the Mandaeans. The dominance of religious discourse in the new regime of Iran made the religious identities the main agent in the sociopolitical sphere of the country. Nonetheless, Mandaic religion was excluded from legal religions in Iran's Constitution. This imposed big challenges on the Mandaean community of Iran, including the restriction for their religious practice and discrimination in education and employment. Even although, local authorities treat them with some degree of tolerance, they never enjoyed the rights of a fully recognized ethno-religious group.*[4]

Both in Iran and Iraq Mandaean children have been spied on in schools and are pressured into converting to Islam. Knowledge of the Mandaic language is also relatively rare, with most Mandaeans speaking Arabic or Farsi and now the languages of their new host countries.

Buckley was very cagey in giving specific details of the current situation of Mandaeans: 'Of course this is very sensitive – and too complicated to answer, and dangerous. Many [in Iraq] are dead, forcibly converted, tortured, have fled.'[5] Since the fall of Baghdad there have been murders, rapes and kidnappings of Mandaeans, estimated by some sources at more than 80 murders just in the few months that followed the Western victory. The November 2009 Mandaean Human Rights Annual Report listed 63 reported murders and 271 reported kidnappings plus reports of rape (many rapes are never reported), assault, forced conversion to Islam and forced displacements.[6] The situation has improved somewhat since then, but the 2014 report continues to list killings, robberies, kidnappings and other atrocities.

Samer Muscati, who was in Iraq observing the current conditions for Human Rights Watch, wrote a report *At a Crossroads: Human Rights in Iraq Eight Years after the US-Led Invasion*.[7]

At the only Sabian Mandaean temple in Basra, community leader Naiel Thejel Ganeen told Human Rights Watch about the evening in 2006 that became the start of his enduring trauma. Masked assailants carrying AK47s and pistols pulled over Ganeen, 55, while he was driving in Basra with his son. They forced his son to leave the car at gunpoint and abducted Ganeen in his own vehicle. He said his kidnappers kept referring to him as 'negis' (impure) and said he had to pay them 'jizya'.[8] His captors tortured him for nine days while keeping him blindfolded and bound in a dark cellar. His right arm is scarred from shrapnel from live rounds of ammunition shot by his kidnappers during a mock execution. Humiliated by what his kidnappers subjected him to, Ganeen refused to further discuss all the things they did to him over the nine days. On the last day, he said, after his kidnappers received a ransom of $40,000, they threw him, blindfolded, in a trash heap. 'The extremists considered us as part of the occupation though we've been in Iraq since before it was a country,' Ganeen said. 'Most of our community has fled Iraq and will never return.' Several Sabian Mandaean elders who listened as Ganeen told his story said they consider him lucky since he made it out alive, even though Ganeen says he is still haunted by the ordeal and continues to see a psychological counselor.[9]

Muscati was able to view a Mandaean purification ritual in April 2010 but only a dozen Mandaeans were in attendance. Their baptism is not an initiation, but is performed every Sunday and at religious festivals by a priest. Photographs and film footage of Mandaean baptisms are now available online.[10] In the aftermath of the war in Iraq Mandaeans have been scattered around the world in a diaspora. In his 2009 BBC television series *Around the World in 80 Faiths*, Peter Owen Jones, an Anglican vicar, travelled around the world researching a wide variety of ancient and modern faiths and taking part, where possible, in their ceremonies. The first episode, shot in Australia, featured a small Mandaean community in Sydney who perform their weekly baptisms in a river in a public park.[11]

The priest explained to Owen Jones: 'Water represents light and radiance and it's the womb from which everything manifests. Anyone who is baptised becomes like an angel in the kingdom of light. All the initiation is to prepare that person to be a spiritual king.'

There are relatively high numbers of Mandaeans in Sweden, Holland, Australia, Canada, Syria and Jordan, plus some in other countries such as the UK 'and what's left in the old countries [Iraq and Iran]'. Buckley estimates that there are around 80,000 surviving Mandaeans worldwide. According to some sources, out of the former population of 30,000 in Iraq, only 5,000 or fewer are thought to be left.[12] The number of priests has been diminishing for some time and isolated diaspora Mandaeans are unable to take part in the weekly baptism or in other rituals such as meals or sacraments for the dead.

Mandaean religious practice has no provision for adopting new members, and therefore the number of Mandaeans is likely to diminish. This issue is discussed privately by Mandaeans, but any suggested changes to this are mere speculation. The conversion issue is not something to be dealt with in public, at all, if you are an outsider. Traditional Mandaeans are even reluctant to talk about people who have married outside of the religion, who may be considered apostates. Young members of the new diaspora tend to be integrated into their new societies to the same extent as other Iraqi exiles. Mandaean refugees have suffered internment at various times, along with refugees of other ethnic groups and from other countries, in Indonesia and Australia.

Few of the Mandaean diaspora communities are large enough to truly preserve their traditions or have a priest to maintain full religious observance, and even those that do have problems with finding unpolluted flowing water. Mandaeans in New York and New Jersey rely on occasional visiting priests and have been able to take advantage of a state park in New Jersey, which contains a clean river that has also been used by Christian Baptist groups.

Yahia Sam, a Mandaean electrical engineer in Sweden, is trying to grow myrtle, which is essential to Mandaean ritual. It grows wild in Iraq but is not native to Sweden. Sweden's cold climate means that outdoor baptisms in running water are nearly impossible for half the year. Salam Gaiad Katia, a Mandaean priest in a rundown housing project in Sodertalje, a Swedish industrial town, which has taken in more Mandaean refugees than the whole of the USA and Canada, has adapted the rituals and conditions to his urban environment, using a public swimming pool and performing his ritual cleansing under a running tap rather than in a flowing river.[13]

Mandaean tradition states that a deceased person should be buried on the day of death or the following day, but the laws and customs of the Western countries to which Mandaeans have migrated do not facilitate this. Nor is it easy to dress the corpse in the required Mandaean manner, which involves washing the body in running water, dressing the deceased in the white baptismal robe and tying a belt around the shirt.[14]

The Mandaean diaspora has resulted in a little more attention in academia being given to the Mandaic language and literature. A project to establish a text for the *Book of John* and translate it into English has recently received funding.[15] A lexicon of Mandaic is now available online,[16] plus material for the study of the *Ginza Rba*.[17]

Buckley's advice for those concerned about the plight of the Mandaeans is to contact the normal channels of human rights organizations, such as Amnesty International, the US Department of State's annual reports to Congress on International Religious Freedom and the website in Germany for the Society for Threatened Peoples.[18]

The last Gnostics

One odd little snippet that indicates that Mandaeans now based in the West have a place in modernity is the following: the *New Horizons* interplanetary space probe examined the dwarf planet Pluto (recently demoted from full planetary status). There was a competition to come up for a mythologically inspired name for any significant mountain that might be discovered on Pluto. Underworld figures were de rigueur for Pluto, so Krun, the giant mound of flesh, was put forward as a Mandaean proposal, with Mandaeans and interested sympathizers urged to vote online for the abominable Krun. Unfortunately, not enough votes were cast, so Krun will not be able to cast his baleful influence over the planetscape of Pluto.

Buckley mentions a nightclub in Madrid ostensibly named after the entertainment district in Tokyo. The club is actually run by Mandaeans. Mandaean culture is renowned for its wordplay: the name of the nightclub is Ginza.[19] The Mandaeans have a presence, however small, in the modern world.

One section of the *Right Ginza* describes the conditions under which the end of the world will occur: 'When Kewan [Saturn] has entered Scorpio and goes from Scorpio to Leo the great Euphrates will empty itself into the Tigris and for fifty years the Babylonian country will remain a desert ... then it will be seen that the mendacious Messiah is coming.' The astrological details might be off, the ecological catastrophe might be imprecise, but I would be surprised if some modern-day Mandaean had not related this passage to Saddam Hussein's draining of the marshes.[20] Likewise, Lady Drower commented: 'Some Mandaeans gaze at the aeroplanes which fly over their heads in modern Iraq, and ask themselves if the destruction of man will come about in that manner.'[21] The Iraq war may have been decades after this, but her comment has a prophetic ring to it in retrospect.

Scholar Nathaniel Deutsch saw the situation in Iraq thus:

Under Sadaam Hussein the Mandaeans were a religious minority, like Yezidis or Chaldeans or Syrians (there's an enormous variety of religious minorities there) who were more or less tolerated but were still in different ways discriminated against, but in general were tolerated. All those people I mentioned had been there for many, many centuries and were really woven into the local fabric. Under Sadaam that continued. So, for example, in a town in southern Iraq you might have a street called the Subi street, where all the Mandaeans had their metalsmith workshops and they knew their Shiite neighbours and people might have stereotypes of one another, and maybe there might sometimes be some tension, but people would, generally speaking, get along. What happened with the invasion was, that fabric, those local connections between peoples, the neighbourhoods, all of those had been, in many places anyway, just torn apart. Neighbourhoods that were integrated at one time are now segregated. People who leave can't come back. Either they don't want to come back or their homes have been taken over, or don't exist any more. For a group like the Mandaeans it's particularly difficult because in many ways they are the most vulnerable of the vulnerable. They don't have a safe haven, as some of the groups in the north in particular have. Their religious rituals are performed by priests who are very distinctive looking, and they are done out in the open in flowing water. That has been the source of harassment, and in some cases violence, when they've tried to perform some of their rituals.

It's one thing if you've lived with your neighbours and you've known them and their grandfather knew your grandfather, etc. There's a certain tolerance that's built on that. But when you're a refugee and you're in a new place and no one knows you from Adam, and you're different and you're from the south and now you're in the north, you're in Baghdad, you become even more vulnerable, particularly at the time when a lot of people there are engaging in different forms of ethnic cleansing based on people's backgrounds, religious and otherwise. Because the Mandaeans have historically been involved in metalwork, which actually may have something to do with religion in the sense that in the Middle East a lot of minority groups, for instance Jews in Ethiopia or North Africa, end up getting involved in metalwork because that profession is seen as polluting, so often the dominant group doesn't want to engage in it. So you end up with a minority group engaging in it. But because they're involved in that profession, they're seen as having a lot of money. Therefore they've also been targeted by people because they think they can get their gold.[22]

The Mandaeans will surely need to adapt their religion and culture to their new homelands if Mandaeism is to survive. Already the Internet has changed the nature of communication between members of a population now scattered among the continents of Asia, Europe, North America and Australia. Probably some accommodation will have to be made within

Mandaeism to the reality of the modern conditions of life, in terms of accepting converts and stabilizing or increasing the population. It is possible that the Mandaeans accepted converts early on in their history. Accepting converts from Islam would have had a deadly result, but the picture would be quite different in the secular West. Yet in the modern world ethnic and religious identities are overlapping and approximate. When a young Mandaean in Britain went to get his hair cut the barber, an Iraqi, asked him if he was Iraqi too. 'Yes,' he replied.

'Are you Muslim?' asked the barber.

'No, kind of like a Christian, but not really.'

'Well, it could be worse. You could be Shia.'

One of the more straightforward challenges is to achieve a local population density great enough to fund, build and support a Mandaean ritual centre, which must be situated by a river under strict religious conditions. For a scattered people who number only in the tens of thousands worldwide, this is no mean task.

For the survival of the religion, our times are already a Mandaean apocalypse. But the Mandaeans have gone from crisis to crisis over the centuries and still held out. Back in 1970, Edwin Yamauchi commented that Mandaeism was facing extinction due to a lack of candidates for the priesthood. Yet it still survives today.

Some younger Mandaeans, having discovered that their religion is seen as a form of Gnosticism, have been investigating other types of Gnosticism. It would be extraordinary indeed if they could represent an uninterrupted thread from antiquity down to a reflowering of modern Gnosticism. Writing this book has convinced me that the Mandaeans truly are Gnostics. Previously, I have contemplated whether a Gnostic religion would ever be able to survive for centuries without losing its bearings. Major exemplars of Gnosticism, such as the ancient Sethians and Valentinians, the Manichaeans and the Cathars, never succeeded as established religions of the majority, although the Manichaeans had a close scrape with respectability for some decades when Manichaeism was the official religion of the Uighur Empire.

If Gnosticism is a religion of the underdog, always in need of a numerically advantaged, dominating oppressor, which worships the wrong god – the false god in distinction to the Great Life of the Mandaeans – then Mandaeism surely must qualify on that count. Perpetually in the shadow of world religions, world events, of empires and tyrants and global politics, the Mandaeans truly are the last Gnostic religion.

Let us hope that the dogged, long-lived Mandaeans, the last surviving group of ancient Gnostics, are still baptising and worshipping the Great Life in another 2,000 years' time.

Notes

Introduction

1 From Mark 1:11, Revised Standard Version (RSV).

2 A chapter in an earlier book of mine, 'The Last Gnostics: The Mandaeans' in *The Secret History of the Gnostics* is still worthwhile as a brief glance at the Mandaeans in the light of the history of Gnosticism, but it only scratches the surface of the subject and is a little more conservative in some of its opinions. In certain places my opinions have developed and I now find the Mandaeans' own traditions of their origins convincing.

3 Buckley, *The Mandaeans* p.122.

4 Mandaic words are usually given various diacritical marks when written in the Latin alphabet. For ease of reading I have eliminated these and used the easiest version for readers of English where possible.

Chapter 1: Strange Religion: Minority Religions in the Middle East

1 Islam has condemned paganism no less than Christianity has. The present author doesn't agree that pagan religions were somehow fair game in a way that monotheistic religions aren't. Pagan religion was at times cruel, but all the Abrahamic religions have waged war and practised oppression at various times in their histories. Most of modern social development and relative equality has developed via secular influence and through accommodation to technological development.

2 Gurdjieff, *Meetings With Remarkable Men*, pp.65–66.

3 Gerard Russell mentions that after the Iraq war the Iraqi prime minister cursed Satan at the beginning of one of his speeches to the parliament. The only Yazidi member of parliament was compelled to object to the use of the word. Russell, *Heirs to Forgotten Kingdoms*, p.73.

4 Drower, Mandaeans of Iraq and Iran, p.258.

5 I have come across no mention of reincarnation in Mandaean material. Lady Drower reports a priest as saying that once the soul has left the prison of flesh it can no longer return to a body. Drower, *Mandaeans of Iraq and Iran*, p.41.

6 Interview with Gerard Russell in *The Gnostic* 6, pp.130–135.

7 It is worth noting that Hinduism, often seen as polytheistic by casual observers, may also be classed as a modal monotheism. That is, each god or goddess is a mode of the one transcendent God.

8 The Samaritans survive as a tiny community in Israel and they are also Abrahamic. They are usually ignored when the Abrahamic religions are mentioned. They may be considered a form of heterodox Judaism but they consider themselves to be a separate religion.

9 Another figure named Bihram, in whose name baptisms are performed, is thought to be a development of an ancient Indo-Iranian divinity. However, myth doesn't respect its sources. See Lupieri, p.163.

10 I am addressing commonly held views on the role of the devil or Satan. There are convincing arguments that the serpent in the Garden of Eden wasn't identified as Satan until the Christian period.

11 Particularly ancient cities like Alexandria, Rome and Antioch.

12 Drower, *Mandaeans of Iraq and Iran*, pp.52–53.

Chapter 2: The Mandaean Myth

1 Drower, *The Haran Gawaita* and *the Baptism of Hibil-Ziwa*, p.xi.

2 Al Saadi and Al Saadi, *Ginza Rabba*, Right Volume (Right Ginza), p.27.

3 Al Saadi and Al Saadi, *Ginza Rabba*, Right Volume (Right Ginza), p.28.

4 Not to be confused with the MMORG (Massively Multiplayer Online Roleplaying Game) of the same name.

5 Al Saadi and Al Saadi, *Ginza Rabba*, Right Volume (Right Ginza), p.28.

6 Al Saadi and Al Saadi, *Ginza Rabba*, Right Volume (Right Ginza), p.29.

7 To my knowledge, Ptahil is not identified with Yahweh. However, given the ins and outs and complexities of Mandaean scripture someone over the centuries has probably come up with the equation Ptahilffi Adonai.

8 Drower, *The Mandaeans of Iraq and Iran*, p.269.

9 Drower, *The Mandaeans of Iraq and Iran*, p.255. Curiously, although pure water is always associated with light and life, the ontological opposite seems to be polluted water rather than dryness and aridity, as might be expected in a land of extreme heat, dependent on irrigation in many areas. To my knowledge there is no tradition of interpretive theology in Mandaeism that attempts to reconcile all these discrepancies. Perhaps the nature of the changes to the religion that will result with the diaspora might produce a new attempt by Mandaeans to sort through their myths and give them different applications. Already some of the more abstract cosmogony and cosmology has been associated with similar ideas in modern physics.

10 See Buckley, *The Mandaeans*, pp.40–48, for an interpretation of Ruha, which draws on the less negative aspects.

11 Drower, *The Mandaeans of Iraq and Iran*, p.149.

12 Al Saadi and Al Saadi, *Ginza Rabba*, Right Volume (Right Ginza), 2012, p.v and

Foerster, *Gnosis Vol II: Coptic and Mandaean Sources*, 1974, p.215.

13 Drower, *The Mandaeans of Iraq and Iran*, p.41

14 Drower, *The Mandaeans of Iraq and Iran*, p.44.

15 Interview with Miguel Conner, to be published in *Other Voices of Gnosticism* (Bardic Press: Dublin, 2016).

16 Arabestani, Mehrdad, 'Ritual Purity and the Mandaeans' Identity' in *Iran and the Caucasus* 16, pp.166–167.

17 Drower *The Mandaeans of Iraq and Iran*, p.30. Once, so the story goes, all Mandaeans wore white, not just the priesthood: *The Mandaeans of Iraq and Iran*, p.36.

18 Drower, *The Mandaeans of Iraq and Iran*, p.35.

19 Drower *The Mandaeans of Iraq and Iran*, pp.110–113, for further details on the baptism and a diagram of the cult hut.

20 Lady Drower uses the delicate and pseudo-medical term 'nocturnal emission', but at one point calls it a wet dream. She is unusually frank for her time and social standing. *The Mandaeans of Iraq and Iran*, p.154.

21 One wonders why nocturnal emission would be considered such a problem that there are such detailed rules for purification if it occurs. One factor is that priests are usually married, and can marry either before or after their consecration. Perhaps a virile young priest who was used to having sex with his wife every night would simply respond in this way.

22 Drower, *The Mandaeans of Iraq and Iran*, p.186.

23 Drower, *The Mandaeans of Iraq and Iran*, p.199.

24 Drower, *The Mandaeans of Iraq and Iran*, p.180.

25 Drower, *The Mandaeans of Iraq and Iran*, p.181.

Chapter 3: The Mandaeans Emerge into History

1 See Koester, Vol I, pp.249–251 for a summary of the situation in antiquity.

2 Buckley, *The Mandaeans*, p.4.

3 My thanks to Dr Anthony Harvey of the Royal Irish Academy for a stimulating discussion about this.

4 Morgenstern in 'Jewish Babylonian Aramaic and Mandaic: Some points of Contact' in *Aram Periodical* 22, pp.1–14.

5 I do not have figures, but I would doubt if the total number of scholars of Mandaic is more than a couple of dozen.

6 This example was given by James McGrath, who has been translating the Book of John into English in its entirety for the first time. http://rogueleaf.com/book-of-john/2011/11/16/30-jesus-comes-to-john-to-be-baptized/

7 See Jorunn Buckley's *The Great Stem of Souls* for a detailed exploration of

several colophons.

8 Lady Drower's intended final book is said, in Morgenstern's review, to have been 'a mystical work that apparently implies that Christianity begins as a Mandaean heresy'. Kurt Rudolph, the great scholar of Gnosticism, tried unsuccessfully to get the book published and it apparently languishes in an archive somewhere. The academics seem to find it embarrassing, but it may be that spiritually interested people would find it appealing, and modern English-speaking Mandaeans doubly so. I have no idea of the quality of the work but Drower can write well. See Morgenstern's review of Buckley's *Lady E.S. Drower's Scholarly Correspondence*. In *Journal of Semitic Studies* 2014. Morgenstern, p.241.

9 Lupieri, *The Mandaeans*, p.114. In Lupieri the Nizaris are referred to as Nusairs, a rendition that I have been unable to discover elsewhere. Lupieri's is a translation from Italian and he is referring to the earlier, unscholarly sources of Conti and Norberg, so I have substituted 'Nizaris', the modern standard English-language term for 'Nusairs'.

10 Buckley, *The Great Stem of Souls*, p.139 – 1,500 was the number Yahia Bihram gave to Heinrich Petermann, a German scholar who stated in Iraq in 1854 to learn Mandaic.

11 I use faith merely as a synonym for religion, and am not suggesting that it is faith rather than *gnosis* that is central to Mandaeism.

12 Although cholera is no longer a problem for Mandaeans, the need for unpolluted running river water remains a difficulty for Mandaeism to this date, with many refugees and migrants now established in big cities. The most important quality of the water is that it is flowing, and if this condition can be considered to be met then it is possible to conduct rituals correctly.

13 The Mandaeans use the Islamic calendar.

14 Buckley, *The Great Stem of Souls*, p.137, italics as per Buckley.

15 Buckley, *The Great Stem of Souls*, pp.133–147.

16 In Suq es-Shuyuk, Iraq.

17 Masco, *The Mandaeans*, p.29. This should be the nasuraiia, the Mandaean priestly class.

18 Merillat, The Gnostic Apostle Thomas, Chapter 17. http://gnosis.org/thomasbook/ch17.html

19 Morgenstern in 'Jewish Babylonian Aramaic and Mandaic: Some points of Contact' in *Aram Periodical* 22, pp.1–14.

20 In 1604 Mandaeans were classified as Chaldeans, a name for Christians of the Syrian Church.

21 Drower, *The Mandaeans of Iraq and Iran*, p.2. She added that 'now that Iraq has a national government [the St. John Christian signs] have disappeared'.

22 Lupieri, *The Mandaeans*, pp.65–66.

Chapter 4: Those Ubiquitous Knights Templar

1 Eco, *Foucault's Pendulum.* p.x.

2 Frale, *The Templars and the Shroud of Christ,* 2011, p.62.

3 The mandylion is a cloth with the face of Christ on it that reputedly belonged to Veronica (who is depicted in one of the stations of the cross wiping the brow of Jesus) and it does indeed have the same first syllable as 'Mandaean' but this has no linguistic significance.

4 Forlong, *Faiths of Man,* Vol I, p.93.

5 According to the Talmud, which was a product of the Babylonian Jewish academies, Rabbi Johanan said, 'One who studies the Torah but does not teach it is like the myrtle in the wilderness'. Talmud – Mas. Rosh HaShana 2a.

6 'Last BSTS Meeting: Norma Weller' in the newsletter of the British Society for the Turin Shroud: Newsletter 32, September 1992.

7 New and Undisclosed Secrets of The Turin Shroud: A letter from Norma C. Weller.

8 New and Undisclosed Secrets of The Turin Shroud: A letter from Norma C. Weller. See also 'Clues and confirmations towards the authentication of the Turin Shroud' by Norma C. Weller and 'Does the Shroud Show a Mandaean Burial?' by Louis C. de Figueiredo at http://earlychurch.org.uk/article_mandaeans.html

9 See Picknett and Prince, *The Turin Shroud,* pp. 313–315.

10 Haag, *The Templars,* 2009, p.68.

11 Haag, *The Templars,* 2009, pp.122–124 and pp.189–190.

12 Thomas, 'Israelite Origins of the Mandaeans' in *Studia Antiqua,* 2007, p.25.

13 Russell, *Heirs to Forgotten Kingdoms,* 2014, pp.56–57 and p.88.

Chapter 5: Harran, the Hermetic City of the Sabians

1 Kriwaczek, *Babylon,* p. 259.

2 References to the Quran from Haleem, *The Quran,* pp.9, 74, 210.

3 The spelling in English can vary considerably. Sabaeans is a popular alternative, as is Sabeans. Even when a particular spelling is used to make a distinction between the Sabaeans of South Arabia and the Sabians of the Quran, for instance, this is not always consistent from scholar to scholar, nor from original source to source, nor from translation to translation.

4 Gündüz, *The Knowledge of Life,* pp.26–27.

5 Gündüz, *The Knowledge of Life,* p.131.

6 Gündüz, *The Knowledge of Life,* p.126.

7 Gündüz, *The Knowledge of Life,* p.131.

8 Adapted from Ibn al-Nadim's quotation in the *Fihrist,* from Gündüz, *The Knowledge of Life,* p.34.

9 Salaman et al, *The Way of Hermes*, p. 55.

10 From Haleem, *The Quran*, p.193.

11 Russell, *Heirs to Forgotten Kingdoms*, pp.62-64.

12 Drower, *The Mandaeans of Iraq and Iran*, p.275.

13 Abu Rayhan al-Biruni on the Sabians in *The Book of the Remaining Signs of Past Centuries*. Translated by Sachau, 1879, p.188, quoted in Häberl, 'Mandaeism in Antiquity and the Antiquity of Mandaeism', pp.267–268.

14 Al Saadi and Al Saadi, *Ginza Rabba*, Right Volume (*Right Ginza*), p.203.

15 Pallis, *Mandaean* Studies, p.19.

16 See Chapter 8 By the Rivers of Babylon.

17 Russell, *Heirs to Forgotten Kingdoms*, p.154.

Chapter 6: 'People of the Book'

1 Picknett, *Mary Magdalene*, p.264.

2 Knowledge of biblical characters was spread by the scriptures of Judaism and Christianity. While many, or even most, characters are specifically Jewish in origin there is also the possibility that stories could have been preserved by other Semitic peoples. Also, some of the stories in the Bible are versions of ancient Middle Eastern tales or myths, the most famous being the Flood. Thus the Mandaeans could have obtained these characters and stories from a number of sources. If their origins are essentially Jewish they may have brought the Bible stories with them and adapted them to their own needs. If they are even more ancient than that then they might have preserved separate versions as, arguably, the Samaritans did. Regardless of their origins, they could have adapted Bible stories that became known to them through contact with Jews, Christians or even Muslims. Finally, there is the possibility that a tradition like the Flood might have incorporated Babylonian elements, which were in their origins much more ancient than the Bible.

3 Pallis, *Mandaean Studies*, p.129.

4 Buckley, *The Mandaeans*, p.5.

5 Häberl, 'Mandaeism in Antiquity and the Antiquity of Mandaeism', p.267.

6 There is an urban legend that the water of the Tigris used for baptism is disinfected by a product produced in the Vatican! Lupieri, *The Mandaeans*, p.xvii.

7 Interview with the author.

8 Pallis, *Mandaean Studies*, p.131.

9 Interview with Nathaniel Deutsch, to be published in Conner, *Other Voices of Gnosticism* (Bardic Press: Dublin, 2016)

10 Lupieri, *The Mandaeans*, pp.9–10.

11 We should also acknowledge that the variety in spellings of these terms is

considerable, adding to the confusion of many authors who identify groups mistakenly because of similar names.

12 Lupieri, *The Mandaeans*, pp.114–115.

13 Bartlett, *The Assassins*, pp.128–130. Hodgson, *The Secret Order of Assassins*, p.204.

14 According to Russell, *Heirs to Forgotten Kingdoms*, pp.160–161, Philip Hitti claimed that the Templars showed signs of being influenced by the Druze.

15 *The Gnostic 5*.

Chapter 7: Mani and the Lost Religion

1 Gardner and Lieu, *Manichaean Texts from the Roman Empire*, p.33. The reference is likely but not absolutely indisputable: there could have been another baptismal sect in the marshes at that time. Most commentators see it as reasonable to identify the al-Mughtasila with the Mandaeans.

2 Masco, *The Mandaeans*, p.23.

3 Waardenburg, Jacques. (ed.) *Muslim Perceptions of Other Religions*, p.37.

4 *The Gnostic 5*, p.170.

5 Drower, *Mandaeans of Iraq and Iran*, p.54.

6 Lady Drower believed 'Elkasaites were once closely related to Nazoraeans'. Drower, *The Secret Adam*, p.97.

7 Aldihisi, *The Story of Creation in the Mandaean Holy Book the Ginza Rba*, p.36.

8 The Medinet Madi discovery contained an extensive collection of Manichaean writings, in Coptic, on papyrus. Some were lost during the Second World War and the rest are housed at the Chester Beatty Library in Dublin and at the Staatliche museum in Berlin. As with the Mandaean scriptures, if these had been discovered now they would be making newspaper headlines.

9 Lieu, *Manichaeans in Mesopotamia and the Roman East*, p.69.

10 Despite Säve-Söderburgh's convincing evidence, some scholars blithely write off the similarities between the 'Psalms of Thomas' and Mandaean material by assuming that the Mandaeans developed out of Manichaeism.

Chapter 8: By the Rivers of Babylon

1 *Canonical Prayerbook* pp.142–143 (Hymn No. 164) quoted by Aldihisi in *The Story of Creation in the Mandaean Holy Book the Ginza Rba*, p.20.

2 Häberl, 'Mandaeism in Antiquity and the Antiquity of Mandaeism', p.98.

3 Smith, (ed.), *The Gnostic 6*, p.130.

4 Aldihisi, *The Story of Creation in the Mandaean Holy Book the Ginza Rba*, p.50.

5 Aldihisi, *The Story of Creation in the Mandaean Holy Book the Ginza Rba*, p.25.

6 Drower, *The Secret Adam*, pp.104–105.

7 Drower, *The Secret Adam*, p.93.

8 Aldihisi, *The Story of Creation in the Mandaean Holy Book the Ginza Rba*, pp.32–33.

9 Yamauchi, *Gnostic Ethics and Mandaean Origins*, p.81.

10 Drower, *The Secret Adam*, p.65. Aldihisi points out: 'Lupieri suggests that the Mandaeans who lived in Characene since the second century must have chosen Bihram (the deity of Maisan) as eponymous deity of their baptism.' (Lupieri, *The Mandaeans*, p.163, from Aldihisi, *The Story of Creation in the Mandaean Holy Book the Ginza Rba*, p.34.)

11 Lupieri, *The Mandaeans*, pp.17–18.

12 Drower, *The Book of the Zodiac*, pp.68–69.

13 Buckley, *The Great Stem of Souls*, pp.319–320.

14 Drower, 'Mandaean Polemics' p.443 quoted by Masco, *The Mandaeans*, p.59. Lady Drower's italics.

15 Aldihisi, *The Story of Creation in the Mandaean Holy Book the Ginza Rba*, pp.39–40.

16 Drower, *Mandaeans of Iraq and Iran*, p.744.

17 Masco, *The Mandaeans*, pp.69–72.

18 Masco, *The Mandaeans*, pp.101–102. See Al Saadi and Al Saadi, *Ginza Rabba*, Right Volume (*Right Ginza*), pp.18–19 as well.

19 Häberl, 'Mandaeism in Antiquity and the Antiquity of Mandaeism', p.267. Aramaic terms omitted.

20 Tammuz, also known as Dummuzi in Akkadian, was paralleled by other myths such as Baal and Adonis. Long seen as an example of the dying and rising god, it has been disputed for some time that he was ever resurrected.

21 Drower, *Mandaeans of Iraq and Iran*, p.318. Unfortunately this section of the *Ginza* is not included in the new English edition.

22 Drower, *Mandaeans of Iraq and Iran*, p.256.

Chapter 9: Alphabets and Incantations

1 Drower, *Mandaeans of Iraq and Iran*, p.50. The colour blue is sometimes avoided and sometimes prescribed in Mandaean culture. This reflects the contradictory attitudes to Ruha who is generally a negative figure, with whom association must be avoided, but she also requires appeasement on the level of practical folk magic

2 Drower, *Mandaeans of Iraq and Iran*, p.150.

3 Aldihisi, *The Story of Creation in the Mandaean Holy Book the Ginza Rba*, p.50.

4 Drower, *Mandaeans of Iraq and Iran*, p.311.

5 Lilith could be used as a term for any female demon so we see references to 'liliths' in the plural. Yamauchi *Gnostic Ethics and Mandaean Ethics*, p.56.

6 Levene, Dan, *Curse or Blessing: What's in the Magical Bowl?* Parkes Institute Pamphlet No. 2., University of Southampton, Southampton, 2002.

7 There are exceptions. Magic was part of ancient Egyptian religion and still is part of African religion, for instance.

8 Drower, *Mandaeans of Iraq and Iran*, p.4.

9 Schneemelcher, *New Testament Apocrypha; I- Gospel and Related Writings*, p.445.

10 Drower, *Mandaeans of Iraq and Iran*, pp.240–242.

11 Monoimos, an Arab Gnostic, also used extensive alphabetic and numerical symbolism.

12 Buckley, *The Mandaeans* , p.130–133.

13 Drower, *Mandaeans of Iraq and Iran*, p.240.

14 Buckley *The Mandaeans*, p.144–145.

15 Masco, *The Mandaeans*, p.21.

16 Al Saadi and Al Saadi, *Ginza Rabba*, Right Volume (*Right Ginza*), p.6; Buckley, *The Mandaeans*, pp.45–46.

17 Buckley, *The Mandaeans*, pp.45–46. The mode of speech in which opposites are proclaimed in the first person is reminiscent of Thunder Perfect Mind from the Nag Hammadi library. See Meyer, *The Nag Hammadi Scriptures*, pp.367–377.

Chapter 10: Among the Gnostics

1 The identification of each of these figures as a 'demiurge' seems to be due to the Church Fathers recognizing the similarity between the Gnostic creator God and Plato's benign demiurge. I cannot think of any Gnostic scripture, whether Sethian, Valentinian, Manichaean, Mandaean, Cathar or anything else, in which this figure is actually tagged as 'demiurge'. Still, it is a useful convenience.

2 Conner, *Voices of Gnosticism*, p.87.

3 Conner, *Voices of Gnosticism*, p.289.

4 Turner, John D. 'Sethian Gnosticism: A Literary History' in Hedrick, Charles W. and Hodgson, R. (eds.), *Nag Hammadi*, Gnosticism and Early Christianity, 1986. According to an account by Hippolytus the Sethians specified that the 'Saviour' washed in sacred water and drank flowing water after his descent to the abyss, recalling the practice of the Mandaean priest who must drink the water that the people are baptized in. (Pallis, *Mandaean Studies*, p.196.)

5 Buckley, *The Great Stem of Souls*, p.303.

6 Yamauchi, *Gnostic Ethics and Mandaean Origins*, p.18.

7 Buckley, *The Great Stem of Souls*, p.260.

8 Lewis, *Introduction to 'Gnosticism'*, p.64; see also Gaddis, *There is No Crime For Those Who Have Christ*, pp.194–196.

9 Gospel of Thomas saying 23 in Smith, *The Gospel of Thomas*, p.77.

10 For a translation and commentary see my *Gnostic Writings on the Soul*.

Chapter 11: Sects, Sects, Sects

1 Lupieri, *The Mandaeans*, p.158; also Drower, *The Mandaeans of Iraq and Iran*, pp.273–280.

2 See Pétrement, *A Separate God*, p.472.

3 Koester, *Introduction to the New Testament*, Intro Vol II p.205.

4 Gündüz, *The Knowledge of Life*, p.99.

5 Ehrman, *Lost Christianities*, p.103.

6 Pétrement, *A Separate God*, p.233. The Pauline epistle to the Colossians was once believed to attack Gnostics in the Lycos valley in Samaria, thus suggesting another link between Samaria and Gnosticism.

7 See, for example, Lupieri, *The Mandaeans*, p.171 n.22.

8 Gündüz, *The Knowledge of Life*, p.1.

9 For some comparisons between Simonians and Mandaeans see Drower, *The Secret Adam*, p.89f.

10 Drower, *Haran Gawaita*, p.7. The parentheses are Drower's.

11 Wise, Abegg and Cook, *The Dead Sea Scrolls*, p.421.

12 Drower, *The Mandaeans of Iraq and Iran*, p.56.

13 Apparently the Essenes didn't defecate on the Sabbath. Russell, *Heirs to Forgotten Kingdoms*, p.196.

14 Yamauchi, *Gnostic Ethics and Mandaean Origins*, p.59.

15 http://www.crosswinds.net/fiessenes/theiring.html

16 Masco, *The Mandaeans*, p.123. See also Lupieri, *The Mandaeans*, pp.50–51. It is difficult to rationalize this with the account of the four Mandaean ages in which the First Age began with Adam and the Fourth Age with Shem.

Chapter 12: At Last, John the Baptist

1 Lupieri, *The Mandaeans*, pp.125–126.

2 Yamauchi, *Gnostic Ethics and Mandaean Origins*, pp.39-40. Recall that letters from another realm are a common motif in Gnosticism.

3 Brown, 'What Was John the Baptist Doing?', pp.37–38.

4 Brown, 'What Was John the Baptist Doing?', p.38.

5 Brown, 'What Was John the Baptist Doing?', p.42. The Damascus document is a central text from the Dead Sea Scrolls.

6 Robinson, *The Priority of John*, p.136.

7 There are many different versions of these names in English-language translations and scholarly resources. Buckley, for example, uses Yuhana and Yahia.

8 See Smith, *Lost Teachings of the Cathars*, for more on this.

9 From Josephus's *Antiquities of the Jews*, 18.63, the Earl Doherty translation online at http://jesuspuzzle.humanists.net/supp16.htm

10 Admittedly, arguments for a historical core of the Testimonium are not all just hacking and slashing away at the text but make arguments according to Josephus's typical vocabulary and so on. See http://earlywritings.com/forum/viewtopic. php?fffi3&tffi1237&sidffi3d5a1db4d04b1190c47792897d9dce15#p27374

11 See Funk, Robert W. and the Jesus Seminar, *The Acts of Jesus*, for an assessment of the historicity of the incidents that occur in the gospels, and Funk, Hoover and the Jesus Seminar, *The Five Gospels*, for the authenticity of the sayings attributed to Jesus.

12 Mead, *Gnostic John the Baptizer*, p.129.

13 Farmer, *The Oxford Dictionary of Saints*, p.215.

14 Meyer, *The Nag Hammadi Scriptures*, p.26.

15 John the Baptist appears briefly in the Gospel of Thomas. Although the Gospel of Thomas is found in codex II of the Nag Hammadi library, which was clearly used by Gnostics, it is not considered Gnostic in any Sethian or Valentinian sense.

16 Meyer, *The Nag Hammadi Scriptures*, pp.613–628.

17 Layton, *Nag Hammadi Scriptures*, p.616.

18 Meyer, *The Nag Hammadi Scriptures*, pp.663–678.

19 Al Saadi and Al Saadi, *Ginza Rabba*, pp.121–124.

20 John the Baptist is represented not only in the *Book of John*. Book 6 of the *Right Ginza* describes John's encounter with Manda d-Hayyi and John's death (John is given as Yahia in Buckley).

21 Lupieri, *The Mandaeans*, p.125.

22 Buckley, *The Great Stem of Souls*, p.305.

23 Eusebius, *The History of the Church*, 1.11.1–6.

24 Drower, *The Secret Adam*, p.101. Yuhiu referred to here appears elsewhere in this book in the form Yahia.

Chapter 13: The Apostate Jesus

1 Jesus' status may have been diminished in certain ways. Many Valentinians believed that when Jesus came to Earth he had no real physical body. To Sethian Gnostics, Jesus was just the latest avatar of Seth, the third son of Adam and Eve. But none of the ancient Gnostics made Jesus into an evil figure, or even a misguided one.

2 Davies, *Spirit Possession and the Origins of Christianity*, pp.3–5.

3 Drower, *The Mandaeans of Iraq and Iran*, p.176.

4 The Mandaean attitude to Jesus as an apostate is an ancient one and doesn't seem

to have much relevance these days. As far back as the first half of the 20th century Lady Drower was told, 'But Prophet [sic] Moses never suffered himself to be circumcised, neither did the prophet Jesus, for Jesus was of our sect, and they do not allow mutilations.' Drower, *The Mandaeans of Iraq and Iran*, p.268.

5 Brown, *The Community of the Beloved Disciple*, pp.29–30.

6 The mysterious figure who does occupy a privileged position in the fourth gospel is the so-called Beloved Disciple, or 'the disciple whom Jesus loved' (John 13: 23). This is conventionally assumed to be John but there are certainly other candidates: Mary Magdalene is probably the most controversial alternative, but the case for Mary as the Beloved Disciple is not without its merits.

7 Luke's prologue is very much a rule-proving exception, but the prologue has little to connect it with the main body of the gospel.

Chapter 14: Home of the Baptisers

1 www.nabataea.net/Nabataea_Early_History.html

2 Masco, *The Mandaeans*, p.14.

3 Drower, *Haran Gawaita*, p.3.

4 The attentive reader will have noticed that the spelling of Harran is not standardized. The spelling of the city of Harran in northern Mesopotamia is at odds with that in the *Haran Gawaita*. Another variant is Hauran.

5 These are all attempts at transliteration into English so not too much should be made of the differences.

6 Roux, *Ancient Iraq*, pp.382–384.

Chapter 15: Survival: The Last Gnostics

1 I have known Mandaeans in the West to be shy about their religion even after they have spoken in public or to the media about the situation.

2 *The Religion Report*, 'Mandaeans in Australia,' 11 June 2003, www.abc.net.au/rn/talks/8.30/relrpt/stories/s877145.htm

3 Institute for War & Peace Reporting (IWPR). See http://iwpr.net/report-news/mandaean-faith-lives-iranian-south. Mandaeans are not allowed to attend university. www.abc.net.au/cgi-bin/common/printfriendly.pl?http://www.abc.net.au/rn/talks/8.30/relrpt/stories/s877145.htm

4 Arabestani, 'Ritual Purity and the Mandaeans' Identity', p.158.

5 Quotations from Jorunn Buckley are from my email interview with her on 27 Jan 2011. Additional quotations are taken from her podcast interview 'Discovering the Mandaeans' available at http://www.bowdoin.edu/podcasts/

6 Human Rights annual reports can be downloaded from the Mandaean Associations Union website www.mandaeanunion.org. The annual

report lists the names of all the murdered and kidnapped Mandaeans. The abuses are summarized in the article 'Who Cares for the Mandaeans?', which can be found at www.islammonitor.org/index. php?optionffiicom_content&viewffiarticle&idffi3198:who-cares-for-the-mandaeans&catidffi190&Itemidffi59] For instance, in 2009 three Mandaean jewellers were massacred in Baghdad (www.humanrightsdefence.org/save-the-mandaeans-of-iraq.html).

7 See www.hrw.org/en/reports/2011/02/21/crossroads where a PDF of his extensive report can be downloaded. More of his photographs can be seen on Flickr (www.flickr.com/photos/sultan/sets/72157623907031141/ with/4622605961/)

8 *Jizya* is the poll tax, a head tax that early Islamic rulers demanded from their non-Muslim subjects in return for communal autonomy and military protection.

9 His description of the Mandaeans is found in the 2011 report, pp.65–68.

10 A search on YouTube for Mandaeans gives several examples of filmed baptisms. There is even a recipe for Mandaean spiced duck available. Muslims are only permitted to eat wild duck, so the presence of ducks in a farmyard is a good indication that the family is Mandaean.

11 The section on the Mandaeans in Sydney begins around 33:30 in the first episode.

12 See article at www.gfbv.de/pressemit.php?idffi1420 Other estimates place the figure as low as 3,500. Jorunn Buckley has been an expert witness for Mandaeans in immigration courts since the 1990s. 'It's very hard to convince American legal authorities and the INS [Immigration and Naturalization Service, now subsumed within the Department of Homeland Security] that there are credible reasons for fearing persecution, torture, jailing, etc. when you are sent back to your own country,' Buckley said. She was first called on as an expert witness for the US Department of Justice in an immigration court in San Diego in 1995. There are particular difficulties in representing such little-known people. 'You need to educate the judge. You need to be on very good terms with your own lawyer. Your own lawyer may not know anything about this unless he's worked with Mandaeans before.' She found that US officials had trouble understanding the nature of Islamic law and the lack of representation for Mandaeans in Iraq and Iran because of the separation of Church and state in America.

13 See article at www.nytimes.com/2007/04/09/world/europe/09iht-mandeans.4.5202220.html.

14 See the video interview 'Iraqi Refugees in Sweden: A Mandaean Priest Speaks' at www.minorityvoices.org/news.php/en/281/iraqi-refugees-in-sweden-a-mandaean-priest-speaks.

15 http://mandaeanbookofjohn.blogspot.com/ The translation by Mead published

in The Gnostic John the Baptizer consisted only of selections translated from a German version of the source text.

16 http://www.mandaic.org/Mandaic/lexicon/main.htm

17 https://sites.google.com/site/ginzarba/ginza-rba-download

18 The Society for Threatened Peoples in German is Gesellschaft für bedrohte Völker, or GfbV (www.gfbv.de). The central website for the Mandaean community is the Mandaean Associations Union (www.mandaeanunion.org).

19 Buckley, *The Mandaeans*, p.151.

20 Pallis, *Mandaean Studies*, p.20. This passage is not part of the selections from the Ginza that have recently been translated into English.

21 Drower, *The Mandaeans of Iraq and Iran*, pp.92-93.

22 Interview with Miguel Conner, to be published in *Other Voices of Gnosticism* (Bardic Press: Dublin, 2016).

Glossary

The scholarly convention in transliterating Mandaic to the Western alphabet involves various diacritical marks, most of which are unfamiliar to a general audience. I have chosen to exclude these in the interest of readability. There are several variations in spelling in the standard academic texts. I render 'sh' rather than 's' and 'th' rather than 't' where appropriate. For a wide range of Gnostic terms see my earlier book A *Dictionary of Gnosticism* (Quest Books, Wheaton, Illinois, 2009).

abaga Mandaic alphabet

Abathur 'keeper of the scales', the Third Life, sometimes called Bhaq Ziwa, Emanated by the Great Life. Father of Ptahil.

Ada Adam – see also Hawa

Adonai according to the Mandaeans, an evil god who was also the sun and the God of the Hebrews.

andiruna cult hut built for weddings and the initiation of priests, distinct from the *manda*.

Anosh an *uthra*, saviour or revealer figure, equivalent to Enosh in the Bible.

Bahram Abraham

Bhaq Ziwa see Abathur

demiurge The lower God responsible for creating the material world. In Gnosticism the demiurge is usually ignorant or evil.

diwan a scroll

Diwan Abathur A Mandaean text that describes the journey of the soul.

Dmuta the ideal image or heavenly counterpart in the world of light.

drabsha a wooden cross-shaped standard for Mandaean ritual on which is draped a cloth and wrapped a myrtle cutting.

ganzibra a high priest, sometimes likened to a bishop.

Ginza One of the sacred books of the Mandaeans and perhaps the most important. *Ginza* means 'treasury' and the full title is *Ginza Rabba*, sometimes transliterated as *Ginza Rba*. The *Ginza* actually consists of two books bound together as one. The *Left Ginza* and *Right Ginza* are bound upside-down to one another such that you can open one and read, then flip the book over to begin reading the other.

Left Ginza The smaller of the two books of the *Ginza*, which contains hymns for the dead and is concerned with the ascent of the soul.

Right Ginza The larger of the two books of the *Ginza*, which contains a collection of myths and other material.

The Book of John Also known as the *Book of the Kings* this is a collection of discourses ascribed to John the Baptist, translated by Mead as the *Mandaean John Book*.

Hawwa Eve – see also Ada

Hiia raba 'Great Life', the supreme being in Mandaeanism.

Hibil Abel. In Mandaean mythology he is also an *uthra* from the Lightworld. He baptised Adam.

himyana a ritual belt or girdle

Ishtar Babylonian goddess of love, war and death.

kasia hidden, secret, mystical

klila myrtle wreath

Krun underworld figure, a great mound of flesh

kushta A ritual Mandaean right-handed handclasp representing the union with this world and the world of light; also the qualities of truthfulness, etc. that it represents.

lilith a female demon, common to Semitic cultures (from Lilith).

malka king; also used for *uthri*.

Malka Dhshuka king of darkness –a lion-headed lord of the dark waters who creates demons.

mana the soul; vessel

manda The root of the name Mandaean is *manda*, which means 'knowledge' or *gnosis*. The religious space used for the regular baptisms of the Mandaeans is known as the *mandi*, from the same root. Thus the Mandaeans are the people of *gnosis* and their mandi is the place of gnosis.

Manda d-Hayyi 'knowledge of life', the chief Mandaean revealer figure, who is also translated as 'son of life' or 'image of life'.

mandi Mandaean cult huts

Mara drabuta 'the lord of greatness' the supreme being in Mandaeanism, another name for the Great Life.

margna staff 'of living water'

masbuta weekly baptism with multiple immersions followed by eating of ritual pitta bread, drinking of water and anointing by sesame oil.

masiqta mass for the dead

mshunia kushta the world of ideal forms; paradise.

Musa Moses

nasuraiia member of the Mandaean priesthood's inner circle.

nishimta the soul

pagra body

Panja the five-day festival between the end of the year and the New Year.

Ptahil the Fourth Life, sometimes also called Gabriel, a demiurge created Adam, inanimate until Adakas (Adam Kasya, 'hidden Adam') his soul arrives from the world of light.

Qolasta prayers, hymns and other liturgical material used at the rituals and ceremonies of the Mandaeans. Also known as the *Canonical Prayerbook* or *Mandaean Liturgies.*

rasta ritual robe

ratna the spoken Mandaic language or neo-Mandaic

rish ama the spiritual head of the Mandaeans, the highest clerical rank – no *rish ama* has existed for some time.

Ruha 'spirit' Mandaean equivalent of Sophia, she falls from the realm of light to darkness. Ruha is the equivalent of soul in other Gnostic traditions, not of spirit.

Sabians an unknown 'people of the book' mentioned in the Quran as deserving tolerance from Muslims. The Mandaeans were identified as Sabians, and they were thus acknowledged as 'people of the book' (for their *Ginza* scriptures) within Islam, despite periodic persecutions.

sheikh – Arabic term used for an elder, leader or priest; used widely in the Middle East in many religions.

shganda a lay helper or acolyte in ritual

skandola iron seal

tarmida priest

Tibil the physical world.

Ur a dragon, lord of darkness, son of Ruha.

uthri light beings, heavenly priests who are the models and ideals of Mandaean priests.

yalufa literate layman

Yama dsuf the 'sea of the end', into which imprisoned souls will be cast on the final day.

Yardna the Jordan River; the river of light; the running water used for baptism.

Yoma rba ddna the Mandaean day of judgment, on which trapped souls will be cast in to the Yama dsuf ('sea of the end').

Yoshamin Second Life, emanated by the Great Life.

ziwa radiance; sometimes used as an epithet for *uthri*, particularly Hibil Ziwa and Bhaq Ziwa.

Bibliography

Aldihisi, Sabah, *The Story of Creation in the Mandaean Holy Book the Ginza Rba*. Ph.D. University College London. Proquest, Ann Arbor, 2013.

Al Saadi, Qais Mughashghash and Al Saadi, Hamed Mughashghash, *Ginza Rabba*. Drabsha Publishing, 2012.

Arabestani, Mehrdad, 'Ritual Purity and the Mandaeans' Identity' in *Iran and the Caucasus* 16, Brill, Leiden, 2012, pp.153–168.

Baigent, Michael, *Astrology in Ancient Mesopotamia*. Bear & Company, Rochester, VT, 2015.

Baker, Karen, *The Hidden Peoples of the World: The Mandaeans of Iraq*. VDM Verlag, Saarbrücken, 2009.

Baker-Brian, Nicholas J., *Manichaeism: An Ancient Faith Rediscovered*, T & T Clark, London, 2001.

Barnstone, Willis, and Martin Meyer, *The Gnostic Bible*, Shambhala, Boston, 2003.

Barber, Malcolm, *The Trial of the Templars*, Cambridge University Press, Cambridge, 1978.

Barber, Malcolm, *The New Knighthood*, Cambridge University Press, Cambridge, 1995.

Bartlett, W.B., *The Assassins: The Story of Medieval Islam's Secret Sect*, Sutton, Stroud, 2001.

BeDuhn, Jason David, *The Manichaean Body: In Discipline and Ritual*, The Johns Hopkins University Press, Baltimore, 2002.

Birks, Walter, *The Treasure of Montségur: Study of the Cathar Heresy and the Nature of the Cathar Secret*, Aquarian Press, London, 1987.

Boyce, Mary, *Textual Sources for the Study of Zoroastrianism*, Manchester University Press, Manchester, 1984.

Brighton, Simon, *In Search of the Knights Templar*, Orion, London, 2008.

Brown, Colin, 'What Was John the Baptist Doing?' in *Bulletin for Biblical Research* 7, 1997, pp.37–50.

Brown, Raymond E., *The Community of the Beloved Disciple*. Paulist Press, New York, 1979.

Buckley, Jorunn Jacobsen, 'Two Female Gnostic Revealers' in *History of Religions* 22, no. 1, 1982, pp.60–84.

Buckley, Jorunn Jacobsen, *The Great Stem of Souls: Reconstructing Mandaean History*,

Oxford University Press, New York, 2002.

Buckley, Jorunn Jacobsen, 'Turning the Tables on Jesus: The Mandaean View' in *A People's History of Christianity*, edited by Richard Horsley, Vol. 1: *Christian Origins*, Fortress Press, Philadelphia, 2005, pp.94–109.

Buckley, Jorunn Jacobsen and Albrile, Ezio, 'Mandaean Religion' in *Encyclopedia of Religion, Second Edition*, Vol. 8, Macmillan reference USA, Farmington Hills, Michigan, 2005, pp.5634–5640.

Buckley, Jorunn Jacobsen, *The Mandaeans: Ancient Texts and Modern People*, Gorgias Press, Piscataway, New Jersey, 2010.

Burke, Alexander J., Jr., *John the Baptist: Prophet and Disciple*, St Anthony Messenger Press, Cincinatti, 2006.

Churton, Tobias, *The Gnostics*, George Weidenfeld & Nicholson, London, 1987.

Churton, Tobias, *The Golden Builders*, Weiser, New York, 2005.

Churton, Tobias, *Gnostic Philosophy: From Ancient Persia to Modern Times*, Inner Traditions, Rochester, Vermont, 2005.

Churton, Tobias, *The Mysteries of John the Baptist: His Legacy in Gnosticism, Paganism, and Freemasonry.* Inner Traditions, Rochester, Vermont, 2012.

Conner, Miguel, *Other Voices of Gnosticism*, Bardic Press, Dublin, 2016.

Conner, Miguel, *Voices of Gnosticism: Interviews with Elaine Pagels, Marvin Meyer, Bart Ehrman, Bruce Chilton and Other Leading Scholars*, Bardic Press, Dublin, 2010.

Couliano, Ioan P., *The Tree of Gnosis*, HarperSanFrancisco, San Francisco, 1992.

Davies, Stevan L., *Spirit Possession and the Origins of Christianity*, Bardic Press, Dublin, 2014.

Dentzer, Jean-Marie and Augé, Christian, Petra: *The Rose-Red City.* Thames & Hudson, London, 2000.

Doresse, Jean, *The Secret Books of the Egyptian Gnostics.* MJF Books, New York, 1986.

Downes, Richard, *In Search of Iraq: Baghdad to Babylon.* New Island, Dublin, 2006.

Drower, E.S., *A Mandaean Book of Black Magic in The Journal of the Royal Asiatic Society of Great Britain and Ireland*, No. 2 (October 1943), pp.149–181.

Drower, E.S., *The Book of the Zodiac: Sfar Malwasia*, Murray, London, 1949.

Drower, E.S., *Diwan Abatur or the Progress Through the Purgatories*, Studi e Testi 151. Biblioteca Apostolica Vaticana, Vatican City, 1953.

Drower, E.S., *The Haran Gawaita*, Studia e Testi 176. Biblioteca Apostolica Vaticana, Vatican City, 1953.

Drower, E.S., *The Canonical Prayerbook of the Mandaeans*, E.J. Brill, Leiden, 1959.

Drower, E.S., *The Secret Adam*, Clarendon Press, Oxford, 1960.

Drower, E.S., *The Thousand and Twelve Questions: A Mandaean Text*, Akademie Verlag, Berlin, 1960.

Drower, E.S., *The Mandaeans of Iraq and Iran*, E.J. Brill, Leiden, 1962.

Eco, Umberto, *Foucault's Pendulum.* Vintage, London, 2001.

Ehrman, Bart, *Lost Christianities*, Oxford University Press, Oxford, 2003.

Eisenman, Robert, *James, the Brother of Jesus*, Penguin, London, 1998.

Eisenman, Robert, *The New Testament Code*, Watkins, London, 2006.

Eliade, Mircea and Couliano, Ioan, T*he HarperCollins Concise Guide to World Religions: The A-Z encyclopedia of all the major religious traditions*, HarperSanFrancisco, San Francisco, 2000.

Endress, Gerhard, *Islam: An Historical Introduction*, Edinburgh University Press, Edinburgh, 2002.

Eusebius, *The History of the Church*, Penguin, London, 1989.

Faivre, Antoine (ed.); Hanegraaff, Wouter J. (ed.); van den Broek, Roelof (ed.); Brach, Jean-Pierre (ed.), *Dictionary of Gnosis and Western Esotericism*, E.J. Brill, Leiden, 2006.

Farmer, David Hugh, *The Oxford Dictionary of Saints*. Oxford University Press, Oxford, 1982.

Foerster, Werner. *Gnosis: A Selection of Gnostic Texts. Volume II: Coptic and Mandaean Sources*, Oxford University Press, Oxford, 1974.

Forlong, J.R.G., Faiths of Man: *A Cyclopædia Of Religions*, Volume I, Celephaïs Press, Leeds, 2006.

Frale, Barbara, *The Templars and the Shroud of Christ*, Maverick House, Dunboyne, 2011.

Funk, Robert W., Hoover, Roy W., and the Jesus Seminar, *The Five Gospels*, HarperSanFrancisco, San Francisco, 1997.

Funk, Robert W. and the Jesus Seminar, *The Acts of Jesus*, HarperSanFrancisco, San Francisco, 1998.

Gaddis, Michael, *There is No Crime For Those Who Have Christ: Religious Violence in the Christian Roman Empire*, University of California Press, Berkeley, 2005.

Gardner, Iain and Lieu, Samuel N.C., *Manichaean Texts from the Roman Empire*, Cambridge University Press, Cambridge, 2004.

Gibson, Shimon, *The Cave of John the Baptist*. Arrow, London, 2004.

Gilbert, Adrian, *Magi*. Montpelier, Invisible Cities Press, Vermont, 2002.

Gill, Anton, *The Rise and Fall of Babylon*, Quercus, London, 2011.

Gündüz, Şinasi, *The Knowledge of Life*, Oxford University Press, Oxford, 1994.

Gurdjieff, G.I. *Meetings With Remarkable Men*, E.P. Dutton, New York, 1976.

Haag, Michael, *The Templars: History and Myth*, Profile Books, London, 2009.

Häberl, Charles G., 'Mandaeism in Antiquity and the Antiquity of Mandaeism' in *Religion Compass*, Volume 6, Issue 5, Blackwell Publishing, Hoboken, 2012, pp.262–276.

Häberl, Charles G., 'The Demon and the Damsel: A Folktale in Iraqi Neo-Mandaic' in 'Through Thy Word All things were Made' by Rainer Voigt (ed.), 2nd

International Conference of Mandaic and Samaritan Studies 2013.

Haleem, M.A.S. Abdel, *The Quran*, Oxford University Press, Oxford, 2005.

Hedrick, Charles W. and Hodgson, R. (eds.), *Nag Hammadi, Gnosticism and Early Christianity*, Hendrickson Publishers, Peabody, Massachusetts, 1986.

King, Karen L., *What Is Gnosticism?*, Harvard University Press, Cambridge, Massachusetts, 2005.

Hodgson, Marshall G.S., *The Secret Order of Assassins*, University of Pennsylvania Press, Philadelphia, 2005.

The Holy Bible: Revised Standard Version, Oxford University Press, Oxford, 2005.

Hopkins, Keith, *A World Full of Gods*, Phoenix, London, 1999.

Koester, Helmut, *Introduction to the New Testament*, (2 volumes), De Gruyter, New York, 1982.

Kriwaczek, Paul, *Babylon: Mesopotamia and the Birth of Civilization*, Atlantic Books, London, 2010.

Kriwaczek, Paul, *In Search of Zarathustra*, Phoenix, London, 2002.

Lachman, Gary, *The Quest For Hermes Trismegistus*, Floris Books, Edinburgh, 2011.

Laidler, Keith, *The Head of God*, Orion, London, 1998.

Legman, G., *The Guilt of the Templars*, Rudos and Rebes Publishing, San Francisco, 1994.

Leick, Gwendolyn, *Mesopotamia: The Invention of the City*, Penguin, London, 2001.

Lewis, Nicola Densey, *Introduction to 'Gnosticism'*, Oxford University Press, New York, 2013.

Lieu, Samuel N.C., *Manichaeans in Mesopotamia and the Roman East*, E.J. Brill, Leiden, 1999.

Lupieri, Edmondo, *The Mandaeans: The Last Gnostics*, Wm. B. Eerdmans Publishing Co., Grand Rapids, Michigan, 2002.

Maalouf, Amin, *The Gardens of Light*, Abacus, London, 1997.

Martin, Richard C. (ed.), *The Encyclopedia of Islam and the Muslim World*, Macmillan Reference, New York, 2004.

Martin, Sean, *The Knights Templar*, Pocket Essentials, Harpenden, 2004.

Masco, Maire M., *The Mandaeans: Gnostic Astrology as an Artefact of Cultural Transmission*, Fluke Press, Tacoma, Washington, 2012.

Mead, G.R.S., *The Gnostic John the Baptizer: Selections from the Mandaean John-Book*, The Gnostic Society Library, 1924.

Mead, G.R.S., *Simon Magus: His Philosophy and Teachings*, The Book Tree, San Diego, 2003.

Meier, John P., *A Marginal Jew: Rethinking the Historical Jesus. Volume I: The Roots of the Problem and the Person*, Doubleday, New York, 1991.

Meier, John P., *A Marginal Jew: Rethinking the Historical Jesus. Volume II: Mentor, Message, and Miracles*, Doubleday, New York, 1994.

Meier, John P., *A Marginal Jew: Rethinking the Historical Jesus. Volume III: Companions and Competitors*, Doubleday, New York, 2001.

Merkur, Dan, Gnosis: *An Esoteric Tradition of Mystical Visions and Unions*, SUNY Press, New York, 1993.

Meyer, Marvin, (ed.), *The Nag Hammadi Scriptures: The International Edition*, HarperOne, New York, 2007.

Montgomery, James A., *Aramaic Incantation Texts From Nippur*, University Museum, Philadelphia, 1913.

Morgenstern, Matthew, 'Jewish Babylonian Aramaic and Mandaic: Some points of Contact' in *Aram Periodical* 22, pp.1–14. ARAM Society for Syro-Mesopotamian Studies, Oxford, 2010.

Olsen, Oddvar (ed.), *The Templar Papers*, New Page Press, Franklin Lakes, New Jersey, 2006.

Pallis, Svend Aage, *Mandaean Studies*, Philo Press, Amsterdam, 1974.

Partner, Peter, *The Knights Templar and Their Myth*, Destiny Books, Rochester, Vermont, 1990.

Pétrement, Simone, *A Separate God: The Christian Origins of Gnosticism*, HarperSanFrancisco, San Francisco, 1990.

Picknett, Lynn, *Mary Magdalene*, Robinson, London, 2003.

Picknett, Lynn and Prince, Clive, *Turin Shroud: In Whose Image?*, Corgi, London, 2000.

Picknett, Lynn, and Prince, Clive, *The Templar Revelation: Secret Guardians of the True Identity of Christ*, Transworld, London, 2007.

Picknett, Lynn and Prince, Clive, *The Masks of Christ*, Sphere, London, 2008.

Picknett, Lynn, and Prince, Clive, *The Sion Revelation: Inside the Shadowy World of Europe's Secret Masters*, Sphere, London, 2008.

Picknett, Lynn and Prince, Clive, *The Forbidden Universe*, Constable, London, 2011.

Pollard, Justin and Reid, Howard, *The Rise and Fall of Alexandria*, Penguin Books, New York, 2006.

Ralls, Karen, *The Templars and the Grail*, Quest Books, Wheaton, Illinois, 2003.

Ralls, Karen, *Knights Templar Encyclopedia: The Essential Guide to the People, Places, Events, and Symbols of the Order of the Temple*, Career Press, Franklin Lakes, New Jersey, 2007.

Read, Piers Paul, *The Templars*, Phoenix Press, London, 2001.

Robinson, J.A.T., *The Priority of John*, (Bampton Lectures 1984), SCM Press, London, 1985.

Roux, George, *Ancient Iraq*, Pelican, Harmondsworth, 1966.

Russell, Gerard, *Heirs to Forgotten Kingdoms*, Simon & Schuster, London, 2014.

Salaman, Clement; van Oyen, Dorine; and Wharton, William D. (trans.), *The Way of Hermes*, Duckworth, London, 2001.

Schneemelcher, Wilhelm (ed.), *New Testament Apocrypha. Volume One: Gospels and Related Writings*, revised edition, James Clarke & Co. Ltd, Cambridge, 1991.

Schonfield, Hugh J., *The Pentecost Revolution*, MacDonald, London, 1974.

Schonfield, Hugh J., *The Essene Odyssey*, Element Books, Shaftesbury, 1985.

Scott, Walter, *Hermetica*. Solos Press, Shaftesbury, 1993.

Smith, Andrew Phillip, *The Gospel of Thomas: A New Translation Based On the Inner Meaning*, Ulysses Books, Oregon House, California, 2002.

Smith, Andrew Phillip, *The Gospel of Philip: Annotated & Explained*, Skylight Paths, Woodstock, Vermont, 2005.

Smith, Andrew Phillip, *Gnostic Writings on the Soul: Annotated & Explained*, Skylight Paths, Woodstock, Vermont, 2006.

Smith, Andrew Phillip, *The Lost Sayings of Jesus: Annotated & Explained*, Skylight Paths, Woodstock, Vermont, 2006.

Smith, Andrew Phillip, *A Dictionary of Gnosticism*, Quest Books, Wheaton, Illinois, 2009.

Smith, Andrew Phillip (ed.), *The Gnostic: A Journal of Gnosticism, Western Esotericism and Spirituality 1*, Bardic Press, Dublin, 2009.

Smith, Andrew Phillip (ed.), *The Gnostic: A Journal of Gnosticism, Western Esotericism and spirituality 2*, Bardic Press, Dublin, 2009.

Smith, Andrew Phillip (ed.), *The Gnostic: A Journal of Gnosticism, Western Esotericism and spirituality 3*, Bardic Press, Dublin, 2011.

Smith, Andrew Phillip (ed.), *The Gnostic: A Journal of Gnosticism, Western Esotericism and spirituality 4*, Bardic Press, Dublin, 2011.

Smith, Andrew Phillip (ed.), *The Gnostic: A Journal of Gnosticism, Western Esotericism and spirituality 5*, Bardic Press, Dublin, 2012.

Smith, Andrew Phillip (ed.), *The Gnostic: A Journal of Gnosticism, Western Esotericism and spirituality 6*, Bardic Press, Dublin, 2015.

Smith, Andrew Phillip, *Lost Teachings of the Cathars*, Watkins, London, 2015.

Smith, Andrew Phillip, *Secret History of the Gnostics*, Watkins, London, 2015.

Smoley, Richard, *Forbidden Faith: The Gnostic Legacy from the Gospels to the Da Vinci Code*, HarperCollins, New York, 2006.

Säve-Söderbergh, Torgny, *Studies in the Coptic Manichaean Psalm-Book*, Almqvist & Wiksells Boktryckeri, Uppsala, 1949.

Stoyanov, Yuri, *The Other God: Dualist Religions from Antiquity to the Cathar Heresy*, revised edition, Yale University Press, New Haven, 2000.

Tabor, James, *The Jesus Dynasty*, Harper Element, London, 2006.

Tardieu, Michel, *Manichaeism*, University of Illinois Press, Chicago, 2008.

Thesiger, Wilfred, *The Marsh Arabs*, Penguin, London, 1967.

Thomas, Richard, 'The Israelite Origins of the Mandaean People' in *Studia Antiqua*

5.2, Fall 2007, pp.3–27.

Turner, John D. 'Sethian Gnosticism: A Literary History' in Hedrick, Charles W. and Hodgson, R. (eds.), *Nag Hammadi, Gnosticism and Early Christianity*, 1986, pp.55–86.

Valantasis, Richard, *Religions of Late Antiquity in Practice*, Princeton University Press, New Jersey, 2000.

Waardenburg, Jacques (ed.), *Muslim Perceptions of Other Religions: A Historical Survey*, Oxford University Press, Oxford, 1999.

Wasserman, James, *The Templars and the Assassins*, Destiny Books, Rochester, Vermont, 2001

Wilson, Ian, *The Turin Shroud*, Penguin, Harmondsworth, 1979.

Wise, Michael; Abegg, Martin; and Cook, Edward, *The Dead Sea Scrolls: A New Translation*, HarperSanFrancisco, San Francisco, 1996.

Yamauchi, Edwin M., *Gnostic Ethics and Mandaean Origins*, Harvard University Press, Cambridge, Massachusetts, 1970.

Yamauchi, Edwin M., *Pre-Christian Gnosticism: A Survey of the Proposed Evidences*, Tyndale Press, London, 1973.

Index